DESERT BATTLES

Other titles in the Stackpole Military History Series

THE AMERICAN CIVIL WAR
Cavalry Raids of the Civil War
Pickett's Charge
Witness to Gettysburg

WORLD WAR II
Armor Battles of the Waffen-SS, 1943–45
Australian Commandos
The B-24 in China
Backwater War
Beyond the Beachhead
The Brandenburger Commandos
Bringing the Thunder
Coast Watching in World War II
Colossal Cracks
D-Day to Berlin
Exit Rommel
Fist from the Sky
Flying American Combat Aircraft of World War II
Forging the Thunderbolt
The German Defeat in the East, 1944–45
Germany's Panzer Arm in World War II
Grenadiers
Infantry Aces
Iron Arm
Luftwaffe Aces
Messerschmitts over Sicily
Michael Wittmann, Volume One
Michael Wittmann, Volume Two
The Nazi Rocketeers
On the Canal
Packs On!
Panzer Aces
Panzer Aces II
The Panzer Legions
Retreat to the Reich
The Savage Sky
Surviving Bataan and Beyond
The 12th SS, Volume One
The 12th SS, Volume Two
Tigers in the Mud

THE COLD WAR / VIETNAM
Flying American Combat Aircraft: The Cold War
Land with No Sun
Street without Joy

WARS OF THE MIDDLE EAST
Never-Ending Conflict

DESERT BATTLES

From Napoleon to the Gulf War

Bruce Allen Watson

STACKPOLE
BOOKS

AUG 2 3 2007

Published in paperback in 2007 by
STACKPOLE BOOKS
5067 Ritter Road
Mechanicsburg, PA 17055
www.stackpolebooks.com

DESERT BATTLE: COMPARATIVE PERSPECTIVES, by Bruce Allen Watson, was originally published in hard cover by Praeger, an imprint of Greenwood Publishing Group, Inc., Westport, CT. Copyright© 1995 by Bruce Allen Watson. Paperback edition by arrangement with Greenwood Publishing Group, Inc. All rights reserved.

Cover design by Tracy Patterson.

Cover illustration: Destroyed German Pz Mark III tank. Courtesy of The Tank Museum.

Printed in the United States of America

10 9 8 7 6 5 4 3 2 1

FIRST EDITION

Library of Congress Cataloging-in-Publication Data

Watson, Bruce, 1929–
[Desert battle]
Desert battles : from Napoleon to the Gulf War / Bruce Allen Watson. — 1st ed.
    p. cm. — (Stackpole Military history series)
Originally published by Praeger in 1995 under the title: Desert battle.
Includes bibliographical references and index.
ISBN-13: 978-0-8117-3380-9
ISBN-10: 0-8117-3380-7
1. Battles. 2. Desert warfare—History. I. Title.

D295.W38 2007
355.4'7154—dc22
                                        2006018316

Table of Contents

Maps

Preface

I watched the television coverage of the 1991 Gulf War, appropriately impressed by the coalition's domination over the Iraqi Army, a domination attributable—so it seemed—to high-technology weapons. My impression soon waned, however, replaced by a concern that the war was isolated, sanitized, and offered as a paean to the future. The explications of the war emphasized its unique qualities but largely ignored those that made it ordinary—in short, they lacked historical context. I offer this study of the development of desert battle as a means to fill the void and, simultaneously and in a curmudgeonly spirit, throw down the historical gauntlet before those who think desert battle a great romance.

My central question is simple enough: What connects desert battles regardless of time or place? To answer the question I review seven desert campaigns, beginning out of chronological order with Erwin Rommel's entry into North Africa. Rommel is familiar ground and what he did, in reality and as legend, conditioned much of our thinking about desert battles. Next is a chapter on deserts—unfamiliar ground to most of us—as the physical context of battle. I then explore Bonaparte's Egyptian adventure, British operations on Indian's Northwest Frontier, 1850–1852, the 1917 British Tigris River campaign, the British counter-offensive against the Italians in Libya, 1940–1941, the 1973 Arab-Israeli War and, of course, the 1991 Gulf War. Comparisons, conclusions, and speculations appear in a final chapter.

Each campaign is discussed in relation to its political and military origins, revealing a remarkable record of errors, arrogance, and ignorance. Oblations are made to weapons development and the organization of the combatants. But running through the narratives of all the campaigns is the story of human endurance in a treacherous environment.

The campaigns were fought in exotic places. Hence, I must give a warning. The names of places and people can be a nightmare. There are always variations. For example, Shubkudur, a village on the North-west Frontier, is spelled five different ways, the modern maps—when such obscure places can be found—showing considerable variance with historical usages. Saddam Hussein has at least eleven different spellings. My selections were based on what would be the most help to the reader spurred to read further.

Acknowledgments

I wish to acknowledge the assistance of the following libraries: the Scottish National Library and the Scottish Records Office, Edinburgh; the India Office Library and Records, and the British Library, London; the Doe Library and the Richmond Northern Regional Research Library of the University of California, Berkeley. For very special help with photographs I must thank the following persons: David Fletcher, Librarian of the Tank Museum, Royal Armoured Corps Centre, Bovington; Riaz Hasan Khan of Islamabad, Pakistan; the staff of the Information Office, Pakistan Embassy, Washington, DC; Colonel Ron Niv, military attaché, Israeli Embassy, Washington, DC; and Dr. Ralph Cross. For reading all or part of the manuscript I am grateful to Dick Dudley, Morey Fine, George Blanchard, and Thomas Davies. I must also thank Joe Sexton, acquisition librarian in my college, for his years of friendship and endless assistance. At a more personal level, my friend Bill Perry generously shared with me many of his experiences as an officer in the Western Desert Force. As always, my wife, Marilyn, and youngest sons Brian and John provided the environment within which I could work by reading and criticizing early drafts, arguing often esoteric points, and just listening.

CHAPTER 1

Erwin Rommel:
Birth of a Desert Legend

ROMMEL'S FIRST ADVANCE IN CYRENAICA, APRIL 1941

Mersa Brega, 31 March 1941, 1400 hours. German Stuka divebombers plunged toward the British infantry positions below, their engines filling the sky with a terrible and all-too-familiar scream. The young British troops, members of the 1st Tower Hamlets Rifles, half their men already lost in three days fighting, stared upward helplessly as bombs splintered the earth. There was no sanctuary from the onslaught as great geysers of sand and rock hurtled upward with each explosion. Jagged bomb fragments cut across the barren landscape like scythes. Smoke and flame rose from Bren Gun carriers and trucks. An acrid, reeking stench hung over the battlefield, a mixture of burning gasoline, oil, rubber, paint, and human flesh.

1630 hours. German infantry of the 5th Light Division, supported by tanks and machine gun units, filtered through the sand hills to the north and west of Mersa Brega, overrunning British forward positions. The main defensive line bent under the German attack. British artillerymen, seeing their positions threatened, lobbed some shells in the general direction of the enemy, then packed up their guns and moved east. The infantry quickly followed. No armored units supported the British defense or covered the retreat. British aircraft were conspicuously absent. The withdrawal was confused and hurried.

Lieutenant General Erwin Rommel watched the battle unfold, pleased with his troops' swiftness as they pressed their attack, overcoming any opposition. He also noted with particular satisfaction how quickly his armored and transport vehicles refuelled. Men and machines worked together with artillery, tanks, and aircraft supporting the infantry. This combined arms maneuvering was not the result of

1

special desert training, but of tactics worked out in the Nazi assaults in Europe, especially during Rommel's advances around Arras in France. Once in Tripoli, one order prevailed: attack! Now Rommel stood on the shore of the Gulf of Sidra, near El Agheila. Ahead stretched miles and miles of undefended desert. The road lay open to Benghazi, Tobruk, and Bardia. Beyond, possibly within reach, were Sidi Barrani, Alexandria, Cairo, and the Suez Canal. Was such a campaign possible?

The answer to that question is found both in the circumstances that brought Rommel to the Western Desert and in what he decided to do once he arrived. On 6 February 1941, Rommel reported to Field Marshal Walter von Brauchitsch at Berchtesgaden, Hitler's retreat in southern Bavaria. Brauchitsch informed him that he was to command an army corps—still forming—in North Africa to support the Italian Army being mauled by the British. Some units of the 5th Light Division would be in Tripoli by mid-February, the entire division transported within two months. Meantime, battalions from the 15th Panzer Division would join them, the entire division embarking by mid-May.

11 February 1941. Rommel, now in Catania, Sicily, received reports describing the magnitude of the Italian defeat. Four days earlier, the British Army's Western Desert Force (also designated XIII Corps), Richard O'Connor commanding, took Benghazi on the east shore of the Gulf of Sidra. The British now dominated Cyrenaica, as eastern Libya is known, defeating ten Italian divisions. O'Connor was poised for a strike into Tripolitania. Knowing that O'Connor had to be derailed as quickly as possible, Rommel ordered Luftwaffe Lieutenant General Hans-Ferdinand Geissler, commanding Fliegerkorps X in Sicily, to attack Benghazi harbor and British forces around El Agheila. Geissler refused. Rommel telephoned headquarters in Berlin and reported the air commander's reluctance. Geissler's bombers took off the next day. German air raids continued for a week, even turning back a British supply convoy near Benghazi.

Rommel went to Tripoli on 13 February. He pushed every man, every gun, every machine immediately east toward El Agheila. The urgency of thwarting further British attacks consuming him, Rommel badgered his fledgling corps until they, too, were infused with the same energy.

Simultaneously, Rommel secured two important command changes. Stephan Frölich, assuming the title *Fliegerführer Afrika,* replaced the reluctant Geissler. Rodolfo Graziani, supposed to be Rommel's superior, resigned. He realized the Germans would soon be in control and was personally unable to accept subordination to ambitions that Rommel took no pains to disguise. Italo Gariboldi took command of all Italian troops in North Africa but, as Graziani anticipated, was directed by Mussolini to put all his motorized units at Rommel's disposal. In effect, Rommel took full control of the North African theater.

On 19 March, Rommel flew to Berlin, reporting to Brauchitsch and Colonel General Franz Halder, chief of staff, that Italian troops were demoralized by the British advance and he doubted their fighting ability. He wanted more men, tanks, artillery, and supplies; he believed that only a brisk advance would stop the British. But an attack on El Agheila was only a first step. Rommel outlined a campaign to retake Benghazi, Tobruk, and push beyond to the Egyptian border. Nothing less than knocking the British completely out of Cyrenaica would do (Map 1). Given the open terrain and the position of harbors, he realized that neither the Germans nor the British could hold only a piece of the region. Rommel threw down a gauntlet. It had to be all or nothing.

Barrie Pitt, in *The Crucible of War: Western Desert, 1941,* makes the important point that Brauchitsch and Halder did not tell Rommel of plans, wrapped in secrecy, to open a Balkan front and yet another in the Soviet Union, plans that would ultimately limit manpower and supplies sent to North Africa. Instead, they reminded their eager general that he was in Libya merely to support the Italians. He could retake Benghazi, but under no circumstances was he to launch a major offensive.

Rommel returned to North Africa on 21 February and, as Pitt stresses, immediately ignored the orders given him in Berlin. The 3rd Reconnaissance Battalion and other units of the 5th Light Division marched to El Agheila on the twenty-third, taking the town with a surprise attack. What made the attack, indeed the entire advance to follow, surprising was that both the general staff in Berlin and the British commander, Archibald Wavell, and his staff in Cairo thought Rommel

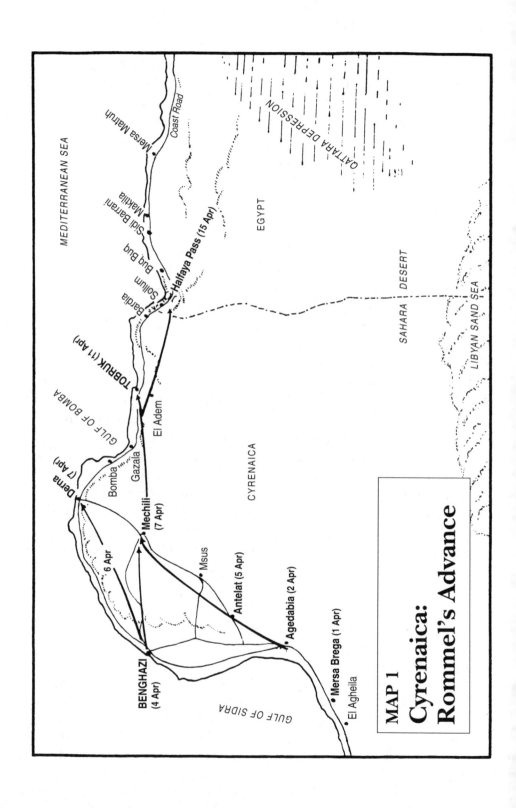

MAP 1
Cyrenaica:
Rommel's Advance

would not be ready for operations until at least mid-April and perhaps not until early May.

General Wavell, commander in chief, Middle East, brought O'Connor's brilliant campaign to an end on 13 February, a blow to O'Connor, who believed his men, despite a pervasive fatigue and badly worn machines, could take Tripoli. But Wavell was under pressure from London to take the offensive in Somalia, Ethiopia and, on the Red Sea, in Eritrea (then part of Ethiopia). Most importantly, the Italian invasion of Greece, with subsequent German intervention, called on all Wavell's resources. The Western Desert Force was literally dismembered. The battalions of the famous 7th Armored Division, the most experienced armored unit in the entire region, were parceled out to various fronts, and O'Connor reassigned to Cairo as general officer commanding, Egypt.

The British units in Cyrenaica shifted from an offensive posture to one of defense. And these were thin defenses. The 3rd Brigade of the untested 2nd Armored Division was equipped with fifty-two cruiser tanks, half under repair. In desperation, the British used captured Italian M11/39 tanks, one of the worst machines ever conceived. Two Australian infantry brigades were near Benghazi, another at Tobruk, and a motorized Indian brigade deployed around Mechili, all under the command of Lieutenant General Philip Neame. Wavell was not at all pleased with Neame's deployments. An Australian brigade south of Benghazi lacked support on its flanks and had no transport. They were, as Wavell observed, "completely useless and prey to any armored vehicles that broke through at Agheila" (Pitt, 1941, 250). Neame did his best but, in comparison to O'Connor's recent campaign, he fell short.

Rommel wrote his wife in early August that "we've been attacking since the 31st [of March] with dazzling success" (Pitt, 1941, 257). Despite repeated protests from General Gariboldi that he was exceeding his authority, and despite having ignored his orders from Brauchitseh and Halder, Rommel would not be stopped. But no scathing messages arrived from Berlin. Instead, Adolf Hitler gloated over Rommel's success and gave him complete freedom of action.

By 6 April, the Italians, feeling a new confidence wrought by the vigorous Rommel, sniffed victory in the offing. On 7 April, units of the Italian Ariete Division and of Rommel's 5th Light Division threatened Mechili, south of Derna. Wavell, uncertain of Neame, sent O'Connor back to Libya. It was a fateful decision. Arriving at Neame's headquarters at Maraua, O'Connor found Neame preparing to evacuate. They drove off together into the black night. Stopping to rest, they were surrounded by a German reconnaissance unit and captured (and eventually interned in Italy).

Mechili fell despite a determined British resistance. The Germans and Italians captured Derna on 8 April, then took Gazala, Bardia, and Sollum. By 28 April, Rommel's Africa Corps stood on the Egyptian border.

Rommel's advance, a lightning stroke rooted in the man's boldness, imagination, and impetuousness, filled with high risk, was not a walk-over. For Rommel discovered, as O'Connor before him, that desert heaped cruelties on machines and men. Trucks, gun carriers, and tanks ran out of fuel, and attacks occasionally stalled for want of support. Ammunition supplies were severely depleted. Water reserves ran dry and some captured German soldiers were near crazed with thirst.

Even though the Africa Corps reached the Egyptian border, Tobruk, vital because of its fine harbor, still held out. The British garrison numbered about 24,000 men. These included the 1st Australian Division and remnants of units that found their way into the city during the retreat from Benghazi and Derna. The basis of their defense was the old, obsolete, and incomplete Italian defensive line. This included anti-tank ditches and an incomplete barbed wire barricade. British shortages of tanks and artillery further compromised defensive efforts. Rommel surrounded Tobruk by 11 April. The 5th Light Division, given the task of breaching the defenses, attacked again and again. Again and again they failed. The 5th Panzer Regiment then attacked and lost eleven of twenty-four tanks. The 8th Machine Gun Battalion attacked, only to get bogged down in a trench. A British tank lumbered in upon them, forcing the battalion to withdraw. The 8th lost 700 men, three-quarters of its strength. On 16 April, British anti-tank fire destroyed eighteen Italian tanks. On 1 May, the 1st Battalion, 104th Rifle Regiment, newly arrived from Germany, launched a 2:00 A.M. attack into withering machine gun fire that crushed the battalion. Volkmar Kühn states that Tobruk became a Verdun of the desert, referring to the great World War I siege that ground up thousands and thousands of troops from both sides. The comparison is rather an overstatement. But regardless of interpretation, Rommel was forced to bypass the stronghold, his hopes for a quick victory dashed by the Australians.

Wavell's RAF squadrons and tank force were seriously weakened both by losses during the German advance and demands from other Middle Eastern fronts. He cabled London for help and Prime Minister Winston Churchill responded boldly, ordering a convoy to sail the full length of the Mediterranean from Gibraltar to Alexandria. The convoy made it, despite attacks by the Luftwaffe and Italian Navy, and off-loaded forty-three Hawker Hurricane fighters and 238 tanks. The Royal Navy also established on Malta a much needed squadron of Bristol Beaufighters, a twin-engined craft suitable for night operations. At sea, three destroyers and the cruiser HMS *Ajax* raided a German convoy. They sunk at least one ammunition ship, creating a critical shortage among Rommel's units.

Under pressure from London, Wavell ordered Operation Brevity. This was not a major offensive but a means of taking pressure off Tobruk by recapturing Sollum, taking Halfaya Pass, where the coast road cut through the dominating escarpment, and subduing Fort Capuzzo. The badly planned operation failed against strong German counterattacks.

Brevity's main achievement was to alert Rommel to the possibility of another British attack. He reinforced his front by bringing the 5th Light Division from the Tobruk siege. He also strengthened his anti-tank units. Two batteries of 88mm guns were added to the standard 37mm and 50mm batteries. The 88s were originally designed as anti-aircraft weapons, but experience in the Spanish Civil War and France demonstrated their versatility against armor. Firing a 16.5-pound explosive projectile, they stopped any armor the British possessed.

The planning for the second British attack, known as Operation Battleaxe, was, as Correlli Barnett states in *The Desert Generals*, hasty and amateurish. The reassembled 7th Armored Division was no longer the veteran unit of O'Connor's earlier campaign. Its ranks were now filled with young and inexperienced troops. The main problem, however, was that the commander of the operation, Lieutenant General Sir Noel Beresford-Preise, who earlier commanded the 4th Indian Division with considerable distinction against the Italians, lacked experience commanding armored units. As he saw it, Battleaxe was to be a frontal assault against Halfaya Pass by two Indian Army Brigades. Then the 4th Armored Brigade and 22nd Guards Brigade were to move north toward Sollum, thus out-flanking the Germans. Meanwhile, the rest of the 7th Armored Division would draw Rommel's armored units into a major tank battle. Upon defeating the Germans, the 7th would move toward Mechili and Derna, the RAF lending support.

Because Churchill wanted a clean and speedy victory in the Western Desert, Wavell reluctantly approved the operation. But he harbored serious reservations. He cabled General Sir John Dill, the imperial chief of staff, that the initial attacks would succeed but could not be sustained, much less exploited. When Churchill heard this, he wrote off Wavell as an obstructionist. As Barnett states, Wavell was not one of Churchill's generals.

On 15 June, the RAF attacked air bases, supply depots, and convoys. Then the Indian brigades assaulted Halfaya Pass, but the Germans destroyed most of their supporting tanks and hung on. On the escarpment, the 2nd Camerons advanced toward their objective, but the Germans pushed them back with heavy losses, immobilizing eleven of twelve supporting tanks. The 4th Armored Brigade's advance northward also stalled. At 9:00 A.M., thirty Matildas clanked through the morning mist toward Hafid Ridge. They turned away under intense fire from 50mm and 88mm guns. At 11:00 A.M., the Matildas attacked the ridge again. The German 88s opened fire at 1,100 yards, destroying eleven tanks. The British attacked later in the afternoon but, once more, they were turned away by anti-tank gunfire and a counterattack by units of the 5th Panzer Regiment. On a positive note, the 7th Royal Tank Regiment broke through the defenses at Fort Capuzzo, but they could not hold their ground without infantry support. Yet, they did keep German counterattacks, threatening to sweep around their southern flank, at a distance.

Wavell flew to 7th Armored Division headquarters to assess the situation. His worst fears were confirmed. He ordered the 22nd Guards to withdraw and canceled an attack order for the 7th Armored Division. The Indian brigades also withdrew, protected by their remaining armor and the RAF Action was broken off on 17 June. Operation Battleaxe, the blade badly dulled, failed.

According to the *Official History*, the British lost 122 killed, 588 wounded, and 259 missing. Of some 190 tanks engaged, 91 were lost. The German losses included 93 killed, 350 wounded, and 235 missing. Estimates put their tank losses at fifty.

Churchill, angered by a second successive defeat, decided that Wavell, too independent and too gloomy, was not the kind of general he wanted. He had to go. General Sir Claude Auchinleck, in India at the time, but with experience fighting the Germans in Norway, replaced Wavell. Wavell, in turn, replaced Auchinleck as Far East commander in chief. He soon presided over Singapore's fall to the Japanese under conditions as appallingly unprepared as any he found in the Middle East.

AND THE LEGEND WAS BORN

The war in the Western Desert continued as a series of battles producing indifferent results. In November 1941, Auchinleck launched Operation Crusader, catching Rommel by surprise and forcing him out of Cyrenaica. In January 1942, the British were pushed back to Gazala but, with both sides missing tactical opportunities, with water and supply lines too long and too vulnerable, with men and machines worn out, contact was mutually broken off.

The indecisive desert campaigns frustrated both German and British high commands. Yet, from all the fighting there burst forth one clear result: the birth of the Rommel legend—part devil, part hero, always the Desert Fox. No other Nazi general acquired the same respect, and the reasons for his reputation are as fascinating as was the man.

Rommel held a unique place in history, ripe for legend building even among his enemies—the quintessential professional soldier, daring, imaginative, having an independent streak, a leader who suddenly appeared on the battlefield where needed, a man who cared about his soldiers. But the number of officers possessing like qualities are numerous. More than these few personal qualities form a legend like Rommel's.

Very important was the larger context of the war. World War II in Europe began with Hitler's deceits, exemplified by his cynical betrayal of the Munich Pact when he swallowed Czechoslovakia and then Poland. As the war unfolded, as Europe collapsed beneath the Nazi military machine, the meaning of total war came into focus. The German air raids on Warsaw, Rotterdam, and London, for instance, disregarded the line between civilians and the military. Everything and everyone was a target. The Luftwaffe destroyed homes as well as factories, transforming cities into burnt-out hulks. Roads and bridges were bombed and strafed, and so too were the long-struggling masses of refugees that clogged them. And into the shredded lives and blackened cities marched Hitler's SS units and the Gestapo, imposing a state-sanctioned terrorism.

This dark picture of brutal war was absent in North Africa. Rommel may have been a German general, but he was quickly cast more as a noble soldier than a willing servant of Hitler. Make no mistake, the desert war was not kind. The British and Germans took turns bombing Tobruk, Benghazi, Sollum, and Bardia, and they did so with as much destructive force as they could muster. True, their raids were small stuff compared to the London blitz. But death was just as real in the desert as in Europe. A tank driver died as cruelly in the desert, splattered all over the furnace-like interior, as did one in France. But no clouds of refugees jammed the roads leading away from the remnants of their lives, only to be set upon by the Luftwaffe. Neither side took a town for its prestige, such as a Paris or a Warsaw. Air bases and harbor facilities were measures of a desert town's importance. Neither side wanted territory. That was a worthless impediment. Above all, no SS troops marched with the Africa Corps, and no Gestapo lurked in the shadows.

The Rommel legend also emerged more narrowly from a complexity of circumstances that, themselves, deserve special study. I shall briefly offer here only three elements behind the legend, as it were a heuristic spur. First, because Adolf Hitler gave him a free hand, Rommel shaped the Africa Corps to his own purposes. As many historians point out, the corps was uniquely his. Removed from Europe to a secondary front, more a sop thrown to the distraught Italians, Rommel dared to conduct warfare with the dash of old-fashioned cavalry, drawing from his men a personal loyalty that sent them charging across the desert with great élan. Next, even though blitzkrieg warfare secured earlier Nazi victories across Europe, Rommel's North African campaign brought the strategy into focus as never before. Not only did the British initially yield to the lightning strokes, but an entire generation of Europeans and Americans, their concepts of warfare shaped by the useless repetitive slaughter of World War I trench warfare, were mesmerized by what Rommel accomplished in the desert—a legacy, I suggest, that remains intact over a half-century later. Finally, Rommel himself contributed to the legend building by idealizing desert battle. He called it *Krieg ohne Hass*, war without hate. The implication is that the desert somehow cleansed the armies of their ideological baggage, allowing the armies to do battle at its most essential level in the vast arena of the desert, as if an epiphany of war had been reached. The British historian Correlli Barnett reified Rommel's quite Germanic romanticism when he wrote in *The Desert Generals* that the desert provided the context for pure warfare. Thus, with no great cities to conquer, with few civilians to get in the way, ideological issues set aside, and in the absence of hoary relics of past epochs, the armies could get on with what they were trained to do—kill each other. In short, if one had to have a war, what better place than the desert?

This romantic setting could be created only by sanitizing the desert, making it part of the legend-building process. For, indeed, there were civilians in North Africa, most of them Arabs together with a large Italian colony. These people were regularly bombed, strafed, and shelled by both sides if they got in the way. The Arabs, the more nomadic population, seemed to get in the way more than the Italians. Their villages might be overwhelmed by a battle. Sometimes, seen wandering across the desert, they were shot because they were not trusted, and sometimes for the mere sport of it. True, there were no large cities in the battle zone, but Sidi Barrani and Tobruk, for instance, were important, and Benghazi, although not Florence, was the centerpiece to the Italian North African empire. And there certainly were hoary relics from past epochs dotting the coast, the remains of Roman antiquity, such as Lepcis Magna. The claim is made that the ideological baggage was left on the docks of Europe when the troops departed for North Africa, but that is a point proven more often by its repetition than by any objective evidence.

Nonetheless, a prevailing belief surfaced that desert battles could be fought on their own, perhaps unique, terms across the sweeping sands and that the killing, so massive and arbitrary in Europe, was confined and made more endurable, a little more honorable, for its alleged avoidance of the innocent. The soldiers were recast as a carefree, jolly lot, racing about in a variety of vehicles, looking like so many sand-borne pirates than regular troops. The photos of the young warriors—affecting a variety of hats, often sporting beards, frequently shirtless, wearing only shorts and boots—smile out at us in silent confirmation of what we want to believe: Desert warfare was a lark, a great dashing adventure, filled with danger, even death; but maybe the desert was a better place to die than the mud of France.

The Rommel legend emerged from this mélange, a blend of truth and myth. He was the enemy but the way he conducted himself fit the stereotypical image of the honorable warrior, the teutonic knight, amidst the Nazi horror and degradation. Rommel reconfirmed, within the framework of a new war against an old enemy, a belief system about the nobility of war that had drowned in the blood of World War I and its nihilistic aftermath. That Rommel became the focus of such legend building is not surprising. His quick intelligence and tactical sense, his command flexibility, and his ability to integrate his weaponry—armor, infantry, artillery, and air power—contrasted sharply with the inept war carried out by the Italians and against which O'Connor's command so swiftly and successfully reacted. Moreover, isolated from Europe, Rommel's campaign was carefully watched because the North African desert was the only place where the British and German armies were fighting. In that isolated, desolate arena, he audaciously tweaked the noses of his superiors by launching a major campaign, an unheard-of behavior in a society that demanded great conformity, overrode the local Italian command and, in the process, endeared himself to his enemies.

Rommel was responsible for shaping much contemporary popular and scholarly thinking about the nature of desert battle. That is why I start this study with his first advance into Cyrenaica. Not surprisingly, and whatever is said in this study notwithstanding, many of our subsequent judgments of desert battle may still be measured against the model he provided, whether that model be legend or truth.

BEYOND LEGEND

My purpose in exploring the Rommel legend is not to excoriate him. Rather, it is to demonstrate the way fact and fancy are sometimes confused, as if floating in a desert mirage. More practically, Rommel's initial campaign also provides a kind of case study, familiar enough, by which to finally identify the common elements of desert battle.

One constant in Rommel's campaign and the British reaction to it that needs immediate recognition is the desert itself. It provided nothing but the playing field, all the more cruel for its unrelenting and objective character. The desert neither loved nor hated. But it could never be taken for granted. The implicit invitation it offered was the illusion of unlimited mobile warfare. The reality was overextended supply lines, a surface that savaged vehicles, and the certain knowledge that nothing moved without fuel and no one moved without water. This was not an ideal arena for war because, paramount among all the other battle elements, human error was magnified. In any war, judgment is only as good as the intelligence system that feeds it. In desert warfare, that problem expands exponentially. Information pours into a center. A tank column moves here, an infantry unit digs in there. Planes are seen here, there, and then everywhere. Each facet must be organized, sifted, and judged. In an era before digital computers, the buildup of information could be very rapid but its evaluation very slow. Errors were made—constantly. Thus, the British were surprised at the rapidity of Rommel's attack, fully a month before it was expected. Likewise, Rommel was taken off-guard, by Operation Crusader when, in November 1941, Claude Auchinleck fought him to a standstill. Why did Rommel or Beresford-Preise or Auchinleck make the assumptions they did? Could tanks destroy tanks? Were frontal attacks viable? What accumulated knowledge of desert warfare did these men inherit? Or did each start from scratch, trapped by a technology never before tested in the desert? But there is more to understanding desert battle than the recitation of technological changes. There is also a human side. Fighting is bad enough but to fight in a desert, without any place to hide, using constantly upgraded, ever more sophisticated weapons, must take a unique toll on the human spirit.

These questions and issues take us to the historical perspective of this study. Beginning with Rommel, as it were, in the middle of things, we move away from him in both directions. First, we shall go back in time to Napoleon's Egyptian campaign, then move to India's Northwest Frontier between 1849 and 1852, and on to the British Mesopotamian campaign of 1916 to 1917. We reach the Western

Desert in 1940 and the campaign that brought Rommel on stage. The Arab-Israeli War of 1973 demonstrates post–World War II developments, and the Gulf War illustrates contemporary trends.

Before addressing these campaigns, we would do well to have some understanding of the desert environment by first reviewing some general features of deserts and second by looking specifically at the desert regions represented by the campaigns to be studied. In short, deserts are the physical context of battle, and whether soldier, student, or scholar, we must come to terms with them.

CHAPTER 2

Deserts:
The Physical Context of Battle

MIRAGES

Intellectual curiosity and honesty urge the conclusion that the desert is not a pure arena for war. This argument has been pursued by Bryan Perrett in his *Desert Warfare*, about the only readily available survey, and in various chapters in *Armoured Warfare* by J. P Harris and E. N. Toase. Viewing deserts as vacant ground simply feeds a legend. I suggest that in images of desert battle the picture should be less that of Rommel dashing about in his *kübelwagen*, desert goggles around his neck, than the omnipresence of the desert itself. The desert is the common enemy of all who march upon it. The sensible alternatives are to embrace the desert or get out as soon as possible. The armies described in this study, unable or unwilling to choose between those alternatives, fought in deserts anyway.

Sand, sand, and more sand! The young American soldiers and marines who went to Saudi Arabia as part of Operation Desert Shield in 1990 stood in awe of the thousands of square miles of nothingness. Sand—in every crevice of clothing, in eyes, boots, and food, in fuel filters, gun breaches, and helicopter rotors. And with the sand comes great heat, climbing to 125°F in the afternoon—throbbing head, aching eyes, skin turning to inflamed parchment. Nothing metallic can be touched with bare hands, and even heavy fabric, like canvas, is too hot to touch. With the heat comes a great need for water. As A. Leopold tells us, an average adult will lose a quart of salty water during a hot desert morning. By midafternoon, he will have lost about eighteen pounds and will feel weak. By nightfall he will be dead. Even with a water allotment of one gallon a day, he will be dead in a week. But the average adult of Leopold's scenario is probably unprepared for desert activity. Prepared or not, there is no escaping the flies. Any waste, however small, be it human waste, kitchen garbage, or a dead animal, will attract huge swarms. Wounds must be covered or they will be crawling with maggots. Sand and heat, seemingly aseptic, spawn ugly creations of their own.

Exceptions to Leopold's grim analysis can be made for many military operations. Soldiers are usually in good physical condition, often have time to acclimatize, and may be fortunate enough to have additional time to train for desert battle. At that, an army may still not be equipped for the task because the unforgiving environment skews even the best plan. The scene turns horrific: A column of French Foreign Legion infantry marches across a sand sea, each step tracked by the merciless sun. The men carry monumental backpacks because everything they need for survival must be brought with them. Their greatcoats are buttoned back from their knees to make walking easier, and sun flaps at the back of their white *kepis* help guard against sunstroke. But nothing can protect them from the stirring sand. It moves in riffles at first but soon is whipped into great billowing yellow clouds. The sergeant orders the men to kneel and keep shifting about to prevent them from being buried alive by the *khaseem*, the sandstorm. But one soldier leaps to his feet, screaming curses and loading his rifle. The sergeant orders him to kneel but the man lunges at him. The sergeant fires a bullet into his head. *Cafard*, the desert madness, has taken the soldier. The storm subsides. The column moves on. March or die.

Is this scenario the product of a film-fed imagination, or did it really happen? Both. The scene and so many like it are cinematographic clichés of desert fighting. Films such as the *Lost Patrol* (1934), *The Thirteen* (1937), *Nine Men* (1943), and three versions of *Beau Geste* (reprised on television), have created the cliché. But Percival Christopher Wren, who wrote *Beau Geste*, told his readers in 1926 that his characters and the incidents in his novels of life in the Foreign Legion were fact based and yes, the sergeant did shoot the desert-maddened soldier.

The point of this exercise, which nears self-indulgence, is to demonstrate that there is a fine line between reality and imagination when trying to understand desert battle, a line as ephemeral as a mirage. Events and forms of human interaction are magnified, exemplified by the Rommel legend. But the smallest things taken for granted in conventional situations suddenly become vitally important. John Strawson, in *The Battle for North Africa*, quoted some rules, taken from the notes of an Indian Army officer, for getting along in the Western Desert. Among the correct behaviors listed were that a cup of tea offered a stranger is always good form and that one must be courteous and hospitable to all (something the Arabs understood for hundreds of years). One must never do anything to endanger another, such as using his slit trench. No messes can be left about lest they attract flies. One can complain about his own officers, but never about another's. The list was lengthy, its purpose to remind the soldier that the desert lacks those familiar signposts by which European-based peoples guide human conduct. Military life is filled with enough discontinuities from normal civilian behavior. Place soldiers in a desert where civilization is nowhere to be seen, and the attention to behavioral detail becomes crucial for survival. It is ignored at the soldier's peril.

Fortunately, most of us have never been in a battle of any kind, much less a desert battle. If, however, we are to discover the reality of desert battle, we must first find the reality of deserts.

DESERTS: A SYNOPSIS

Nearly 20 percent of the earth is covered by deserts. One string of deserts runs along the tropic of Capricorn. This group includes the lava deserts of Chile and the Patagonian deserts, the Namib and Kalihari in southern Africa, and the Great Australian Desert. Around the Tropic of Cancer are the Sahara and Arabian deserts. The Arabian links with the Iranian and Indian deserts further east. To the northeast is the Turkestan Desert. Branching out from all these locations are near-desert conditions. There are also some exceptional desert regions beyond these belts, such as the Mongolian Desert and those of the American Southwest and Southern California.

The common thread among all deserts is their aridity. They receive less than ten inches of annual rainfall. The Sahara is the largest of them all—3.5 million square miles, with an annual rainfall of less than an inch. The Arabian Desert is a million square miles of sand and is the only desert without a river flowing through it or a mountain watershed.

There are also polar deserts, Antarctica and the Arctica being the most obvious. Although covered with ice and snow, their aridity results from lack of rainfall and very low temperatures. Consequently, water in a usable form is scarce. There are also high mountain deserts where, in extremity, altitude and subzero temperatures produce similar conditions to those in the polar ice caps. Parts of the Sierra Nevada Mountains in California above the 12,000-foot level, parts of the Rocky Mountains into New Mexico and Arizona, and the Hindu Kush in northern Pakistan exemplify high mountain deserts.

The campaigns discussed in this study took place in three different desert or near-desert regions: The northern Sahara from the Nile to the Gulf of Sidra, and east of the Suez to the Sinai; India's (now Pakistan's) Northwest Frontier; and Lower Mesopotamia to the Persian Gulf. Each of these regions has their own geographical and climatic peculiarities that influenced the military operations that ranged over them.

The Sahara: The Western Desert and Cyrenaica
The northern Sahara is conveniently subdivided into the Western Desert, extending from the Nile to the Libyan border; Cyrenaica, or eastern Libya; Tripolitania, or western Libya; and on into Tunisia, Algeria, and Morocco. Three campaigns discussed in this study took place in the eastern regions. Napoleon arrived in Egypt in 1798, taking Cairo, then moving north toward Syria and south up the Nile. Mussolini decided in 1940 to invade Egypt. The British then mounted a counterattack that ranged across the Western Desert and ended with the conquest of Cyrenaica. That is when Rommel entered the picture.

The Mediterranean rim of the Sahara from Egypt into Cyrenaica has a narrow coastal belt along which are most of the water wells and several towns, a few with good ports. In 1940, few roads existed, and they varied in quality from poor to nothing more than sand tracks. Even though the hottest Saharan temperature ever recorded was 136°F in 1922 at Al Aziziya, just south of Tripoli, the summer temperatures along the coastal belt, hot by northern European standards, are bearable, from 90°F in Egypt to 100°F in Libya. Rainfall also varies along the coastal belt, from ten inches through much of the area to as much as twenty inches around Benghazi on the Gulf of Sidra.

Paralleling the coastal belt is a long escarpment, with elevations from 300 to 500 feet. Halfaya Pass, just inside the Egyptian border, is the major passageway east from Libya. Behind the escarpment in Egypt is the Qattara Depression, a great hole in the ground, ranging in depth from -70 feet below sea level to -234 feet. It zigzags its way behind El Alamein in the east, where it is about twenty miles inland, to seventy miles inland from Mersa Matruh in the west. Behind the escarpment is a plateau. Surfaces vary from fine sand to clay to pebbles and small boulders.

Beyond the plateau are the vast Egyptian and Libyan sand seas, the latter not on any maps until World War II. Sand dunes, always moving, vary in elevation from 300 feet to 600 feet, forming a great natural barrier to the interior. The British found they could cut through the dunes in only a few places and then only for a short time because the tracks disintegrated under the weight of their vehicles. The plateau and sand seas get very hot, reaching 125°F. Rain, when it does fall, usually evaporates before hitting the ground.

The deadly interior climate with its difficult terrain ordained that most battles would be fought along the coastal belt. Necessarily then, as mobility increased, military planners had to contend with that restricted space and narrow front, rethinking tactics and the feasibility of wide flanking maneuvers. No one could enter the interior deserts, away from water resources and logistical support, without very special preparations and men trained to the task. Anything short of that was suicide.

East of the Nile and the Suez is the great shoulder of the Arabian Desert. Part of this is the Sinai Peninsula over which the modern Egyptians and Israelis have battled since the latter nation was formed in 1948. Barren, with mountains ranging up to 8,000 feet, its value is more strategic than economic.

The Northwest Frontier

The exact boundaries of the Northwest Frontier are always disputed. For our purposes, it should be known that the Frontier is shaped by an enormous mountain rim that begins west of Peshawar at the Khyber Pass, leading into Afghanistan through the Sufed Koh range. These mountains extend northerly to the Hindu Kush mountains which, in turn, join the western Himalayas. That juncture forms the

Pamir Knot, 36,000 miles of barren peaks, whose average elevation is 14,000 feet, though individual mountains such as K-2 exceed 25,000 feet. Smaller mountain chains, with peaks gradually descending to as low as 1,000 feet, form valleys as they run in a southerly direction. Sprawling south from the low mountains is the Peshawar Plain. In 1850, it was not an especially fertile area and was the battleground for many Anglo-tribal wars.

The Swat Valley is above the Peshawar Plain. Anyone visiting Swat today would not find a desert. Indeed, it is more akin to a mountain retreat, tempting tourists with its great beauty and modern amenities. Much of this alpine idyll did not exist in the nineteenth century. Swat is subdivided and separated from the Punjab to the south by three barriers. The most southerly is the Kabul River, which flows east from Afghanistan across the Peshawar Plain and joins the Indus River. The second barrier is a low mountain chain some thirty miles north of the Kabul River. Four passes cut through the chain, the most important being the Malakand. The third barrier, a few miles farther north, is the Swat river, tumbling from the Hindu Kush, its 200-mile length flowing south, then radically turning east to join the Kabul near Charsadda.

The Swat Valley is a land of vivid contrasts. Snow covers much of the northern area in winter, bringing temperatures into the 10°F to 30°F range. Snow falls in the lower valley only a few times a year. Light fogs are more persistent. During the hot season, from April to October, temperature in the lower valley often reaches 90°F In many places it can soar to 120°F, an extreme that is characteristic of deserts. The annual rainfall in the north is above thirty inches. In the lower valley and across the Peshawar Plain the average is closer to ten inches, but in some years the rainfall is much less because storms completely bypass the area, creating conditions of extreme aridity.

Most agriculture in the lower valley and the Peshawar Plain was, in the 1850s, confined to the river banks and along the crude canals dug through the tough, rocky soil. The villagers herded animals and grew corn, rice, and wheat. Thus, the lands adjacent to the Swat and Kabul rivers were much like the Nile Valley and its delta, as it were so many green ribbons run out along the valley floor. However, farming was not consistently bountiful because, in dry years, crop failures were frequent. That forced the tribes to find other ways of subsisting in the rough, ragged, rock-strewn mountains that abruptly thrust from the valley and which in the mid-nineteenth century offered only danger to the unwary.

The Mohmand, Yusafzai, Utman-Khel, and Sam (plains) Ranizai tribes—all Sunni Muslims—were among the most important in the lower Swat Valley. They often supplemented their mean agricultural livelihood by charging across the Peshawar Plain and raiding villages to the south. The Sikhs, whose Punjab kingdom eventually bordered the Frontier, battled the tribes sporadically but cared little about the raids as long as they continued to receive taxes. The British arrived in 1849, established a new system of regional protection, and battled the tribes for a hundred years.

The British were faced with two main problems along the Frontier: first, how to survive in the near-desert environment and, second, how to develop successful tactics. These problems were compounded by the fact that few British knew anything about the Northwest Frontier, much less about Swat. Yet, they marched north from Peshawar into that uncharted land over narrow and broken tracks against a people who were shadows in the landscape.

Mesopotamia: The Road to Baghdad

Lower Mesopotamia, the region between the Tigris and Euphrates rivers south of Baghdad, is our third geographical area and the setting for two examples of desert war. The first was the British campaign in 1916 and 1917 of General Stanley Maude against the Turks, and the second was the Gulf War of 1991.

To use Lower Mesopotamia as a place for desert war may seem a contradiction because those familiar with ancient history know the region as the birthplace of such civilizations as Sumer, Babylon, and Assyria. Yet their great accomplishments withered and died. The Turks finally took over the region, ruling until the end of World War I. The river plain gradually degenerated from a vast park, as it was once described, into a desert.

Agriculture in ancient Mesopotamia, as in the Nile Valley and Swat, was made possible by the two rivers and the irrigation canals extending from them. That is still true today. But in 1914, the canals were in severe disrepair. Also, because most of the land between the rivers is below sea level, dikes called bunds were built to control the rivers, which swelled with water in March and again in April from the melting snows of the northern mountains. Unfortunately, the bunds were not maintained, breaks regularly occurred, and 10,000 square miles of land flooded, turning the compacted soil into a glue-like ooze.

Annual rainfall, averaging 6.5 inches, arrives in sporadic and violent downpours between October and April. Dry river beds, called *nullahs* from Mesopotamia to India, fill rapidly, overflow, and rush away to nowhere or feed the marshes that are not far from the rivers. Snow often arrives in December, and snow showers and temperatures below freezing last into February. April to October is the hot season, just as in Swat. Temperatures can climb to a steady 100°F At Amara on the Tigris River during the British campaign of early 1916, the temperature was 110°F in the shade and 120°F in the full sun. The intense heat is generated by two adjoining deserts. Southwest of the Euphrates River is the shoulder of the Arabian Desert. Winds blowing across its sands continue into Lower Mesopotamia, carrying heat and dust. East winds blowing across the Iranian desert also carry heat into the region.

Annual flooding, a collapsed irrigation system, and poor drainage created excessive salinization in three-quarters of the land. Thus occurred further reduction of crop-growing capacity, and these conditions also contributed to the desert effects.

The expeditionary force from India that landed in Lower Mesopotamia in 1915, much like their forebearers on the Northwest Frontier, knew nothing about the region, lacked reliable maps, and were ill equipped to fight a sustained campaign in the difficult environment. They, too, paid for their ignorance.

By the time of the Gulf War in 1991, high technology weapons were commonplace. Many so-called experts assumed these weapons would neutralize the impact of the desert on battle or, conversely, that the desert would choke the weapons into obsolescence. Thus, the western armies, bristling with untried arsenals, had to adapt to the desert just as all those who went before.

WHO FIGHTS IN DESERTS?

Who, indeed, fights in deserts? One might think it so overwhelming that it calls only for a lunatic fringe. Fortunately, Bryan Perrett leads us toward a more definitive answer in his book *Desert Warfare*, in which he notes that there are two main types of military operations.

The first type of desert warfare is low intensity confrontations between regular army troops and guerrilla warriors, exemplified by the fighting between the French Foreign Legion and the tribes of Algeria and Morocco. Such actions are characterized by guerrilla raids, ambushes, and hit-and-run fights. The guerrillas, realizing they cannot match the firepower of the regulars, resort to such small unit actions. The hope is that this kind of fighting will wear down the regulars and force a political resolution or cause them to retire altogether.

The fighting can go on for years because, able to confront only small groups, the regulars have little opportunity for a decisive, victory. Then, impatient, frustrated by insubstantial results costing substantial manpower, money, and supplies, and usually under enormous political pressure to achieve a meaningful victory, the regulars resort to extramilitary sanctions against the native population. This barbaric behavior is rationalized by the belief that the regulars cannot distinguish between a guerrilla and a true civilian. Sanctions may include burning villages, mass internment of civilians, and bribery and torture as means of extracting needed information. Sometimes outright murder is used as the ultimate weapon of state terrorism. The guerrillas often retaliate in kind. The situation in Algeria, for example, escalated into a general revolt against French rule in 1954. An estimated 25,000 guerrillas took up arms against a half-million French regulars. The war dragged on as the guerrillas blew up convoys, ambushed military columns, destroyed communications centers, cut roads and bridges, and murdered key French officials. The regulars also committed terrorist acts against the native population, particularly kidnapping, torture, and murder. The end came in 1962 with Algerian independence.

The second form of desert war is between large regular forces. The ancient Egyptians, Assyrians, Persians, Greeks, and the Romans all fought their share of desert battles. Medieval European armies marched against Muslim armies in Judea in a series of wars called the Crusades, using weapons and tactics not much different from those used in ancient times. Swords, bows and arrows, catapults, and battering rams were some of the common hardware.

Armored war in the desert surfaced during World War I when the British fought the Turks in Lower Mesopotamia, in Gaza, and in Palestine, finally taking Jerusalem. In World War II, the British fought across North Africa against the Italians and the Germans. After the war, continuous fighting erupted between the newly founded Israel and its Arab neighbors, particularly Egypt and Syria. A war between Iraq and Iran consumed most of the 1980s. In 1990, Iraq took Kuwait, precipitating the Gulf War. With each conflict, the technology of war became more sophisticated and efficient, exemplified by the obvious development of aircraft from World War I open frame putt-putts that could barely make 80 mph to late twentieth-century supersonic jets that deliver weapons systems more powerful than a World War II battleship.

Perrett's distinction between low intensity and high intensity confrontations is useful within limits, for it tells us the types of armies that have engaged in desert warfare. It does not, however, tell us why they chose to do their fighting in the desert. 1 think there are three principal reasons.

First, desert warfare belongs primarily to people who live in deserts. Once again, the notion that deserts are empty environments is a fiction. The people most associated with deserts are the Arabs, and their clan and tribal warfare across North Africa and into the Middle East is as ancient as their presence. By modern standards, their intramural conflicts were in the class of Perrett's small-scale confrontations, mostly along the lines of guerrilla warfare, and were technologically low grade. But as the twentieth century unfolded, as populations grew, as cities developed in the sands—all made possible by modern transportation and trade and by industrial and petrochemical exploitation—and as nation-states emerged in these regions to supplant tribal loyalties, regular armies were founded that possessed destructive capacities equal to those of any European power. These massive changes created circumstances in which tribal ethics of patient revenge, of an eye-for-an-eye, were subsumed within nationalistic ideologies related to state security. Thus, there was an apparently endless cycle of conflict-reprisal-conflict in the Middle East, exemplified by the Arab-Israeli conflicts, the Iran-Iraq war, and Iraq's invasion of Kuwait.

Second, desert warfare often followed the course of empire. Historically, a European power needed the natural resources, usually oil,
in lands on which desert nomads grazed their flocks. Or the European power needed harbors and military installations along patches of
desert coastline. Or perhaps the European nation wished to enhance
its prestige among other imperialistic nations by grabbing what available lands were left—and deserts were usually last on the list of desir-
able colonies. For instance, Britain decided before World War I to
shift from coal- to oil-driven naval vessels. That placed their interests
in the Persian Gulf, influencing imperial policy during and after the
war and sending British troops into the deserts of the Middle East and
the Horn of Africa. The French took Algeria, among other reasons, to
secure their southern flank in the Mediterranean and rationalized the
conquest by making the territory part of metropolitan France. Therefore, any native anti-French sentiments were not merely ingratitude,
they were outright subversion. The Italians simply grabbed what they
could—Libya and Italian Somaliland.

In the end, the imperial nation might be granted a measure of
prestige in European corridors of power by conquering a stretch of
sand. If that was not sufficient, as in the example of the Italians, who
were thought to be second-raters among colonial powers, they could
always use their existing territories as excuses to further extend their
imperial ambitions. Thus, Italy held two separated regions, Libya and
Somalia. The Italians then broadcast that it was their destiny, or at
least Mussolini's, to link the territories by taking Ethiopia (Abyssinia).

The European powers, to their eternal shame, never asked the
native populations how they felt about becoming subjects of faraway,
strange, and sometimes not very benevolent masters. The Italians'
behavior toward the Libyan Arabs was inhuman, and their treatment
of Ethiopian natives was, if possible, worse. And the French shot the
Riffs whenever possible in the same way the British chased after the
Frontier hill tribes. The United States, not to be left out, expanded
into the southwest deserts, where any dead Indian was a good one.

There were squeaks of moral indignation by other colonial powers but, in the end, they came to nothing because no one really cared
lest the moral microscope be focused on them. Anyway, so went the
hushed excuse, the recipients of the abuse, only ignorant savages,

were a long way from the real power centers. In some instances, as the Senussi in Libya, the Riffs in Algeria, the Ethiopians, and the Mohmands of the Northwest Frontier, the natives fought back in savage guerrilla wars.

The third reason for engaging in desert warfare is perceived strategic necessity. This theme has three variations.

First, the perception of strategic necessity may be the result of logical military requirements exemplified by the British move into Lower Mesopotamia in 1915 to secure their oil interests and to curb German expansion toward the Mediterranean. Unfortunately, the logic of that move was soon forsaken, as we shall see, in favor of unanticipated goals that skewed the entire campaign.

Second, strategic necessity can also emerge unexpectedly, a consequence of unforeseen circumstances. When the British conquered the Punjab in 1849, they rubbed against the borders of the Northwest Frontier, unintentionally committing themselves to warfare against neighboring tribes. Frontier defense, as such, became a much larger strategic necessity in 1915, when the Indian Army found itself initially responsible for the Mesopotamian campaign. The Indian viceroy complained that a continual withdrawal of troops from India would weaken the Frontier, spawning massive revolt among the hill tribes and that movement would spread south, inflaming Indian nationalism and a reprise of the Great Mutiny of 1857. Thus, the very security of India was at risk.

Third, strategic necessity may be not a military fact but an idea more important for its symbolic value. Rommel's arrival in North Africa was predicated on the simple premise that he was to stop a further British advance toward Tripoli and support Italian colonialism. But his rapid advance against the British escalated the war in Cyrenaica and the Western Desert to new heights unanticipated by both the British and German leaders, making out of the campaign an event more immediately important for its symbolic than military value. For a case could be made that North Africa was an early World War II distraction, consuming men and supplies at a rate greater than the product of any victory.

The campaigns chosen for this study demonstrate why different nations at various periods fought in deserts; hence the interest in political motivations. But whether they were digging for oil or planting a flag is less important to this study than the manner in which they fought their battles. Necessarily, the examples illustrate changes in war technology and how that technology did and did not work under desert battle conditions. However, it would be remiss to think that the development of desert battle is simply a study of machinery in the sand. Also to be considered is the impact of desert battle on the men who did the fighting. This human element, to what extent a constant or a variable remains to be seen, is central to understanding the development of desert battle.

CHAPTER 3

Bonaparte in Egypt, 1798 to 1799

A PRIVATE LITTLE WAR
The General in Control

Napoleon Bonaparte, a major general at age twenty-eight, sequestered himself at home in the Rue de la Victoire during the spring of 1798, planning a campaign in Egypt. The Directory, France's ruling body, gave its blessing to the expedition on 5 March and backed it with a grant of 4.5 million francs, funds looted from the city treasury at Berne, Switzerland. Of course, the Directory required that Bonaparte provide them with an accounting of how he spent the money. The young general adamantly refused and also slammed the door on the Directory's stipulation that their commissioners oversee the expedition. Bonaparte chose his own senior officers, the troops he needed, and was given a fleet of naval vessels, including thirteen ships-of-the-line (the sailing ship equivalent of battleships), to escort his convoy of 200 transports.

How could a man so young be so disdainful of the government he was sworn to serve? How could he ignore the War Ministry and plan the campaign in his own house? Why did the government acquiesce to his demands? What conditions made this near-private adventure possible? Even though there was nothing very mystical about it all, the answers to these questions are quite as fascinating as the expedition.

Bonaparte trained his eye on the Egyptian prize in 1797. The Directory offered him command of the army at the English Channel but, when they could not secure a loan to finance the invasion, he refused the position. Instead, he resurrected an old Royalist idea to strike at Egypt. The Directory was captivated by the concept. Such an expedition would be a major distraction to the British, the only country still at war with the Republic, by causing havoc in the Turkish Ottoman Empire, upsetting the Middle Eastern power balance, and perhaps bringing the Russians into the arena. These disruptions would place Bonaparte in a position to threaten British India—Bonaparte's suggestion that he could lead his army there was not entirely foolish. Why, a canal might be dug between the Mediterranean and the Gulf of Suez, making the march an even greater triumph. Having conquered Egypt, and perhaps beyond, Bonaparte would then return to France, assume command of the Channel army, and invade England. Or so he let the Directory believe. He was rapidly developing his own agenda.

If Bonaparte was dissembling, so too was the Directory. These men may have been unimaginative lawyers, gray little bureaucrats, but they were not stupid. Bluntly put, they wanted Bonaparte as far from Paris as possible. Egypt was a good place. For Bonaparte was a visible and tangible threat. In 1797, he had concluded a brilliant Italian campaign. Paris stood in awe of the man. Whenever he appeared in the streets, cheering crowds gathered about him, the quintessential Republican general. From humble circumstances, he served the revolution, rose through the ranks, and brought victory and glory to the Republic. Not an imposing figure by any measure—rather sparse in those days, unkempt, his sword dangling awkwardly at his side—he nonetheless exuded ability and power. He was indeed the charismatic leader on the ascendance—and the Directory was afraid of him.

If the Directory tried to distance him from Paris, the National Institute welcomed him. In electing him a member, these artists, poets, writers, scientists, and scholars found in Bonaparte a man of outward intellect who, in discussing Egypt, welcomed his fellow members as part of the enterprise, offering them a page, or at least a footnote, in history. They were to be the modern explorers of an ancient civilization, revealing its secrets and reshaping history. As Alan Moorehead clearly states in his *Blue Nile*, the Institute became "another corps of cadets following young Caesar into battle" (64).

In truth, the Directory could not have stopped Bonaparte. By 1797, the French army was a power unto itself, the Directory impotent against its generals. As Jean-Paul Bertaud points out in his excellent study *The Army of the French Revolution*, the separation of the army from state authority began in 1795 in a legalistic manner. A law was passed that changed the composition of courts martial proceedings, replacing civilian judges with military men. The generals were still not satisfied because the juries retained enlisted men. The end result was that each division within the army established its own military tribunals composed entirely of officers.

There was more. Closet Royalists were making political inroads. Fearing for their own safety, the Directory purged the ranks of civil commissioners appointed to oversee army operations lest some Royalists be among them. That pleased the generals, who never particularly liked the men sent to spy on them. Henceforth, generals were free to loot conquered territories as they wished and use any confiscated gold in any manner they judged necessary. They were also empowered to offer and to accept peace terms with defeated governments.

As Bertaud concludes, the army was now entirely in the hands of the generals. The door was open for Bonaparte's ascendancy to power. He but needed to extend the reputation he gained in Italy. Egypt was the means he chose.

The French Army of Egypt: A Background

Bonaparte's force, as Moorehead notes, was led mostly by officers whom he had appointed or promoted and composed of veterans of various Republican wars, many from the Italian campaign. That they were, generals and soldiers alike, scattered about France and Italy was of little concern to Bonaparte. He sent out a flurry of orders from his home, putting troops in motion and placing his generals in key embarkation points.

One of the earliest recruits to the Egyptian plan was Louis Desaix. He did not serve under Bonaparte in Italy but met him there in 1797 while on a tour. Bonaparte discussed the proposal with the young general—he was only a year older than Bonaparte—and was impressed with his insights. In early 1798, Desaix was with the Army of the Rhine. Signing on with Bonaparte meant he would only command a division but, convinced that Bonaparte would achieve so much glory that some of it was bound to reflect on his generals, he did not mind.

Among the thirty-one generals serving in Egypt, several earned high honors and the confidence of Bonaparte and would serve him loyally in the empire to follow. One of these was Andache Junot, age twenty-seven. He was with Bonaparte at the siege of Toulon and then was an aide-de-camp during the Italian campaign. Another was Jean Lannes, age twenty-nine, who started life as a dyer's apprentice but found a new life in the Revolutionary army. During the Spanish War of 1793-94, he rose to brigadier general. Two years later he was out of the army, considered redundant under army reforms. He re-enlisted for the Italian campaign and became a colonel in time for the Battle at Lodi and, at Mantua, was a brigadier once again. Never brilliant, he was a journeyman soldier and commanded a brigade in Egypt. Joachim Murat, an innkeeper's son, was age thirty-one in 1798. He had enlisted in the royal cavalry, turning his back on church law studies, but was dismissed from the army in 1790 for insubordination. Through political influence, he was back in the army in 1795, assigned to the new Constitutional Guard of Louis XVI. He first met Bonaparte in 1795 and joined him as an aide-de-camp in Italy. Three years later, Murat was commander of the Rome garrison but left that post to join the Egyptian expedition as a division commander.

And so the list continued: Jean-Baptiste Kléber, at forty-five one of the older generals, did not really like Bonaparte but came out of early retirement to accept a post as a division commander; Pierre Berthier, also forty-five, was a workaholic and detail man who proved himself an indispensable chief of staff in Italy; Louis-André Bon, another division commander, also served in Italy; and ex-baron Jacques Menou, a maverick under both Royalist and Revolutionary banners, went to Egypt as a division commander, converted to Islam, and married a bathhouse owner's daughter. These were officers whom Bonaparte knew and trusted. He cared less about whether they were gentlemen in the Wellingtonian sense, or whether they had served in the royal army—in fact, twenty-seven of them had. He accepted them for their achievements. They won battles. In Egypt, facing a strange culture in a strange environment, he needed every advantage.

As early as the Italian campaign, Bonaparte willfully, one might even say cynically, laid the foundations of the self-anointed charisma that later emerged as a full-blown cult of personality. As Bertaud tells us, Bonaparte published two intra-army newspapers that informed his soldiers of their leader's diplomatic skills, as well as dropping the latest gossip, as it were *nouvelles brèves d'Armée*, to snake the troops believe they shared information few others possessed. Additionally, battalion letterheads were redesigned to feature Bonaparte, thus symbolically attaching the army to him rather than to the French state. Regimental flags were also redesigned, all with the same color scheme but with individual regimental numbers emblazoned on each together with an appropriate Napoleonic motto. All these calculated gestures created an esprit de corps among the troops, etching in their minds the source of their shared glory—Napoleon Bonaparte. Thus, he widened the gulf between army and government, whose instrument it was supposed to be. And the point of it all? The troops gathered for the Egyptian campaign did not rally to the call of France. They heard Bonaparte's voice and rallied to him.

The Egyptian expeditionary force numbered 36,000 army men. There were eleven demi-brigades of infantry and four of light infantry. Three thousand artillerymen manned 171 guns. Each gun was supplied 300 rounds of shot. Six cavalry regiments were included, but they experienced difficulties getting a sufficient number of horses ashore in Egypt. Nearly 1,000 noncombatants accompanied the army, their numbers so few because, in a moment of prescience, Bonaparte decided the army would probably have to live off the Egyptian economy; therefore, he did not need much of a commissariat. The largest part of the force was, then, infantry. And an infantry army it remained.

The French army from which the expeditionary force was formed, Bertaud notes, underwent significant changes from early Revolutionary days. In 1789, the army was composed of soldiers from the Royalist army and volunteers. In 1798, former Royalist soldiers comprised only 3.3 percent and old volunteers 18.2 percent of the rolls. Fully one-third of the army were draftees from 1793. In aggregate, over half the army was made up of hardened veterans. Bonaparte's Army of Italy was arguably the most experienced. The Revolutionary mass army was gradually replaced with divisions that had regional identities, but were soon replaced by a battalion and demi-brigade organization that dispensed with regionalism in favor of a truly national army. French army officers were typically young men, the generals averaging age thirty-eight. Their youth and vitality represented all that was thought good in the young Republic. Bertaud sampled the records of more than a thousand officers from infantry demi-brigades and found that over 64 percent within each rank of captain, lieutenant, and sublieutenant were under age thirty-five. Yet, he also discovered that within the Army of Egypt 18 percent of the sublieutenants were between ages forty and fifty. It is interesting to speculate on this apparent anomaly. Was there something peculiar or special about the units in Egypt, or were these men veteran noncommissioned officers rewarded with commissions? But such questions fail to address the issue of what it was that was peculiar or special about them. To understand, we will have to know more about those units and individual officers.

Bonaparte knew the value of having about him officers and men he trusted, and among whom there existed a strong camaraderie. Battalions and demi-brigades had fought side-by-side and knew what to expect from one another. That familiarity gave the army great confidence.

But to think that one and all marched to the docks arm in arm, singing Republican songs under banners declaring noble thoughts is so much romantic folly. Most of the officers and men knew only that they were going abroad. They had marched about Europe—Spain, the Rhineland, Italy—without hesitation, defending their homeland. A sea voyage meant real distance from home and suggested great unknowns. The soldiers' morale, as J. C. Herold tells us, in *Bonaparte in Egypt*, was already low from not being paid at the same time the generals' handpicked commissioners lived in luxury produced by illegal activities that somehow never were reported. For many, the march into the unknown of overseas service was the limit of their loyalty. Desertions skyrocketed. Herold wryly concludes that if the rest of the men had known where they were going and what they would have had to endure once there, they too would have deserted.

EGYPT IN 1798: THE CONTEXT OF THE CAMPAIGN

The Nile River flows north from the east central African highlands through the Nubian desert and cuts the long narrow valley that has been the lifeblood of Egypt. The river passes the remains of the once magnificent ancient civilization—Abu Simbel, Luxor, Karnak, the cluster of the Great Pyramids at Giza with, in Bonaparte's time, a great head jutting above the sands, to name only some of the more prominent monuments. Then the river divides above Cairo to form the soil-rich delta that supports endless crops of rice, barley, wheat, cotton, and flax. The rhythm of life established by the river appeared timeless.

. The timelessness is a historical conceit for, as the Egypt of the pharaohs collapsed, outsiders imposed new rhythms upon the old. The most influential if not permanent of those were the Ottoman Turks who conquered the region in 1517, nominally taking over from the Mameluke Turks who controlled Egypt from the mid-thirteenth century. But the Ottomans were less interested in Egypt as a territory than as a source of tax revenues. Consequently, they left the Mamelukes in charge of Egypt's numerous districts, subject only to a Turkish pasha, or provincial governor. By the eighteenth century the pasha was little more than a figurehead and a sometimes useful tool of the Mamelukes.

The Mamelukes were a professional warrior caste, purchased as children by the Turks from their Caucasian peasant parents. They were converted to Islam and trained to fight. Although similar to the famed janissaries, the lives of the Mamelukes were not nearly as ascetic. Many were quite wealthy and possessed large harems. Yet, they failed to routinely sire their own replacements. Infant mortality and the practice among the harem women of aborting to preserve their youthful appearance required the Mamelukes to continue purchasing boys, mostly from southern Russia, Albania, and Greece.

The size of the Mameluke population depends on how they were counted. Moorehead, including dependents in his estimate, indicates there were as many as 100,000. Herold, discounting the dependents, concludes that there were about 10,000 Mameluke warriors in Egypt in 1798. The warriors owed their allegiance to local district princes or beys. Jealousy, jurisdictional disputes, family quarrels, and the sheer love of fighting left Egypt in a state of constant internecine warfare. The Ottoman Turks were in no mood to control it.

As soldiers, the Mamelukes were throwbacks to the Middle Ages. Each man bristled with weapons: knife, mace, axe, scimitar, bow and arrows, spear or lance and, as a concession to modernity, a pair of pistols at his waist and a carbine across his back. They wore large turbans, often decorated with feather clusters, voluminous pantaloons, leather boots and, beneath the upper body apparel, chain mail. Over all were brightly colored light robes. Their wild cavalry charges led more than one observer to write them off as nothing more than bloodthirsty and undisciplined desert butchers. That assessment proved to be too quick and too easy. For all Egypt's agricultural wealth, the 300,000 people who lived in Cairo made the economy work, and it was there that the Mameluke leaders met in councils, called divans, to determine policy. The city's population was cosmopolitan even then. Most Mamelukes and most Turks in Egypt lived there. But so too did Syrians, Jews, Greeks, Russians, Albanians, Armenians, Georgians, and a host of tribal people now lost to memory. This rich social mosaic, like an early-day Singapore, was devoted to profit. It mattered little who one was or where they came from—all bowed before gold. And gold could only be produced by trade. The city was a great bazaar where anything could be bought if the price was right, giving Cairo an exotic, erotic, and downright degenerate character in the shared wisdom of those Europeans who had visited the place and the many Frenchmen who would occupy it. But lurking beneath the smirking condemnations was much misunderstanding of Muslim customs. Doubtless, there was a complete ignorance of those customs within the French army—and not a little guilt for being attracted to them.

Beyond the Nile Valley is the vast Western Desert, the home of the Bedouin Arabs. Only they knew how to live in that barren environment, and interlopers were often murdered and stripped of all their belongings. With Bonaparte's invasion, French stragglers were usually never seen again, and that put fear into the hearts of the survivors of the long marches.

CAIRO IS THE GOAL
First to Alexandria
The French Army of Egypt embarked from Toulon, Genoa, Ajicco on Corsica, and Civitavecchia north of Rome. Bonaparte, most of his troops, his staff, and members of the Institute departed from Toulon on 19 May 1798, sailing into heavy seas.

The British were aware of the military buildup and knew that a fleet was gathered at Toulon. They feared an imminent invasion of England, and if not England then certainly Ireland. The British Royal Navy was utterly bewildered. Lord Horatio Nelson, who commanded the Mediterranean squadron, put in at Naples, where he received word that the French were about to leave Toulon. But the storm into which the French sailed screened their departure. Nelson arrived off Toulon on 27 May. He was too late.

The French fleet went first to Genoa and then to Ajaccio. Sailing to Civitavecchia, they found that Desaix, charged with gathering armaments, and his division had left for Malta. By the time Bonaparte arrived at Malta with the convoy on 9 June, Desaix was already ashore and had skirmished with the Knights of St. John, also known as the Hospitallers. The Knights immediately surrendered. The once unconquerable brotherhood lost all will to resist.

Within six days, Bonaparte dismantled the Order of St. John, expelled most of its members from the island except for the younger French knights whom he volunteered for his own army, looted the treasury of 7 million francs, commandeered 35,000 muskets and some galleys, freed the 600 slaves held by the knights, ordered the Maltese regiment absorbed into his army, ordered all the sons of these soldiers who were over age ten to be made seaman apprentices in his fleet, and garrisoned the island with 3,000 men of his own army.

However much the dismantling of the knightly order may have reflected the anti-Royalist, anti-Catholic ideologies of the French Revolution and the Republic that followed, Malta itself was a key base by which to secure lines of supply and communication along the Mediterranean to Egypt. It was vital if the French fleet was to challenge the Royal Navy's domination of the sea, useful if they decided to keep the Russians bottled up in the Black Sea. The Knights were a minor bother.

Nelson, not finding the French at Toulon, returned to Naples. Correctly assuming that the French were headed for Egypt, he set sail to find them. There then interposed one of those strange moments in history. Nelson's squadron was much faster than the French convoy, which necessarily maintained the speed of the slowest transport. Thus, on the night of 22 June, Nelson sailed right past the French and did not know it. He sped to Alexandria, still thinking the French were ahead of him, but found only an empty harbor. Frustrated and embarrassed, he sailed west to Sicily to discover that the French were not there either. Where were they? Had Nelson waited another hour at Alexandria on 1 July, the French fleet would have sailed into his guns.

Bonaparte found the Egyptians at Alexandria in defensive positions so, not wanting to land under fire or waste time looking for another favorable site, he ordered a landing at Marabut, west of Alexandria. The sea was running high and the wind was up. The troops started ashore around noon. The disembarkation was a mess. Even though the ships of the line formed a protective screen out to sea, the transports within the ring were jumbled together in the rough water. Some were only 800 yards from shore while others were three miles offshore. Without any system, the men piled into pitching boats and made for shore amid rocks, reefs, and through breakers. Some landed in a half hour. Others took eight hours to land. The soldiers who stumbled onto the beaches were drenched and stiff with cold, exhausted and hungry. No supplies were ashore to relieve their distress. No artillery and no cavalry horses were put ashore in the initial landing. Most importantly, there was no water. After fifteen hours, some 6,000 men had landed. Bonaparte, growing impatient by the minute, reviewed the men, organized them into three divisional columns, and marched seven miles to Alexandria.

Bonaparte deployed his troops around the city, placing Menou's division on the east side, Kléber's on the north, and Bon's on the west. Bonaparte did not rest the men but ordered an immediate attack against the city's outer defenses. Without benefit of artillery, the men clambered over the walls, scattering the defenders who fled to the inner city. There was some desultory street fighting but, after three hours, Alexandria was in French hands.

Bonaparte realized he could not stay long in Alexandria. He needed to secure port facilities at the mouth of the Nile and, at the same time, march against Cairo. The success of the campaign depended on speed. The Mamelukes could not be allowed time to react (Map 2).

To the Nile

On 3 July, Desaix marched his division from the outskirts of Alexandria toward the Nile River (Reynier's division soon followed). The objective was the village of El Rahmaniya, forty miles from the sea on the Rosetta fork of the Nile and forty-five miles southeast of Alexandria. Desaix's division of 4,000 men still lacked artillery and cavalry support. They carried a four-day biscuit ration, but no provision was

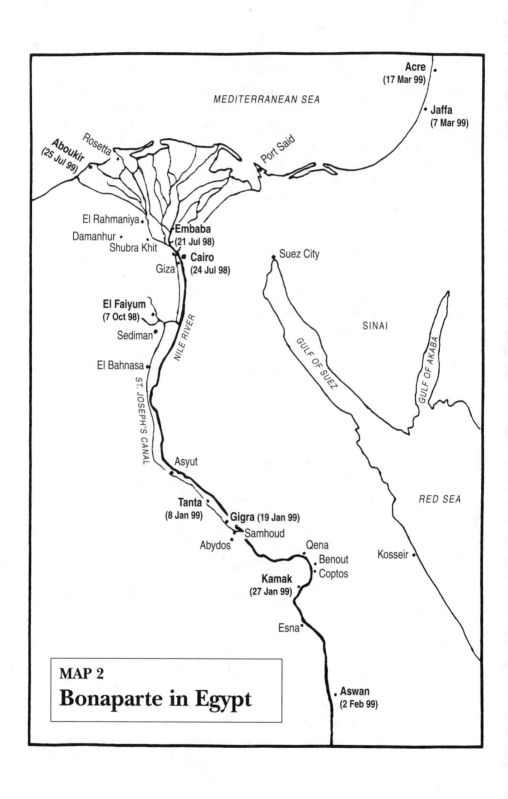

MAP 2

Bonaparte in Egypt

made for a regular water supply. No one in the French army, including Bonaparte, had any idea what it was like to cross open desert without sufficient water. Burdened by heavy backpacks, wearing serge uniforms suitable for European service but wildly inappropriate for the desert, the men suffered a three-day march. Some died of heat exhaustion. Some sat down, unable to take another step, and others straggled behind, losing ground with every step. They never saw their comrades again. They were set upon by the lurking Bedouins, killed, and stripped. Desaix sent one message after another to Bonaparte, pleading for suitable rations, water, transport animals, and the promised artillery batteries. Nothing arrived. Once at El Rahmaniya, his men broke ranks and splashed into the river. Then they raided the local melon patches, gorging themselves on the fruit.

As Desaix and Reynier marched inland, General Charles Dugua, a barrel-shaped little man who looked more like an English publican than a high-ranking French officer, led another column around the delta coast to Rosetta. His seaward flank was covered by gunboats that also carried supplies. They took Rosetta without much difficulty and pressed up the Nile, the gunboats screening the troops who marched along the west bank. They reached El Rahmaniya on 11 July, linking up with Desaix and Reynier. Bonaparte, meantime, marched across the desert, bringing with him two more divisions, the artillery, and what little cavalry he could scrape together. The horses that did get ashore at Alexandria were in wretched shape; consequently, most cavalrymen marched with the infantry, their sabers, now unwanted burdens, dragging uselessly in the sand. All the army's divisions met at Damanhur, then headed south to Shubra Khit, seven miles below El Rahmaniya.

Bonaparte ordered his divisions to form squares, each side six ranks deep, with artillery at the corners. This formation, looking much like the British infantry formations at Waterloo, was in the French training manuals of 1776 but, as Jean-Joel Brégeon points out in *L'Égypte français*, no one had made use of it. At sunrise, 13 July, the French arose to a spectacle few would ever forget. Aligned before them were 3,000 Mameluke cavalry. Behind them were an estimated 10,000 foot soldiers. Mounted on beautiful Arabian horses, the Mamelukes wore colorful robes and turbans which, like their weapons, were encrusted with jewels and silver and gold. The French stared in awe. Here was the living evidence that Egypt was everything they thought, hoped, it would be. Captain Vertray wrote in his journal that the thoughts of every French soldier turned to booty.

The Mamelukes were emboldened by what they saw. Facing them was an infantry army. Some horses could be seen inside the squares, but that positioning rendered them useless. Infantry was scum—sometimes necessary, but always inferior to the mounted warrior. The lexicon of Mameluke tactics had not changed in hundreds of years, despite the introduction of gunpowder weapons. Typically, they first engaged an enemy with a furious cavalry charge designed to disorganize infantry and cavalry formations. During the charge, they hurled spears and lances, then fired their pistols, and closed on the enemy with scimitars. As the enemy formations disintegrated, the Mamelukes, now supported by their infantry, isolated small units and destroyed them. These tactics, as Brégeon notes, were known to Bonaparte, at least on paper. Having studied the Russo-Turkish wars, he concluded that the infantry square was the most effective countermeasure to the Mameluke charge.

Murad Bey, the Mameluke leader, did not know what to make of the French dispositions. His horsemen circled and circled the squares, looking for any weak spots. After three fruitless hours, the Mamelukes charged en masse. It was then they discovered the purpose of the squares. As the Mamelukes drew within range, they were met by one disciplined musket volley after another as the six ranks laid down a virtual wall of lead. The French artillery joined in, firing grape shot. The Mameluke ranks thinned. They could not get close enough to follow through with their charge. After an hour of slaughter, the Mamelukes pulled back to reorganize.

The French gunboats on the Nile River did not enjoy similar success. The French had five boats, the Mamelukes seven. So precise was the Mameluke gunfire that three French boats were abandoned. But luck prevailed for the French. One shot hit the Mameluke flotilla leader's boat in the magazine and blew it out of the water. The remaining Mameluke boats sailed upriver.

The explosion panicked the Mameluke land forces, and they quickly withdrew from the field. The French lost twenty men killed and fifty wounded, most of them on the gunboats. The Mamelukes left several hundred dead on the battlefield.

The Battle of the Pyramids

The French continued their march toward Cairo, now seventy miles farther south, the troops encouraged by their easy victory. They marched smartly in their squares, retaining the formation lest the enemy reappear. Flags boldly identified each regiment and bands played patriotic tunes from the centers of the squares. Seventy miles is a long distance to march. Heat pounded the soldiers and diarrhea was rampant, a gift from the El Rahmaniya melon patches. Dysentery broke out. The mouths of many soldiers were bleeding and sore from bloodsuckers living in the Nile water they drank. The little beasts attached themselves to cheeks and palates and had to be torn out with tweezers. The desert, an unkind host, harbored flies, fleas, and all manner of other biting insects, including some very large scorpions. Worse was to come.

The line of march moved inland from the river bank to shorten the distance to Cairo. This Pythagorean efficiency only increased the suffering. The desert dragged at their feet. Men collapsed from heat prostration, dehydration, and exhaustion. Bedouins shadowing the march soon put them out of their misery. The ground became rougher, cut by gullies and canals that slowed the march and taxed the equipment. Supply carts broke down under the strain, gun carriages lost wheels, and draft animals collapsed. Discipline also collapsed. At first, a few soldiers broke ranks to forage for food and water; then small groups wandered off. Then larger groups broke away. Any village unfortunate enough to be in the way was looted, its women raped, and the men killed. Some villages were burned. The officers were helpless to stop the marauding. The troops moved farther south, with each step becoming less an army and more a mob. They sighted Embaba, a village across the Nile from Cairo, at 2:00 P.M., 21 July.

Murad Bey was waiting with his army. There is a debate over its size because no exact figures exist. Owen Connelly, in *Blundering to Glory*, states the Murad Bey had 6,000 Mamelukes under his command (a figure about which there is consensus) and that Ibrahim Bey, on the east bank, had another 6,000. Yet, Herold tells us that there were not 10,000 Mamelukes in all of Egypt. Estimates of infantry strength also vary, Connelly putting the number with Murad at 14,000 with another 20,000 across the Nile. These figures may be overstated because no distinction was made between combatants and noncombatants, who were all mixed together. Arab horsemen, a great uncounted mass, waited behind Murad's soldiers. Omitting Ibrahim's forces across the Nile, irrelevant to the battle, and discounting the Arabs and most of the Egyptian infantry, few of whom were used, Herold correctly concludes that Murad's effective combat force was smaller in size than was Bonaparte's. Bonaparte therefore must have exaggerated when he claimed that 78,000 faced him.

Bonaparte named the engagement the Battle of the Pyramids. But they were ten miles farther south at Giza. Yet, the choice of name seemed logical to Bonaparte: who ever heard of Embaba? Invoking the pyramids lent immortality to the struggle and made it grand, grander than reality. One is unsure whether Bonaparte actually told his troops that forty centuries looked down upon them—in other words, that they stood in the shadows of the pyramids. The possibility is that he did not but instead inserted the remark into his record of the battle, making certain the immortality was registered. If he did make the statement, then it is doubtful he addressed his entire army, something that would have been quite impossible given their deployment, but he could have said it to his staff.

Bonaparte committed his men to battle after giving them only one hour to rest. The five divisions remained in their squares. Vertray described the deployment:

> The artillery was placed in the intervals between the squares and what little cavalry we had was placed within the squares themselves. In that way, they did not risk being toppled by the shock of the formidable charge of the Mameluke cavalry squadrons and remained available and in good position to throw the Mamelukes into confusion. (Vertray, *Journal*, 56–57)

Desaix's and Reynier's divisions advanced from the French right, that is, on the west side of the line. Murad ordered all his cavalry to counterattack. The French divisions quickly realigned from six to ten ranks deep to better absorb the shock of the charge. They fired volley after volley into the packed Mamelukes. Horses and men, row on row, were brought down by the unrelenting fire of musket and cannon. But the charge had so much momentum that some Mamelukes were literally launched into the first rank, where they were killed by the infantry's crossed bayonets.

The battle revived French discipline. Officers coolly gave orders, and the troops responded. Gaps in the squares were quickly filled from the rear ranks. Once again, the incredibly brave Mamelukes, endowed with the *élan* of medieval warriors, met an anonymous wall of disciplined infantry that functioned like a great killing machine. Individual dash and courage were obsolete battle tactics that could not prevail.

General Dagua's division, accompanied by Bonaparte, advanced against the Mameluke camp at Embaba. Defeating a cavalry charge, the troops attacked the poorly handled Mameluke artillery, and then those in camp were slaughtered.

Confusion plagued Murad Bey. This was not battle as he knew it. Every time his main force fell back from a failed attack against the squares, every time they paused to rest and regroup, the French formations advanced. Impenetrable, unswerving, the firepower of the French infantry dominated the battlefield. Murad Bey realized he could not win and retreated with what cavalry he could extricate from the carnage. The Egyptian infantry and Arab horsemen were only too glad to leave, not wishing to die for the Mamelukes. French troops looted the battlefield corpses.

Ibrahim Bey, still across the river, watched the battle and its aftermath with growing horror. He decided that he was not needed on the west bank; in fact, he was not needed in Cairo. He returned to the city, packed up his treasury, his family, and his entourage, including the Turkish pasha, and fled into the Sinai, headed for Syria. The citizens of Cairo panicked, killing one another as needs be, looting, and burning—including the palaces of Murad and Ibrahim. Many left the city without any idea of where to take refuge. Equally panicked, many peasants from nearby rural districts poured into the city to escape the oncoming French.

DESAIX'S NILE CAMPAIGN

On 24 July, Bonaparte entered Cairo. On 13 August, he received news that Nelson's squadron defeated the French fleet at Aboukir. Bonaparte reacted with equanimity. His transport ships were still intact, he owned Lower Egypt, and the Ottomans stood neutral. Murad Bey, still wandering about Upper Egypt, remained his only threat and had to be destroyed. There was too much for Bonaparte to do in Cairo, so General Desaix would confront Murad.

Louis Desaix, considered a soldier's soldier, was arguably the best-known French general after Bonaparte. Never one for ostentation, he eschewed the wealth that many generals acquired by means fair and foul. He ate the same rations as his men and often slept on the ground among them. In contrast to Bonaparte, who often squandered his troops, Desaix diminished casualties whenever possible through careful planning of his battles. This was not timidity, an accusation that often follows such officers, but a pragmatic realization that he might not be able to replace those lost.

Desaix was a sublieutenant in the royal army at the outbreak of the revolution in 1789. Like many royal officers, he elected to serve in the Revolutionary army. In 1792, France was at war with Austria and Prussia. Desaix, with the Army of the Rhine, was still a sublieutenant. But, by August 1793, he was a brigadier general, a meteoric rise by any measure. He distinguished himself in that war and in subsequent campaigns in 1796 and 1797.

Short, rather sloppy, not good-looking—some would say he was ugly—introvertive, a man lacking political passions of any kind, Desaix coolly linked himself to Bonaparte. He did not personally like Bonaparte when they met in Italy, thinking him too much the dissembler and too unforgiving. Certainly there was no reason for Desaix to warm to Bonaparte during the Egyptian campaign because he received more than one verbal flogging from his master. But Desaix saw glory in the foreign adventure, and that was enough for him. The campaign was an end in itself. For Bonaparte it was a pathway for political opportunity and self-promotion.

The campaign against Murad in Upper Egypt began inauspiciously on the night of 25 August as just under 3,000 infantry with a couple of cannon marched upriver from Cairo, the troops, as R. Michalon and J. Vernet poetically comment, matching the rhythm of the flotilla of gunboats and supply craft accompanying them. The campaign eventually consumed nine months and covered 3,000 miles, visiting on Desaix's men tremendous hardships that Bonaparte was in no mood to relieve.

About fifty miles south of Cairo and inland a few miles from the Nile's west bank is the oasis of El Faiyum, the terminus of Joseph's Canal. The canal paralleled the west bank in a southerly direction for 200 miles. The village of El Bahnasa, halfway along the canal, was where Desaix hoped to catch Murad Bey. Desaix led a column across the flood plain, an enervating ooze, to El Bahnasa, where they found the only evidence of Murad's army—a cloud of dust disappearing into the desert. So it was back upriver to Asyut, then on to Beni Adi, then north again to El Faiyum. By now it was mid-September, and the only clear winner was the desert. The French were showing the wear and tear of a meandering campaign in suffocating heat that thus far yielded only increasing despair, short rations, and galloping dysentery. Ophthalmia also increased at an alarming rate. Desaix sent messages to Berthier, Bonaparte's chief-of-staff, begging for replacements, rations, ammunition, boots, cavalry, and artillery. The only reply was a profound silence.

Desaix reached El Faiyum on 7 October. Nearby, at the monastery of Sediman, Murad Bey waited with 4,000 to 5,000 Mamelukes. Desaix immediately deployed most of his troops in a large square. Two smaller squares, each with about 200 men, flanked the main square. Their purpose was to support the skirmishers sent out to harass Murad.

No sooner were the French in their formations than the Mamelukes charged. They hurled themselves first at the two smaller squares. One of them was comprised mostly of men from the 21st Light Infantry Demi-Brigade. They held their volley fire until the Mamelukes were only ten paces distant. It was too close. The velocity of the charge carried the horsemen onto the front rank of the square, trampling some men and knocking aside others, but the Mamelukes were killed by bayonets and by musket fire from the second and third ranks.

The same scenario was repeated in the other squares as Mameluke horsemen and French infantry collided. The hand-to-hand fighting was ferocious. The Mamelukes, never an easy kill, responded to the French bayonets with knives, pistols, and maces. There was no thought given the wounded. They either rolled over and died or kept fighting until killed. There were no prisoners.

Then Murad ordered an artillery battery hidden behind some high ground to fire on the squares. They did so with a precision the French found surprising. The French guns were too busy firing at the enemy horsemen to switch targets and, in any case, were too light to engage in an artillery duel. Desaix concluded that his Infantry must take the Mameluke battery. Presenting bayonets and in column formation, the French marched into the Mameluke artillery fire. The Mamelukes were taken aback. They had never seen such a maneuver. They broke. Murad managed to restore some order among the survivors and led them further south.

Desaix occupied El Faiyum and then marched southeast to Beni Suef, where he set up camp. He needed supplies and he needed reinforcements—immediately. Even though his casualties were rather light, men were dropping from heat prostration and disease every day. Silence was no longer an acceptable response from headquarters in Cairo. Desaix took a boat north, determined to get what he needed and personally see to it that delivery was made. He was eminently successful, rejoining his division on 9 December, bringing rations, munitions, uniforms, more light artillery, 800 infantry and, of vital importance, a corps of 1,000 cavalry.

On the move once again, morale restored by supplies and reinforcements, the French marched to Asyut, 250 miles south of Cairo. Gunboats screened the advance, at least until the infantry outmarched them. That was not difficult to do because the boats, sail and oar powered, were moving against the river current. On 8 January, Desaix's corps was at Tahta where Murad Bey had erected defensive positions within the village. The French charged, breaking through the barricades and emptying the trenches. The survivors leaped into the Nile, where they were easily shot. But the day was not over. Just as the French were congratulating themselves on another victory, a thousand Mameluke and Arab horsemen attacked them from behind. French discipline prevailed. Doing an about-face, they fired musket volleys rank by rank into the oncoming cavalry. The horsemen, surprised and disorganized, turned and galloped away. The French marched on. The 19 January, the corps was at Gigra. The French stayed three weeks, resting and waiting for their flotilla to catch up with them.

Murad did not retreat up the Nile merely to escape the French. Bonaparte's belief that the Mameluke leader posed a threat was correct. Murad certainly did not think he was defeated. Instead, he built a new army. The cadre remained Mamelukes, reduced to 1,500, but the body of his force was now Arab tribesmen. Most of them were from the Hejaz along the west coast of the Arabian Peninsula and included Yenbo and Meccan tribesmen. There were even some Turkish janissaries. They landed at Kosseir by the thousands and gathered at Hiw, forty miles south of Gigra. In addition, Murad bought Nubians and cajoled Egyptian peasants into his new force, which now numbered 15,000.

Alan Moorehead makes the point that Murad realized after the battle at Sediman that frontal attacks against the French squares were senseless and that guerrilla tactics were more effective, a statement both correct and incorrect. Many engagements, such as at Tahta, were rather small affairs in comparison to Sediman, but Murad still flung his cavalry into waves of musket fire and grape shot. Even though it is true that he drew Desaix's force up the Nile, staying just ahead of them, bleeding the force man by man and exhausting the rest, he knew that victory from such fighting lacked panache. Murad always cherished the idea of a decisive battle, one that would attract the attention of other beys and propel his own ambitions.

Thus, it is not surprising that Murad decided to make a stand at Samhoud, sixteen miles south of Gigra, a decision no doubt encouraged by the arrival of 2,000 janissaries. These were warriors who were the sons of Christian slaves and, like the Mamelukes, were converted to Islam and trained as warriors. Unlike the Mamelukes, the janissaries lived ascetic lives, forbidden to marry and living only to die in battle. That zealousness would soon receive its heavenly rewards.

Approaching Samhoud, Desaix deployed his infantry into two squares, placed his cavalry corps between them and his artillery on the flanks. The Mamelukes attacked from all sides, once again probing for any weaknesses. It was as if Murad had never seen infantry squares. French musket volleys and cannon fire cut down the cavalry with predictable efficiency. Then an infantry column of Yenbo Arabs emerged from a nearby canal, firing into the French left square. Desaix ordered the 7th Hussars forward to outflank the attacking infantry and cut their line of withdrawal. Meanwhile, elements of the 21st Light Infantry Demi-Brigade advanced in column along the canal, enfilading the Arabs with musket fire. The Arab column reformed and counterattacked, but the precise fire of the 21st drove them back with considerable loss. Other Arab and janissary attacks

against the French squares were decimated by French artillery fire.
Murad's new army broke and again fled further south.

Now the real chase was on. The French marched to Abydos and
on to Benout and Coptos, where there were further skirmishes. On
27 January, the magnificence of Luxor and Thebes (or Karnak) came
into view. The troops spontaneously drew to attention, presented
arms and, as the bands played, applauded the great temple sites. They
then marched to Esna. On 2 February 1799, they reached Aswan, 587
miles south of Cairo.

The march to Aswan might have signaled the end of the Nile
campaign but Murad, lurking in the Nubian Desert, did not know he
was supposed to quit. He swung north in a wide arc and back into
Egypt, unleashing on the French the guerrilla warfare that Desaix
hoped would never come. The French were again short of everything
from ammunition to light artillery to boots. Desaix felt he had
reached the end of the earth. Native insurrections broke out, and
Murad's men attacked contingents of French soldiers, raided river
traffic, at one point boarding the gunboat *L'Italie* and slaughtering
the nearly 900 men packed aboard. Week after week over seven
months, Murad struck anywhere he pleased and always managed to
persuade or deceive new fighters into joining him.

Desaix finally took a calculated risk. He sent General Belliard to
occupy Kosseir, the port at which Murad's reinforcements arrived
from Arabia. The plan was risky because Belliard's 21st Light Infantry
was suffering from all the usual shortages and, unsurprisingly, considering how often they stood in the forefront of action, were nearing
exhaustion. Another risk was that even if Belliard succeeded, the
British navy might retake the port. The little French column left
Quena on 26 May with only one artillery piece, 350 light infantry on
camels, and some friendly Arabs. Three days and 150 miles later over
hellish desert mountains, they took Kosseir without opposition. Leaving his troops to garrison the port, Belliard returned to Quena on 1
June. As anticipated, the stream of reinforcements stopped.

Desaix rested his men, distributed supplies, and established a
depot and hospital at Esna. For all intents and purposes the Nile campaign was over. Although Murad was not defeated in the field, skirmishes became less frequent and less intense because the surviving

Mamelukes were exhausted. The beys fell to incessant bickering as they wondered which of them might survive to deal with either the French or the Turks, but it made little difference.

The peasantry showed no enthusiasm for the Mameluke cause. Enough was finally enough.

The End of It All

One reason for Bonaparte's neglect of Desaix's needs was that, on 10 February 1799, he led 13,000 men across the Sinai into Palestine toward an invasion of Syria. The expedition fell apart. On 7 March, the French assaulted Jaffa, now a suburb of Tel Aviv. Breaching the walls, the infantry were confronted by 2,000 Turks wishing to surrender. The French bayoneted them. But nearly 3,000 more negotiated a surrender to some junior officers. Bonaparte certainly did not want all those prisoners. Arguments for and against his subsequent actions surface periodically but the facts are clear enough: on 8 March 800 prisoners were shot; on 9 March another 600 were shot; a final 1,040 were shot on the following day. Vertray emphatically points out in his journal that he did not take part in this, "the saddest part of the campaign" (114).

Then bubonic plague struck the French troops. Gathered together in an abandoned mosque, the sick waited in terror. What they received was unexpected: Bonaparte strolling among them like Christ among the lepers. The moment was not lost on Napoleonic apologists. Antoine Gros did an enormous painting (nearly twenty-four feet wide) commemorating the event. Overlooked in the adulation was Bonaparte's order that the plague-ridden should be poisoned, an order never obeyed.

Bonaparte besieged Acre beginning 17 March but could not breach the ancient city walls because he was missing his siege guns, sent by sea and captured by the British navy. The city was also defended by 250 guns, and the Royal Navy gunboats off shore played havoc with the French troops. Acre never yielded. Bonaparte was defeated.

He found a way out of the debacle when he received word that the Royal Navy was landing Turkish troops at Aboukir. He quickly returned to Egypt, but with only 6,500 of his men. All the others were dead.

On 10 July, Turkish forces, their exact numbers in considerable dispute, landed at Aboukir at the head of the narrow delta peninsula. Without cavalry, lacking artillery, and with no bayonets, they were hardly equipped to take the offensive; consequently, their leader, Mustapha Pasha, opted to defend the peninsula. This was a bad choice because he had no line of retreat if that became necessary. The outer defensive line, a thousand yards down the peninsula, had a small fort on each end with entrenchments between. The second defensive line, about 200 yards behind the first, spanned the peninsula. The third defensive position was Fort Aboukir.

Bonaparte marched to Aboukir with 10,000 infantry, 1,000 cavalry, and 17 artillery pieces, reaching the peninsula on 24 July 1799. They attacked at dawn the next day, engaging the two first line forts and their entrenchments. The Turks were slowly pushed back, a gap opening in their line. Bonaparte pushed his artillery into the gap, and soon the second line wavered. Just after noon, the right side defenses collapsed. General Murat swept through the break with his cavalry and in a few minutes was at Fort Aboukir. The Turks from the first and second lines did not know what to do. Nearly 2,000 were killed by the saber-wielding French horsemen. Those managing to escape that slaughter jumped into the sea, hoping to swim to their transport vessels. Nearly 4,000 drowned or were shot.

Fort Aboukir, defended by 2,500 Turks, held out, the men afraid to surrender. But after a thousand deaths from disease, starvation, and lack of water, they finally capitulated. Turkish losses were around 7,000 dead. The French lost 220 killed and an estimated 750 wounded.

Earlier, while at Acre, Bonaparte received a letter from the Directory, telling him that he could expect no more reinforcements and supplies and that there would be no more communications with him because of the desperate situation in Europe. As far as they were concerned, he was on his own and could stay in Egypt or march to India or attack Constantinople. In short, they wrote him off.

Unknown to the Directory, this was Bonaparte's long-awaited moment. If Europe was getting restless, it needed him. He turned over his command to Kléber, giving him leave to negotiate with the beys and withdraw from Egypt as he might. Within a week of his return to Cairo from Aboukir, Bonaparte departed for France (taking the members of the National Institute with him), the Egyptian expedition and its supposedly strategic implications shed in favor of personal ambition.

AFTERWORD: ALL FOR NOTHING

Whatever else may be thought of the Egyptian campaign, it was a contest in human endurance that ended in butchery, revealing some of the worst in Bonaparte. For a general whose legend was rooted in his devotion to his troops, he cared precious little for them when distracted by events or when the men were no longer useful to him. The march from Alexandria to Cairo was a nightmare of ignorance and neglect. He sent Desaix up the Nile and did little to support his suffering troops. At Jaffa, he ordered the plague-ridden to be poisoned. But neglect is a minor accusation when compared to his inhuman treatment of his enemies. Thus, he executed helpless prisoners at Jaffa, and Aboukir turned into a senseless bloodbath. Considering that litany of monstrous activity, I have no difficulty concluding that Bonaparte's major military accomplishment in Egypt was to introduce to desert warfare the first modern example of battles of annihilation.

It is true that Bonaparte inaugurated many imaginative and effective changes for the governance of Egypt. He also instituted changes to help his men adapt to the strange environment. He ordered new uniforms designed that were not so confining, but the troops ridiculed them. He established French-style bistros, which the men in Cairo took advantage of, but which were of no benefit to those in the field. He was distressed by the diseases that plagued his army, so he established base hospitals. French military medicine was as good as any in Europe, but the army in Egypt had too few doctors and carelessly recruited medical orderlies. Some were criminals and many others were interested only in extracting money from the wounded and sick soldiers. He also expanded his sanitation corps by adding 168 officers and 160 administrators.

Bonaparte planned and schemed on the high road, a thinker of global thoughts; yet he did little at first to help Desaix's division survive the daily rigors of desert warfare. But there is more to the campaign than butchery and neglect.

Bonaparte pushed his men unmercifully after leaving Alexandria. They were not prepared for desert warfare. As Vertray tells us, the men in Reynier's division did not even have canteens. Bonaparte was impatient—lest the Mamelukes have time to organize and retaliate, lest the Nile flood before his conquest of the interior was complete, lest he be denied a victory. As Herold concludes, Bonaparte's impatience was that "of a man who took sacrifices for granted and expected men to do the impossible" (81). Therefore, the men who died along the way were insignificant. Even more would die if his goals were not attained.

The long marches to which Bonaparte subjected the troops were among his expectations of the impossible, his version of mobile warfare. There were only four means of mobility in Egypt: camels, horses, river craft, and marches. Even if Mamelukes were mostly cavalry, it did not follow that the speed and strength of their horses gave them an automatic advantage over the French infantry. Horses, as the Mamelukes knew and the French discovered, necessarily operated near the river for water. But the French knew how to march. Desaix's division marched 120 miles to Asyut in only four days, much to Murad's surprise. Thirty miles a day was not unusual, especially if moving in columns. What enabled the French to move so far so fast was their continued proximity to the Nile and riverboats, and the concomitant absence of a baggage train. Draft animals brought a march to a crawl. The infantry carried their short-term needs on their backs. March or die—many did die but the survivors lived to fight, to do the impossible.

The capacity of the French soldiers to endure meant that they could define the character of the battles. Such endurance is usually credited to Bonaparte's influence, but he was nowhere near Desaix's force during the Nile campaign. Desaix was an excellent general, too, but leadership is only one factor in any military success. Often overlooked in the search for explanations were the French fighting formations, primarily the square. As Ardant du Picq wrote in *Battle Studies*, the square "is not a thing of mechanics [but] a thing of morale" (194). Compact, bristling with firepower, the square could not be broken by the Mamelukes. A division of 4,000 men formed four sides, each side in six ranks. Each rank consisted of 166 men. With every man firing three shots a minute, each side fired 2,500 musket balls a minute. Naturally, ideal conditions allowing that rate of fire seldom existed but, even with the confusions of the battlefield, the effect was deadly.

Moreover, the Army of Egypt was composed mostly of veterans who knew about cavalry charges and what it was like to march into artillery fire; indeed, in those terms, as Michalon and Vernet point out, the French battles with the Mamelukes were very much like battles against European armies. Brégeon notes that the men were aware of what other regiments in the division could do, and they depended on the touch of a familiar elbow to help them face the enemy and their own fears. The square, du Picq said, created a feeling of force that "is power in war." That does not equate with firepower alone. It is, du Picq observed, psychological dominance over one's enemies.

The Mamelukes were a crowd that used, to cite John Keegan's term from *A History of Warfare*, "ossified" tactics left over from the Middle Ages. Their cavalry had no internal organization or discipline. They charged en masse, firing their pistols without system. What happened if a rider penetrated a square was not planned because they lacked the tactical sensitivity and imagination to exploit the opening. Their artillery could be accurate, but it was usually widely dispersed and fired without much coordination. The infantry was generally useless, leaving the battlefield at the slightest provocation. Ironically, because the Mamelukes were a crowd, the French did not decisively defeat them in the Nile campaign. There was no army to defeat. His men shot to pieces in one battle, Murad recruited more.

In the end, Bonaparte's abandonment of his army was a blessing in disguise. Had he stayed in Egypt, he would have led a vanishing command as battles, disease and, inevitably, desertions dissipated his numbers. With the desert covering the corpses, Egypt would merely shrug at their passing.

CHAPTER 4

The Northwest Frontier of India, 1850 to 1852

A DAY ON THE FRONTIER

The plain was a dusty table, broken only by a few patches of cultivated land and low-growing scrub. To the west, dry and rocky hills rose to jagged crests, with not a tree in sight. Lieutenant Miller led a column of the Corps of Guides across the plain to Mutta, a nothing village in the middle of nowhere. As the column approached the village, they saw a dust cloud rising in the west. As the cloud moved nearer, Miller saw that it was caused by a raiding party of Mohmand tribesmen led by Nawab Khan, an unruly clan chief whose banditry plagued the Frontier border.

Miller ordered two infantry companies to hide at the base of the hills and intercept the tribesmen after he scattered them with a frontal cavalry attack. But the Mohmands were not fooled. They attacked the infantry, forcing them to pull back, and chasing them around the hills. The fighting broke into individual and small unit actions as men dashed for what cover they could find. A rout was in the making. But the Mohmands did not count on the Guide's discipline. At Miller's command, the infantry re-formed into lines and fired a volley. Two hundred musket balls crashed into the tribesmen who were massing for an attack. Seeing the Mohmands waiver, the Guides presented bayonets and charged, chasing them for two miles. The skirmish with the Mohmands was a typical patrol action along India's Northwest Frontier (Map 3).

The tribesmen, operating as guerrilla groups ranging in size from a few score to a few hundred, conducted raids into British-controlled territory as economic necessity and mood dictated. However, the tribesmen sometimes gathered by the thousands to confront British authority. Thus, beginning in the 1850s and for nearly a century thereafter, British soldiers, native Indian troops, and tribesmen fought again and again over the same ground.

THE BACKGROUND OF BATTLE

What brought the British to this arid and turbulent land and the reasons that they fought with so much determination at enormous expense for so long and so little are complex. They are found in the bewildering events of the first British encounters with a land most did not know and with a people they did not fully understand. Such lack of information, nay ignorance, would not bode well in Europe's familiar environment. On the desertlike plains and barren mountains of the Northwest Frontier it created the difficult times, if not the outright tragedies, that lay ahead.

The story begins in 1849 with the annexation of the Punjab by British India at the behest of James Ramsay, 10th Lord Dalhousie and the governor general of India. Bright, Oxford-educated, occasionally brash, sometimes mercurial in his judgments, at age thirty-five Dalhousie was the youngest man ever to be governor general. He made the decision to annex the Punjab after the Sikhs, who controlled the region, inaugurated two wars. Following the First Sikh War the British occupied only that part of the Punjab closest to India, and garrisoned the city of Lahore. Total annexation after the Second Sikh War brought them to the Northwest Frontier.

Few Britons knew much about the region. Only a few old hands, such as Philip Melville and Harry Lumsden, had been on the Frontier since the First Afghan War in 1842. Most information was based on dubious intelligence supplied by Afridi tribesmen who traded with the Mohmands north of the Kabul River, a few military patrols that ranged around the border, and a sea of rumor often mistaken for fact.

The Mohmand, Yusafzai, Utman-Khel, and Ranizai were among the most aggressive border tribes. All lived around the plain north of Peshawar and the hills of Lower Swat province. To these people, raiding was a natural part of their economic lives. But British policy guaranteed the safety and well-being of everyone living under their jurisdiction. Harry Lumsden, commanding the Corps of Guides, believed the raiding would not stop until the tribesmen were severely

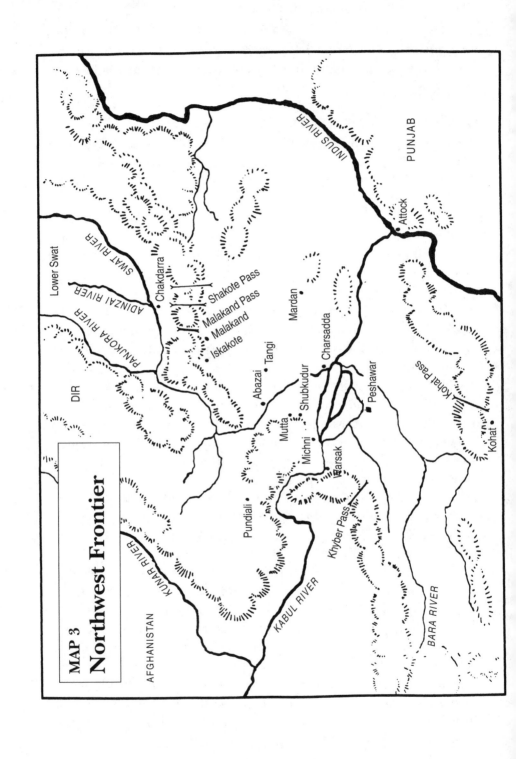

MAP 3
Northwest Frontier

AFGHANISTAN

KUNAR RIVER

DIR

Lower Swat

SWAT RIVER

ADINZAI RIVER

PANJKORA RIVER

Chakdarra

Shakote Pass

Malakand Pass

Malakand

Iskakote

Mardan

Tangi

Abazai

Pundiali

Mutta

Shubkudur

Charsadda

Michni

Warsak

Peshawar

Khyber Pass

KABUL RIVER

BARA RIVER

INDUS RIVER

PUNJAB

Attock

Kohat Pass

Kohat

punished in their own territories, demonstrating the extent and power of British arms to enforce the peace. Dalhousie agreed and sanctioned punitive actions against the tribes.

Dalhousie favored an authoritative approach with all decisions coming from him. He found an ally not only in Lumsden but also in John Lawrence, whom he appointed to the Board of Administration, the Punjab's governing body. Opposing Dalhousie's approach was Henry Lawrence, John's brother. Henry was also on the board but Dalhousie had little faith in him, in fact did not like him, thinking Henry incompetent—probably because they disagreed. Then Sir Charles Napier, hero of the Peninsular War and conqueror of the Scinde, was appointed commander in chief, India. He did not disguise his contempt for civil government and his mistrust of committees. Dalhousie developed an intense dislike of Napier, and Napier returned the feelings in full measure. Moreover, beyond personality clashes and bruised egos, Napier arrived in India with the understanding that he would have sole authority over military affairs. He did not count on Dalhousie's different interpretation of his role.

The ensuing divisiveness, the incessant quarreling, and the torrent of crossed and confused communications created a contentiousness that compromised the ability of civil government to clearly develop coherent policies, and confronted the army with dilemmas, both practical and moral, that made it difficult to function. The near-desert environment of the Frontier was the physical context for the battles between the tribesmen and the army. It also was the environment in which the British authorities played out their intramural conflicts, exaggerating them beyond all reason.

THE PESHAWAR FIELD FORCE, 1850–1852
Cross Purposes
Tribal raids along the Northwest Frontier begged for a permanent and flexible British military presence. The founding of the Corps of Guides in 1847, eventually one of the most famous units in the Indian Army, reflected early and modest efforts in that direction. The Corps recruited native tribesmen who knew the geography and the people they were to police. Their permanent headquarters was at Mardan across the Kabul River some thirty miles northeast of Peshawar. Lieu-

tenant Harry Lumsden founded and commanded the unit. At age twenty-six in 1847, he was already an experienced officer, joining the 59th Bengal Infantry at seventeen. He was among the troops that forced the Khyber Pass in 1842 and he served in both Sikh wars. He spoke Pushtu, the most widely used language in the region, and understood the tribes as well as anyone. The Corps guided the regular army through the Frontier's bewildering landscape and collected intelligence from deep within tribal territories. But a stronger force was also needed.

The Peshawar Field Force was established toward the end of the Second Sikh War, though no exact formations existed in 1849. Regiments were assigned on the basis of availability and were constantly cycled in and out of the force as needs in other regions dictated. Regardless of what particular units served and for how long, they represented three levels of Indian military organization.

Queen's regiments, the first level, were stationed in India for as long as twenty years. Among the Queen's infantry regiments that went to Peshawar between 1850 and 1852 were the 32nd, 60th, 61st, and 98th. The designation "regiment" is one of those British terminological ambiguities that unsettle the uninitiated with great regularity. A regiment in any other army is usually composed of from two to four battalions, but in the British army a regiment was often a single battalion, sometimes two. In war, the number of battalions could be multiplied indefinitely.

The men enlisted for twenty years. Their officers, certainly most in 1849, purchased their commissions and any subsequent promotions. The purchase sometimes required transfer to another regiment because there might not be a higher rank available in their original unit. That meant considerable hopping about for those who could afford further purchases. The officers in the regiments assigned to the Peshawar Field Force were mostly veterans of the two Sikh wars. But they had never trained in any fighting style other than the traditional British line with all its parade ground precision. The 98th Regiment was an exception. Under the command of Colin Campbell, they learned small unit fighting tactics and how to advance in open order over rough terrain, tactics Campbell learned when a light infantry subaltern during the Peninsular War but which were still not in the training manuals.

The native Indian soldiers of the Honourable East India Company—sepoys—formed a second level of troops. That mercantile giant became a potent military force in India because Britain could not provide all the troops necessary to control the vast subcontinent. Like their British counterparts, the enlisted men were long-service volunteers. The regiments—again read "battalions"—serving in Peshawar either came from the Punjab, made up of Sikhs who transferred allegiance to the Company, or were from Oudh. They trained in the same system as the British troops, and many were also veterans of the Sikh Wars. Their officers were British. Some transferred from the Queen's regiments, but others entered the Indian Army directly. Rather than purchasing his commission, the applicant to the Indian Army had to pass a board of review and be recommended. Seniority determined promotion. Thus, many older officers did not obtain high rank by merit, but by outlasting their rivals.

The third level of organization consisted of irregular troops. These were Frontier tribesmen, such as those in the Corps of Guides. Many were Afridis, who seemed to have a penchant for army service. They were among the best light cavalry in the world, men who could ride anything anywhere, tirelessly climb hills, and enter regions where no European could go. Their "uniforms" ranged from the adaptation by Lumsden of khaki to informal combinations of British gear and native dress. Their British officers often "went native," and it is sometimes difficult to pick them from the tribesmen in old photographs. These officers lived in the field with their men, ate the same food, and took the same risks, earning enormous respect from those they led.

Scottish-born Brigadier General Sir Colin Campbell took command of the Peshawar Field Force on 25 November 1849. Recently knighted for service in the Second Sikh War, he was fifty-seven years old. He was introduced to war at the Battle of Vimeiro, Portugal, in 1808, at sixteen years old a lieutenant in the 9th Regiment. His captain took him by the hand and walked him back and forth in full view of French artillery. That day he learned the basic lesson of the British officer: show no fear, setting a courageous example for his men. He fought at Corunna, Bidassao, Vitoria, and Barossa, and served in the first siege of St. Sebastian, where he led the Forlorn Hope, the vain attempt to breach the town walls. He was wounded three times and promoted to captain on merit. He served on Gibraltar, in the

Wallcheren Expedition, Ireland, the West Indies, and commanded the 98th Regiment in the city of Newcastle during the Chartist movement. Then he took the 98th to China, where he became military governor of Hong Kong and then of Chusan Island. During the Second Sikh War, he led a division during the battles at Ramnugur, Chillianwallah, and Gujerat.

Worn by forty-one years' active service, he wanted to go back to England, where prize money from the Sikh War afforded him a comfortable life. On 20 October 1849, he wrote in his private journal, "My dislike of the little annoyances of station or garrison command daily augments. . . . I am only fit for retirement." Sir Charles Napier, his former commanding officer when in Newcastle, prevailed upon him to stay in India and command at Peshawar. Campbell accepted the appointment, hoping it was his last.

He first established a military cantonment just north of Peshawar. He did not want his men quartered in the town, where the narrow streets and congested populace would undoubtedly interfere with troop deployment.

Coincidental to Campbell receiving his appointment, Yusafzai tribesmen raided some villages on the Peshawar plain near the Kabul River. The 1st Battalion, 60th Queen's Regiment made a punitive sweep of three Yusafzai villages, burning houses and crops. Even though 9,000 tribal warriors (probably an exaggeration) watched from the surrounding hills, they made no move against the British soldiers. Campbell hoped the action would deter further raids but disclaimed responsibility because the sweep was planned prior to his appointment. He further noted that the order came directly from the civil commissioner, not from Napier, the commander-in-chief. Napier angrily wrote Campbell that he would not sanction any actions that left "poor women and children to perish with cold in the depths of winter." Campbell was in complete sympathy. The war of words had begun.

Based on his experience in the Scinde, Napier thought that tribal peace and some loyalty could be established by offering subsidies, in effect, buying the friendship of the hill tribes. Lord Dalhousie persisted in his belief that only vigorous military action would bring peace, and he wrote in a memo dated 2 May 1850 that "I will make no concession of any kind to the [Mohmands] or to any other border tribe." Here, as Gordon Martel categorized the attitude, was the imperial imperative—the inherent right of the Great to dominate the small, the savage, the obscure.

Then Afridi tribesmen attacked a unit of army sappers south of Peshawar in the Kohat Pass. Striking in the night, they sneaked up to the sappers' tent, cut the support ropes, and killed the struggling soldiers. Campbell received direct orders from Lord Dalhousie, not from Napier, to punish the Afridis. He organized a column of 600 infantry, the 15th Irregular Cavalry, and two horse artillery batteries. The elusive tribesmen escaped, but Campbell cleared the pass, reinforced the Kohat garrison, and burned a few Afridi villages. In the middle of the operation, Napier himself appeared and took command, furious that Dalhousie ordered a military action without consulting him first.

Dalhousie had written his old friend Sir George Couper in October 1849 that Napier "is very wild and incautious in his talk, and gives me trouble and will give me more, but we are still the best of friends." The final sentiment soon fell away. A journal entry by Napier in April 1850 characterized the growing rift between the two men: "[Lord Dalhousie] is as weak as water and as vain as a pretty woman, or an ugly man. I am sick of him" (Napier, *Life and Opinions*, vol. 4, 254). Several weeks after the Kohat affair, Lieutenant Colonel Frederick Mackeson, Peshawar civil commissioner, ordered another punitive expedition against the Afridis after they attacked a watch tower in the Kohat Pass. But he wanted Campbell to wait until the tribe's crops were ripe and then burn them together with their villages. Campbell contacted Napier, asking that the lines of communications be clearly defined. Could a civil commissioner give him a military order? Napier told Campbell not to move without his express orders. Meanwhile, the commissioner reached a compromise with the Afridis by which the offending tower was removed in return for guaranteed safe passage through the pass. But that did not erase the line drawn between civil and military authority on the Northwest Frontier.

Confrontation followed confrontation, Napier and Dalhousie stubbornly clinging to their positions. Dalhousie insisted that the army was subordinate to the civil government and that, as governor general, he could order military operations at any level without first informing the commander in chief. John Lawrence supported that view and predicted that the army would resist subordination to government, especially if trouble on the Frontier persisted or if the Sikhs became restless.

But Napier already alerted Dalhousie that the Sikhs were not feeling especially pacified, that the Afghans were waiting for the right moment to pour through the Khyber Pass, and that the Peshawar plain north to the Malakand Pass seethed with revolt. In Napier's view, Dalhousie was making a big mistake attempting to control events along the Frontier from faraway Calcutta. Instead, Napier wanted to establish military governorships in the region. Unfortunately, he also allowed arrogance founded in his previous Indian experience to override good judgment by dismissing Dalhousie as an incompetent and pampered aristocrat.

Dalhousie, guarding his prerogatives, equally extended his malice and judged Napier insubordinate, arrogant, and violent. There was not room enough in India for two such men. At last, in December 1850, frustrated, angry, and disappointed, Napier resigned his post and returned to England. General Sir William Gomm replaced him. At seventy, Gomm lacked field experience but once served with Colin Campbell in the 9th Regiment.

Actions against the Mohmands

Major General J. G. Elliott concluded in his study of the Frontier that the Mohmands were the region's most persistent raiders. During a mere five years in the 1850s the Mohmands made forty minor raids and eighty major raids (defined as involving seventy-five or more men) into British territory. To be sure, some Mohmands lived in relative peace and prosperity on the Peshawar plain but others living on the plain and in the hills were neither peaceful nor prosperous. In early April 1851, Lumsden repeated to the Board of Administration that punishing the tribes on their own turf was the only way to stop the raiding. Lord Dalhousie again concurred and wrote Campbell directly, bypassing General Gomm, that he wanted "whole villages devastated." But, he quickly added, such punishment should not be against the entire tribe for the misdeeds of a few. He left it to Campbell to reconcile the differences between devastation and selective punishment. Campbell was also to determine the feasibility of such a campaign.

Accompanied by Lumsden and a small escort, Campbell reconnoitered the area around Mutta and the passes leading into Mohmand territory, then cut northwest toward Pundiali. Campbell had no idea what lay ahead. West of Mutta was the Panj Pao plateau. Only two narrow footpaths led to the crest. "I never saw such a jumble of rough, rugged, irregular hills," Campbell reported to Dalhousie, noting that the hills looked like a crumpled wad of paper. One conclusion was certain: the ground was aptly suited for guerrilla warfare, favoring the tribesmen. They used the matchlock gun, an early form of muzzle-loader, that had a range in excess of 500 yards, ideal for sniping. But the gun's four-foot barrel needed a supporting fork, making it useless in close combat. The tribesmen then used their tulwars—broad-bladed curved swords—and knives. Campbell concluded that his British-trained troops would do very well as long as they fought on the plain, where disciplined firepower gave them the advantage. He further concluded that the punishment inflicted on the tribes might not be worth the casualties his force could suffer during the expedition.

Campbell offered an alternative to a punitive expedition. The Frontier near Mutta could be strengthened by building a bridge across the Kabul River and guarding it with 150 cavalrymen. The bridge would make it possible to respond more quickly to future raids and would be a welcome means to increase local trade, lessening the need for raids. Also, small forts could be established as tangible evidence of British intentions and power. Campbell gave Dalhousie the choice of attacking or defending. Dalhousie opted for the latter course, a curious choice considering his earlier bellicose statements, balking at unnecessary losses. But he discarded the idea of small forts because they were too expensive and a military overstatement. He did not see that the punitive expeditions already conducted were military overstatements.

The Frontier remained quiet for the next several months. But on 10 October 1851 Mohmand tribesmen from the area around Michni attacked villages to the south in British territory, cutting water supplies, burning houses, and destroying crops. Dalhousie fired a letter to Campbell, telling him that he would soon receive orders from General Gomm to punish the offending tribesmen. The populations of twenty-five villages were to be dispersed, their land confiscated and resettled by people more friendly to British intentions. The Michni region would be annexed to British India. Dalhousie had had enough of the Mohmands.

Campbell marched out of Peshawar two weeks later, leading 1,200 troops. He was joined at the Kabul River by five companies of Guides under Lumsden's personal command. Contrary to Dalhousie's expectations, Campbell did not take his troops into Mohmand territory but sent Lumsden ahead to tell the *maliks*, or village headmen, that the people could stay in their villages as long as they banished those responsible for the raids. Campbell thought it counterproductive to disperse the village populations because that would leave them with nothing and only encourage further raiding. Nor did he agree with Dalhousie's resettlement plan, believing that the lives of the new population "would not be worth a night's purchase."

The conciliatory effort, clearly against orders and done without anyone's approval, failed. During the last week of November and the first week of December, Campbell's force moved against the Mohmand villages, toppling houses, pulling down towers, and burning crops. The villagers went into the hills and each night the troops retired to their camp. The result of this mutual reluctance to fight was that zoo lives were lost in what Campbell felt was "a disagreeable task."

To secure the area, Campbell placed garrisons at Shubkudur and Michni. Campbell stayed in a base camp between the two villages. The Queen's 61st Regiment was camped several hundred yards further north.

Sunday, 7 December 1851: Sadat Khan, a leader of the Alumzai, led a force of 4,000 men armed with swords and matchlocks out of the Panj Pao gorges directly toward the 61st's camp. A unit of the 15th Irregular Cavalry was nearby, guarding a flock of pack camels. Fearing the Alumzai would isolate the 15th's men, placing them in grave danger by cutting off any escape path, Campbell gathered together a Guides infantry company, another from the 61st already in his camp, a cavalry troop, and two field artillery pieces. They quick-marched to a small rise halfway between his camp and the Alumzai who were still gathering. Tribesmen atop the heights waved swords and matchlocks, taunting the little British force. Campbell did not want to risk an attack, so he had the gunners fire a few rounds in the tribesmen's general direction to "inform them," as he put it, of the kinds of weapons they faced. The firing worked. Sadat Khan withdrew during the night. Campbell wrote in his personal journal, "If I mistake not, we have upset a hive, and the hornets it contained will not settle in a hurry" (Shadwell, vol. I, 269). The Field Force returned to Peshawar 15 February 1852.

More Fighting, More Confusion

The punitive expeditions against the Mohmands altered Campbell's judgment about what could be ultimately accomplished against such an enemy. He communicated his thoughts to General Gomm on 4 February. Even though the tone of the letter remained factual and objective, there lurked beneath his words a criticism of government policy and the events leading to its formation. Campbell stated that intelligence sources reported that Pundiali was one village. He found it a cluster of thirteen, escalating the number of warriors that opposed him. Moreover, only twelve miles from Pundiali was Kumall, a community that added 1,400 fighters to the tribal forces. And two miles beyond Kumall were the settlements of the Alumzai, the most warlike of the Mohmands. Campbell estimated that the total number of tribal warriors exceeded 20,000.

Campbell felt certain his force could defend the Frontier but that it was inadequate to campaign in Mohmand territory. The mountainous areas lacked water, and roads were so few and so rugged that it was impossible to employ artillery and cavalry. He concluded that "the vast number of hostile mountaineers must be met by infantry only." That necessitated a much larger force than immediately available. The tribesmen, being excellent fighters, having great agility and endurance, and knowing the country so well, were equal, if not superior, to the troops sent against them. Campbell ended by saying that, "there is but one alternative—viz., to preserve the peace of the [Peshawar] valley by rigid attention to the interior lines of defense." That included improving communications, building forts, and extending a military presence in the region by sending out small patrols.

Gomm inexplicably waited three months before transmitting a copy of Campbell's letter, together with his endorsement of its contents, to Lord Dalhousie. He also sent a copy to Peshawar civil commissioner Frederick Mackeson. Mackeson recoiled in disappointment at Campbell's assessment. Seeking to distance himself from Campbell, he wrote Philip Melville, secretary to the Board of Administration, that he regretted ever being influenced by Campbell's doubts, indicating that if the Mohmands had been thoroughly punished a year earlier, they would have ceased to be a problem. Mackeson's letter was a return shot in an increasingly bitter paper war. Confusion existed among civil administrators regarding what Campbell could and could not do and what he actually accomplished. Correspondence went in several directions at once and never did catch up with actual events. Campbell did not help the situation. Confused by his sense of duty as a soldier and his growing moral outrage over the punishment he was ordered to inflict, he unwittingly embroiled himself in government policymaking. That could only draw the fire, indeed the enmity, of Lord Dalhousie.

In mid-April, the Mohmands again harassed Mutta. Campbell doubled the garrison at Shubkudur but, still uncertain of the situation, he left Peshawar on 15 April with a half-battery of horse artillery and a contingent of irregular cavalry. The Queen's 53rd Regiment remained behind on alert. Reaching Shubkudur, Campbell climbed the fort's tower to survey the plain. He saw Mohmands making their way west from the hills, a crowd of 6,000 matchlock men and 80 horsemen. Another body of warriors stood on the heights above as if to screen the movement of those approaching the plain. Campbell ordered his two guns to open fire. The shooting dispersed the matchlock men. Then Campbell took his little cavalry force and the horse artillery guns at a gallop to the top of the heights. The gunners fired on the mass below. The tribesmen withdrew, Campbell noting that they showed great dexterity in using natural cover to avoid the artillery fire. At dusk, the tribesmen returned, rushing forward, using "every accident of ground," as Campbell put it, proving that they were equal to anyone in rugged terrain. Once again, the artillery dispersed the warriors.

Returning to Peshawar, Campbell found a letter from the Board of Administration ordering him to attack the Mohmands. The Board was responding to Campbell's 4 February evaluation. But Campbell did not know that Gomm delayed transmission for three months. He wrote the Board that since he had just fought the Mohmands near Shubkudur, he would not mount another expedition unless ordered to do so by Gomm.

The press, meantime, remained blissfully ignorant of the bureaucratic infighting and confusion and even less knowledgeable of the wholesale destruction wrought by the punitive expeditions. The Bombay *Telegraph and Courier* editorialized on 12 May that "all is being done toward quieting the North West Frontier permanently, effectively, and in a manner becoming civilized men."

More Confusion and More Conflict

The press, however satisfied with events, was not the government. Neither the Board of Administration nor Lord Dalhousie was the least satisfied. Philip Melville wrote a forceful letter to Mackeson, pointing out that matters of policy, namely, how the Mohmands should be treated and what the army should do, were the civilian commissioner's responsibility, not Campbell's. On 17 May, Dalhousie responded to Campbell's 4 February evaluation and Gomm's cover letter, rebuking both soldiers because of their shared views about the Mohmands. He now reversed his April agreement with Campbell to strengthen the Frontier defenses. The Mohmands had to be punished. Dalhousie, possibly uninformed of the old connection between Gomm and Campbell, was surprised by Gomm's support of his truculent brigadier. He wrote Couper that "the normally acquiescent little c-in-c consistently backs Campbell." He did not like the apparent connivance.

The command situation worsened in the flurry of letter writing. Campbell believed he was responsible to Gomm. Dalhousie believed he had direct authority over Campbell, bypassing Gomm, ordering him into the field and requesting personal and confidential reports from him. Dalhousie's circumvention of official communication lines implicitly invited Campbell's criticisms of policy. If the governor general wanted his comments and insights, then he was bound to reply. If Dalhousie really wanted the truth, then some of those replies involved criticism. The two men were thrown into an adversarial relationship.

The conflict between the civil and military authorities deepened when a native official was murdered at Charsadda by a Mohmand named Ajoon Khan. An early report written by Captain H. R. James, deputy commissioner in Peshawar, indicated that Ajoon Khan fled north to escape capture and found sanctuary with the Padshah and Akhund of Swat, the province's secular and religious leaders. Furthermore, the two leaders allegedly encouraged raids into British territory. Dalhousie ordered an immediate invasion of Swat. But Captain James changed his mind, believing the Swat leaders actually stopped some raids and were innocent of any implications in the Ajoon Khan affair. James dutifully reported his new findings to the Board in Lahore and to Mackeson, his immediate superior. He also showed his conclusions to Campbell "at an informal level." That was a serious mistake.

Campbell wrote Gomm that there was no justification for calling out the entire Peshawar Field Force to arrest one murderer. A company or two of guides would do. Then Campbell wrote Mackeson, suggesting the invasion be delayed until the Board reconsidered its position in light of James's new report. Mackeson chastised Campbell, wondering why he was not already marching north, even though approval for the invasion had not yet come from Dalhousie. He further complained that Campbell upset and embarrassed him by using information from Captain James in his letter to Gomm. Blinding himself to Dalhousie's violations of line-staff civilities, Mackeson concluded that Campbell's letter should have first been sent to him because James was a civil commissioner.

Campbell did not accept Mackeson's scolding for what it was: a somewhat justified, if fussy, statement by a man working in the shadow of Lord Dalhousie. Indignation rising like bile, Campbell wrote Mackeson it was hard cheese if he did not like James's giving him information and that he had enough to worry about without learning all Mackeson's pettifogging rules. Then Campbell turned emphatic. He would not invade Swat on the basis of erroneous information. Gomm agreed, ordering Campbell not to invade Swat without more concrete evidence of tribal transgressions.

Dalhousie wrote Couper on 30 May, verbally broadsiding Campbell. "The frontier is troublesome, and Sir Colin Campbell more troublesome than the frontier," furious because he refused to invade Swat. "On what grounds, I ask you? . . . On the avowed ground that . . . he the military brigadier was not himself convinced of the justice of the movement, and therefore would not move!!" (*Private Letters*, 203-204).

Even the press lost patience with Campbell's intransigence. On 9 May, the Bombay *Telegraph and Courier* bemoaned his reluctance to cross the border: "[Campbell] is evidently impressed with an exaggerated idea of number and powers of resistance of the hill men and is . . . bent on not going at them unless considerably re-enforced. We cannot but wonder and regret that [he] should peril his former good name so seriously."

The order to go—that is all it was because no real plan existed—foundered on misunderstanding. The entire cast of characters, only too eager to grab pen and paper and fire epistles at one another, sought self-exculpation. Like so many dust devils dancing across the Peshawar plain, the winds of argumentation and bitterness swirled around the participants.

Real events moved inexorably forward always ahead of the communications. On 10 May, almost three weeks before Lord Dalhousie's letter to Couper, Campbell led a force to the Swat River. His command included a six-gun troop of horse artillery, plus two 8-inch howitzers and two 9-pounder field guns, the 2nd Irregular Cavalry, the Queen's 32nd Regiment, the 28th Bengal Infantry, the 66th Gurkha Regiment, units from the Corps of Guides, and a company of sappers and miners. The force totaled 2,450 men, a strong and balanced operational contingent designed for a long-range punitive expedition. The presence of artillery and cavalry indicated that Campbell did not want the infantry to bear the burden of fighting. He had no intention of chasing the tribal warriors into the hills. He would bring them to the plain.

The column marched toward a group of Utman-Khel villages whose warriors were raiding the border and who allegedly assisted Ajoon Khan. Finding the villages deserted, the force burned them, along with caches of grain. At that point, welcome reinforcements marched into Campbell's camp. Captain Coke led 500 men of the 1st Punjab Infantry and two squadrons of the 1st Punjab Cavalry all the way from Kohat south of Peshawar, to Shubkudur, and then to Abazai. They covered the next forty miles to Campbell's camp in only eighteen hours.

The Field Force marched to Pranghur, considered the stronghold of the Utman-Khel tribe. The village, flanked by ridges, backed onto rugged hills. The tribesmen were waiting, dug in behind the village walls. Under cover of artillery fire, the 66th Gurkhas and the Guides infantry charged forward, easily vaulting the walls, and cleared the village at bayonet point. The defenders and villagers retreated into the hills where Campbell's skirmishers literally chased them from rock to rock. "The artillery made good practice." Campbell wrote in his report, meaning that whenever the tribesmen crowded together, a few rounds either dispersed or killed them. Campbell was impressed with the fighting ability of the tribesmen and admitted that were it not for his artillery, his casualties might have been severe. Only three men were killed and fifteen wounded. Body counts of enemy killed were not required in those days. By order of Lieutenant Colonel Mackeson, the village and a large grain cache found near the top of a hill were burned.

The Battle at Iskakote

On 18 May, the column reached Iskakote (Map 4), a Ranizai village of some 600 houses flanked on the west side by a many-branched jagged range of hills. A wide and deep nullah flanked the south side, then curved east and swept north. Warriors from various Swat tribes, an estimated 6,000, waited at Iskakote. Campbell's force approached from the southeast about two hours after dawn and found the tribesmen arrayed in the nullah and beyond into the village. Campbell formed his troops for battle. The 2nd Irregular Cavalry was deployed on the left to screen the main attack by preventing the tribesmen from enveloping that flank. He placed the Guides cavalry at the front and on the right flank. In between, the infantry deployed in columns, Coke's Punjab Infantry on the left, then the Queen's 32nd, the 66th Gurkhas, and, on the right, the Guides infantry. The 28th Bengal Infantry secured the rear.

Horse artillery fire on the center of the tribal defensive line broke up their concentrations. The Punjab Infantry moved in a northerly arc toward the nullah above the village. The 28th Bengals advanced to support the horse artillery. The 32nd moved south to cut the tribesmen's path of withdrawal. But the main attack was carried out by the Gurkhas and Guides infantry. They stormed into the nullah, charging a large body of tribesmen. Intense hand-to-hand fighting developed, the tribesmen hacking with their tulwars, the Gurkhas stabbing with their bayonets and hubris, their now-famous wide-bladed curved knives. As the battle raged, the horse artillery galloped to the edge of the nullah and opened fire with grape shot directly into the packed tribesmen. The restricted front of the dry river bed forced such congestion that the gunners could not miss.

Unable to withstand the deadly fire, the tribesmen broke into two large groups, one scattering to the hills behind the village, where they came under the fire of the 9-pounders, the other group, a contingent

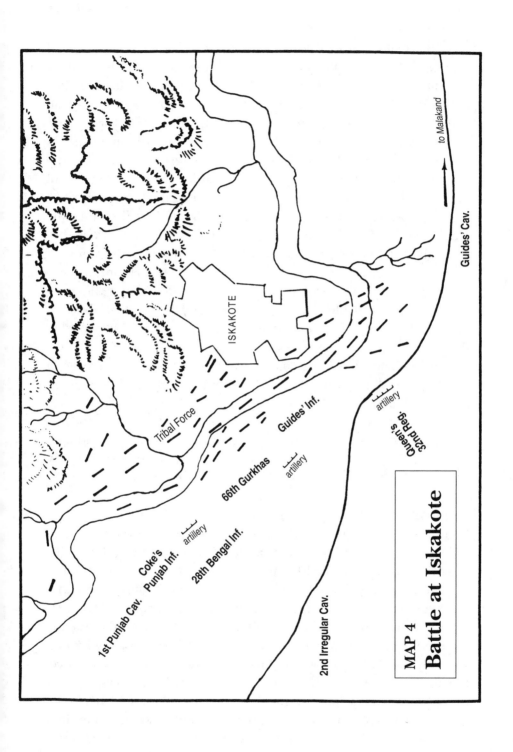

MAP 4
Battle at Iskakote

ISKAKOTE

to Malakand

Guides' Cav.

Tribal Force

Guides' Inf.

66th Gurkhas

artillery

Queen's
33rd Reg.

artillery

Coke's
Punjab Inf.

28th Bengal Inf.

artillery

1st Punjab Cav.

2nd Irregular Cav.

from the Field Force in pursuit, moving east toward the Malakand Pass, the village and all its crops were burned at Mackeson's orders.

The tribesmen at Iskakote surely thought they could overcome the British by force of numbers. But, deploying through the nullah and the village, they threw away their best fighting assets. Given their mobility, endurance, and potential firepower, the tribesmen should have drawn the British into the hills where cavalry and artillery could not follow. But Campbell concluded the battle "was essentially one of the plains and not of the mountains." He shaped the battle to his own ends and overcame the numerical superiority of the tribes. Like the Mamelukes in Egypt before them, the tribesmen knew what they knew about battle but that knowledge was archaic in the context of modern warfare as the British practiced it. The formations and tactics, the disciplined firepower of the British infantry, and the enormous impact of artillery were all elements of battle the tribesmen never before experienced and did not understand. The ensuing slaughter was a foregone conclusion.

The Peshawar Field force marched on, skirmishing with tribesmen and burning nine more villages. The Ranizai clan finally submitted unconditionally. They offered to pay a fine but, in light of the damage done to them, it was never imposed. They also agreed to allow the building of a fort in their territory. Last, they agreed to suspend raiding and to prevent others bent on raiding from crossing their lands.

The Field Force returned to Peshawar.

THE PAPER WAR CONTINUES

Even though Campbell's expedition brought death and destruction, the argument over a full-scale invasion of Swat continued. Letters by the Swat leaders, the Padsha and the Akhund, were discovered at Pranghur, supposedly confirming their involvement with Ajoon Khan. Although no one beyond Mackeson and perhaps a couple of his subordinates ever saw the originals, the letters were declared authentic "by every known text." The nature of those tests is today unknown, and only translations exist in the papers of the Peshawar Field Force. But such an assurance was enough for Dalhousie. The case against the Swat leaders was proven; therefore, Campbell's objections to the invasion were superfluous, objections that Dalhousie indicated in a memorandum of 29 May were directly insubordinate to civil authority.

The Board of Administration, backing Dalhousie, demanded immediate compliance to the governor general's wishes. An editorial from the Lahore Chronicle supporting the government's position was republished in the Bombay *Telegraph and Courier* on 2 June:

> The scruple of Sir Colin Campbell to enter Swat have triumphed over policy that required him making an example of the enemy. . . . We cannot congratulate the Brigadier. . . . He has not added to the laurels that previously encircled his brow.

Then quite suddenly the invasion scheme fell apart. Campbell, finally given orders by Gomm to proceed, requested another 2,500 men based on his assessment of tribal strength observed during the recent expedition. The Board denied the request. Mackeson added confusion, determining that camels were unfit transport for an expedition in mountainous terrain. The commissariat tried to gather elephants, mules, and bullocks, but there were not enough animals and animal handlers available. It was now June and hot weather settled on the Peshawar plain. On 4 June, the Board of Administration ordered that all military activities, including the invasion of Swat, be terminated.

Campbell, seething over what he considered a complete misunderstanding of his views and angered by the attacks against him by Dalhousie and the press, submitted his letter of resignation on 3 June 1852. Sir Charles Napier, always finding the worst in civil authority, particularly in Dalhousie, wrote Lord Ellenborough, "My friend Colin Campbell has been driven from India."

Campbell landed in England in early March 1853 and was immediately invited by Napier to visit him. Hoping that a question would be asked in the House of Lords, Napier again wrote Lord Ellenborough telling of "the unprovoked attacks and cruelties on the tribes around Peshawar," going on to say that "whole districts have been devastated, and the most beautiful villages burned, without any apparent reason but the desire of the politicals to appear 'vigorous' in the eyes of Lord Dalhousie" (*Life and Opinions*, vol. 4, 390). Ellenborough did not rise to the occasion.

General Gomm wrote to Lord Fitzroy Somerset (later Lord Raglan), secretary to the British Army's commander-in-chief, explaining the circumstances of Campbell's resignation and freeing him from the accusation of insubordination. Campbell, grateful to his old friend, probably wondered if the secretary would ever call upon him again to serve Queen and country. The call came sooner than either man expected. The Crimea would test them both.

AFTERWORD: TO MAKE A DESERT
Napier wrote Campbell on 18 April, stating he would have been disappointed if Campbell acquiesced in the Swat invasion because he thought the idea foolish, ill considered, and very unmilitary. He continued in his inimitable fashion:

> Why should you march on these places? What could you have done when you got there? March on to some other two places, and so on, into the heart of Asia!!! and then laid down your arms! . . . March to the top of hill No. 1; lose some men; get there. Enemy waiting on top of hill No. 2; go there; more men killed and wounded; more provisions gone. . . . Now every pass must be carried at the point of the bayonet, whilst the rear-guard is over-powered by a hot pursuing enemy. (Shadwell, vol. I, 303–304)

Campbell, conscience-stricken, all along considered the Swat invasion a potential disaster. This may seem strange considering his operations in May against the Utman-Khel and Ranizai. Success only fed his remorse because he felt the operations against the tribesmen and the proposed invasion were "based on the most cruel injustice." However much his conscience was bothering him, Campbell also believed sound military reasons existed for not invading Swat.

First, there was the matter of transport. Despite Mackeson's poor timing, he was quite right to order that camels be replaced with mules and bullocks. Camels could not operate in rock-strewn mountains because their soft foot pads would be cut to pieces. Furthermore, a column could only move as fast as its slowest animal. Bullocks trundled along at one and one-half miles an hour. Moreover, given the logistics of fighting in that part of the world, the baggage and supply trains for 5,000 fighting men would have included animal handlers for each beast, officers' servants—at least five for each—plus cooks, wood gatherers, water carriers, a full commissariat, a medical facility and orderlies, and more servants and their equipment, a swarm of minor functionaries, and camp followers whose presence was unquestioned if also unnecessary. The column, at the very least 20,000 people, would have been miles long, slow as a snail, and a ripe target for snipers and raiders as it crawled toward Napier's hill No. 1.

Second, the political commissioners offered no plan to guarantee continuous communication between the column and Peshawar. If the expedition ran into serious trouble, there was no way to relay a message to headquarters. Any rider leaving the column would have been shot within a hundred yards. Thus, once across the Peshawar plain, once through the Malakand Pass, the column would have been very much on its own. That did not in itself bother Campbell if the campaign was brief. He volunteered to mount a three-day raid north of the Malakand with a rapidly moving, no-frills, hit-and-run column. The idea was summarily rejected.

Third, and of vital importance, Campbell knew that his Peshawar Field Force, the Guides Corps a possible exception, was ill prepared and ill equipped for mountain warfare. Lord Dalhousie and his commissioners remained confused about this point. They reasoned that since the punitive operations were successful, Campbell could defeat the tribesmen in Swat. Campbell's observation that the battle at Iskakote was of the plains and not of the mountains was a distinction apparently lost on the politicals.

The consequences of ignoring concerns like those aired by Campbell were etched on the memorial tablets of the First Afghan War, 1839 to 1842. In that last year, a column of 15,000 soldiers and civilians, women and children among them, trekked through the mountains from Kabul to Jalalabad, ambushed and sniped at the entire way. Only one man lived to complete the journey (although some were taken prisoner and later returned). Campbell could read. He had the fortitude to say no.

What, now, is the historical importance of these operations above Peshawar? How does wandering about the Northwest Frontier with the Peshawar Field Force and glimpsing the bureaucratic warfare within the British hierarchy advance our understanding of desert battle?

Starting with the application of Bryan Perrett's categories of desert warfare, we find the Frontier battles a kind of low-intensity conflict. From Lieutenant Miller's skirmish near Mutta to the battle at Iskakote, the technology used was at the low end of the scale. Human muscle and draft animals powered the campaigns. Everyone had a gun but these, from pistols to muskets to cannon, were muzzleloaders, weapons with which the Napoleonic soldiers in Egypt fifty years before would have been very comfortable; in fact, the British musket, the Brown Bess, was little different from the model of the same weapon used at Waterloo. Thus, the technology of war did not change much from the Egyptian campaign. Nor had it changed much for the Frontier tribes. Matchlocks, tulwars, and knives often were literally the same weapons used by their grandfathers.

The battle formations used by the two sides were tied to their respective traditions and conditioned by their inherited technology.

The tribesmen, like the earlier Mamelukes, entered battle as a crowd, lacking internal organization and discipline, each warrior carried along by a shared *élan* but very much an individual. They must have looked very impressive as they crossed a plain or emerged from a ravine. But that en masse presentation of power was inefficient. Only those in the first few ranks or along the sides of the mass had clear fields of fire. The rest were all jammed together, the men in the interior and at the rear rendered ineffectual. Consequently, despite large numbers, the tribesmen could not train all their weapons on the British formations, and those that could fired at will. But British artillery fire and musket volleys must have confused those inside the mass. Lacking interior communications, lacking officers to control their movements, lacking any knowledge of British tactics and the sophistication to overcome those tactics with their own new approaches, the tribesmen found it easier to leave the field.

The British formations, line and column, did not change from the Napoleonic Wars, retained partly because the technology of battle did not dictate change and because the formations were continuously effective against enemies such as the Frontier tribesmen. As with Bonaparte's squares, the British line formation was especially efficient in delivering the full weight of the firepower they possessed. Artillery complimented the musket fire and was crucial to British success in the field. Grape shot and round shot were enormously destructive against packed masses. Once again, the tribes were not familiar with such weapons and did not know how to counter their power. As

Campbell's Field Force demonstrated, the number of guns possessed is less important than how they are used. Two cannon shots at Shubkudur were sufficient to turn back a tribal horde.

Campbell also realized that even a small force needed a sound logistical and communications base. This was especially so in a hostile environment. The Field Force carried everything they needed whenever they left Peshawar. Animals were essential, but Mackeson discovered he could not obtain enough draft animals for the Swat invasion. Campbell was concerned that continuous communications with Peshawar were overlooked in the so-called preparations. He stubbornly held his ground against all opposition, a general who put preparations ahead of dash. But this was the mid-nineteenth century, and dash received high marks in influential military circles. They measured Campbell and found him wanting.

The violence visited upon the tribesmen did not have a lasting effect. As Robert Leonhard points out in *The Art of Maneuver*, military strength alone does not translate into civilian compliance. In 1855, barely three years after Campbell's resignation and despite the compromises reached with the British, the Mohmands were again raiding. The British response remained march and burn. Later British policy vacillated between continued punitive expeditions and ignoring the raids in hopes the tribesmen might quit of their own volition. Finally frustrated because neither action nor inaction worked, the British drew an imaginary line around the Northwest Frontier from Kandahar and Jalalabad in Afghanistan, northeast to Chitral in the northern Dir Valley, and ending in the Gilgit Valley of Swat just below the Kara Koram Mountains. Every road leading north was guarded by forts placed in the midst of hostile tribes. A young Winston Churchill, serving in the Malakand Field Force (an updated version of the Peshawar Field Force), saw them for what they were—further provocations for war. Between 1850 and 1910, the British mounted fifty punitive expeditions against the hill tribes. In the 1890s the British garrison at Chitral withstood a forty-six-day siege by hill tribes. The British were still battling to open the Malakand Pass at the turn of the century. From April through October 1916, the Mohmands raided so frequently that the British erected blockhouses and a wire fence to secure the border. Then, on 15 November 1916, some 6,000 Mohmands gathered, threatening Shubkudur yet again. The 1st Peshawar Division, sup-

ported by armored cars, dispersed the tribesmen. The military compound that Campbell constructed outside Peshawar was still there in
1924—encircled by an electrified fence. The fighting went on and on
into the 1930s, all the death and dying and burning predicated on
policies instituted during the confusion of the early 1850s. And what
was accomplished was only that the tribesmen were usually defeated
in the skirmishing. But they were never subjugated. Colin Davies concludes that by punishing the many for the criminal activities of a few,
by burning villages and destroying crops, the British created a desert
and called it peace.

CHAPTER 5

The British Campaign in Mesopotamia, 1916 to 1918

TRAGIC PRELUDE

The British Mesopotamian campaign of 1916 to 1918 began not, with the certain knowledge of eventual victory, but with an unanticipated and tragic prelude. On 5 November 1914, the British declared war on Turkey to halt German expansionism and to protect the oil facilities at Abadan near the Persian Gulf. The London War Cabinet charged the Indian government with securing the area. Elements of the 6th Poona Division landed at the Shattal-Arab and, on 21 November, took Basra. The Indian government was satisfied because a small military investment produced major strategic results. The London War Cabinet was satisfied because the venture cost them nothing and did not divert troops from the Western Front in Belgium and France. The affair seemed a tidy little package (Map 5).

But general orders given the Indian expeditionary force by the Indian high command unlocked a Pandora's box in the Middle East that London did not foresee. The Poona Division could march north along the Tigris River as far as necessary to create a buffer zone around Basra and the oil facilities. Thus, to secure Basra, the town of Qurna was taken on 31 May 1915, a logical choice because it controlled the point at which the Tigris and Euphrates joined to form the Shatt-al-Arab. The British now controlled river traffic in southern Mesopotamia.

The Indian government, meanwhile, without consulting London, sent another division and a cavalry brigade to Mesopotamia. Charles Townshend took command of the Poona Division, and Sir John Nixon was appointed theater commander. Also unknown to London,

Sir Beauchamp Duff, Indian Army commander in chief, told Nixon to develop a plan for taking Baghdad.

Nixon ordered Townshend sixty miles north to Amara, ostensibly as a buffer for Qurna. That was not enough. Amara needed a buffer, so on 28 September 1915, Townshend occupied Kut-al-Amara, 153 miles further north. To hold Kut, the division marched another sixty miles up the Tigris to Aziziyeh. No serious high-level thought was given to the consequences of this incremental move northward, nor was Townshend certain his division could do the job. They lacked proper equipment, supplies, transport, medical facilities, and artillery support and had no plan for reinforcements. But ego triumphed over military reality as he contemplated becoming military governor of the ancient capital and his promotion to lieutenant general. Nixon glibly believed the march to Baghdad was possible. So, too, did Beauchamp Duff. The idea became a brighter reality with each successive move upriver. The London War Cabinet, after much indecision, finally gave their consent at the end of October. Taking Baghdad would revive British prestige in the Arab world. Thus the campaign proceeded on political rather than military grounds.

Nixon ordered Townshend to take Ctesiphon, discounting reports that the Turks were well entrenched and reinforced. Townshend attacked on 22 November. Although inflicting heavy casualties on the enemy, he lost a third of his division. His wounded were evacuated to Amara. There were nearly 3,000 of them, 700 percent more than Nixon estimated for the battle. The men were heaved onto boats and barges, all jammed together in 120°F heat without medical assistance during the journey. Hundreds died. Yet, Nixon reported that the transport and medical systems were working efficiently.

Townshend withdrew down the Tigris to Kut-al-Amara, a dirty little town on a bend of the river. Once there, he decided that his men could go no further and willingly subjected them to a siege. His British and Indian troops repulsed a series of attacks in December but, as the weeks passed, the fighting turned into a waiting game. The real battles were fought further south.

Lieutenant General Fenton Aylmer, V.C., led the newly formed Tigris Corps in the attempt to rescue Kut. Aylmer's corps, lacking howitzers, sufficient mortars and machine guns, lacking supplies and adequate transport, nonetheless attacked the Turks again and again

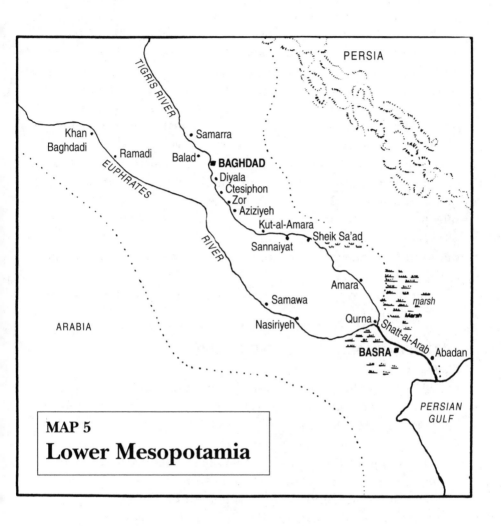

PERSIA

TIGRIS RIVER

Khan
Baghdadi

Ramadi

EUPHRATES

• Samarra

Balad• ■ BAGHDAD
       •Diyala
       • Ctesiphon
       • Zor
       • Aziziyeh
       Kut-al-Amara
              ►Sheik Sa'ad
       Sannaiyat

RIVER

Amara

ARABIA

Samawa

Nasiriyeh   Qurna•

marsh

Marsh

Shatt-al-Arab

BASRA ■   .Abadan

PERSIAN
GULF

MAP 5
Lower Mesopotamia

over open ground. The Tigris Corps lost 22,000 men in four months, twice the number they were trying to save.

London, however shocked by the carnage and ineptitude, became a reluctant partner, sending troops from the Western Front to reinforce Aylmer's corps. Then London took full control of the campaign and made Sir Percy Lake theater commander. But the changes were too late. Aylmer could not break through the Turkish lines in the south. Townshend, his men worn out and malnourished, sick with dysentery, jaundice, cholera, and scurvy, surrendered on 28 April 1916. The Turks sent the British officers by boat to Baghdad. The enlisted men were sent on a death march, whipped, clubbed, bayoneted, and shot by their Kurdish guards. Those who fell by the wayside, too ill or exhausted to move, were tortured, killed, and stripped of their possessions by Arabs shadowing the column. The survivors were sent to forced labor camps in Turkey that, for many, became oblivion.

The British army suffered one of the most humiliating defeats of its long history.

TRANSITION: MAY TO DECEMBER 1916
Stagnant Front
On 30 April, the Imperial General Staff sent a telegram to Beauchamp Duff, stating in no uncertain terms London's position regarding future operations in Mesopotamia:

> At present our policy in Mesopotamia is defensive and we do not attach any importance to the possession of Kut or to the occupation of Baghdad. . . . It is undesirable and impossible to reinforce [the Tigris Corps] owing to the conditions in other theatres of war. (Moberly, *The Campaign in Mesopotamia*, vol. 3, *Official History*, 3)

Beauchamp Duff forwarded the telegram to General Lake, yet added the comment that a further advance up the Tigris would create a greater buffer for the oil facilities and extend British influence from Basra. The man must have been obtuse or blind to the situation, for his addendum was a complete contravention of London's intentions.

In early May 1916, the Tigris Corps numbered 25,450 men, including 2,000 cavalry. They had 143 artillery pieces. Moberly's *Official History* states that Turkish strength was about 16,000 men and 64 guns. But superior numbers did not equal fighting ability. Lord Moran, a front-line battalion medical officer in World War I, stated in his poignant recollection, *The Anatomy of Courage*, "It is not the number of soldiers, but their will to win which decides battles." That will to win, Moran observed, is like a bank account against which combat duty makes constant withdrawals. One day, sooner or later, the account hits zero.

Gloom hung over the Tigris Corps for having failed to rescue the Poona Division. Their relief effort began in the winter of 1916, when snow and sleet brought temperatures below freezing. With spring, torrential rains and the overflowing of the Tigris turned the ground into gluelike mud. Ankle deep, sometimes waist deep, it clung to the soldiers' bodies and fouled their weapons. The men advanced through that muck against Turkish trenches barely disturbed by British artillery, only to be cut down by long-range rifle and machine-gun fire. Casualties mounted: at Sheikh Sa'ad, 4,262; at Hanna in late January, 2,741; at Dujaila in early March, 3,500; at Sannaiyat in early April, 1,807. And this list is not half the battles fought.

Townshend's surrender changed nothing for the Tigris Corps. They stayed in their trenches, staring across no-man's land at the unburied corpses of their comrades. The temperature soared to 115°F by the end of May. Insufferable tents offered no relief. The only water came from the running sewer called the Tigris. The rotting corpses spawned armies of flies that blanketed sweating skin, wounds, food, and drink. Disease ran rampant. According to A. J. Barker, 30,000 sick men required evacuation from the front lines by mid-August. When Major General George MacMunn inspected the troops at Amara, he found the men dirty, unshaven, diseased, and many sleeping in the mud. The camp was poorly laid out. New young officers could not control their men. MacMunn was so appalled that he warned the Indian army colonel in charge that if he found the camp in the same condition three days hence, he would hang him from a flagpole.

These conditions hardly contributed to building an esprit de corps among the remaining veterans and the young half-trained replace-

ments. The purpose of this front was not at all clear, and some definitive message from those in command was desperately needed.

Fortunately, General Lake knew that any attempt to move upriver
invited disaster. Wide-ranging changes were needed in logistical support and medical facilities. The corps needed enlargement and support by more artillery, machine guns, and mortars. A full explication
of the logistical and organizational changes undertaken would interest no one but an accountant, so I shall summarize those in place by
September 1916.

1. Three narrow-gauge railways were nearing completion. One ran
   between Basra and Nasiriyeh, another from Qurna to Amara,
   and a third between Sheikh Sa'ad and Es Sinn. Additionally, a
   metalled road was constructed between Basra and Sheikh Sa'ad
   for trucks, carts, and troops on foot.

2. Sir George Buchanan, a port expert brought from India,
   improved the Basra harbor facilities. Docks for unloading ships
   were constructed—in contrast to unloading on to river craft.
   New dry docks and machine shops employed 6,000 Chinese
   mechanics specially brought in to service river craft and the
   growing motor pool.

3. Sir George MacMunn, new inspector general of the theater,
   developed a systematic approach to river transport, establishing
   the River Transport Service, 7,171 men strong. The service
   included experienced river pilots who understood the sub-
   tleties of the two great rivers. Their efforts increased the tonnage delivered to the front.

4. MacMunn realized he needed more boats. In 1915, there were
   only six steamers and eight tugs, together with a motley array of
   native river craft, available for transport. MacMunn increased
   the number to 446 steam tugs and launches, 774 barges, and
   414 motor boats. This increase was not easily accomplished. Seventeen vessels sank on tow from India, and many built in Britain
   for later assembly at Basra had to be drastically modified. Also,
   the 6,200 miles trip from the Cornwall dockyards to Basra was
   frought with danger. MacMunn developed a relay system to
   speed passage of the small boats during favorable weather.

5. Facilitation of river transport enhanced medical treatment
   because the wounded were delivered to the base hospital at

Amara much faster and under more gentle conditions than experienced after the battle at Ctesiphon. Furthermore, each division was supplied field ambulances. Sanitary units helped reduce losses caused by disease. Battalion and brigade medical facilities were increased, and corps medical facilities included a stationary hospital, two casualty clearing stations, and two advanced medical store depots.

6. Artillery ammunition, especially high explosive projectiles, was stored in the forward area. Mountain batteries from India arrived, as did Royal field Artillery howitzer batteries armed with 4.5-inch and 6-inch guns. Six trench mortar companies, using 2-inch weapons, were organized, and Stokes mortar batteries, used for firing smoke bombs, were also added. Corps level support included 12- and 13-pounder anti-aircraft guns.

7. Every brigade (three battalions) included a machine gun company armed with sixteen Vickers .303 weapons, and every battalion now had six Lewis guns, eminently portable light machine guns. The Lewis guns relieved machine gunners from trying to use the 96-pound Vickers guns in a close support role.

8. The Royal Flying Corps sent Major J. E. Tennant's 30 Squadron to the area. They flew twenty-four B.E. 2Cs, useful for either bombing—they carried 330-pound bombs—or aerial photography. That increased the precision in map making and intelligence assessments. The biwing two-seater, a very stable plane that flew 72 mph, stayed aloft over three hours. Toward the end of 1917, 63 Squadron was added to the theater, flying the famous Spad fighters, a French aircraft capable of 138 mph, and RE 8s, another two-seater reconnaissance craft. The RE 8s flew at 98 mph, carried a 224-pound bomb load, and were armed with two .303 machine guns.

No new offensive could be reasonably considered without these changes. But the purpose of the buildup, if all the men and weapons were eventually going to be thrown away by unimaginative leadership, was at best unclear. On 16 July 1916, the Tigris Corps command passed to one of the most junior major generals in the theater, Sir Frederick Stanley Maude. Then, on 2 August, he was promoted to lieutenant general and replaced an ailing and exhausted Percy Lake as commander-in-chief in Mesopotamia. Historians often note that

Maude enjoyed the confidence of his London masters and so received most of the supplies, weapons, and manpower he requested.

Unlike Lake, Nixon, and Townshend, Maude did not come from the Indian Army. Following his education at Eton and Sandhurst, he entered the prestigious Coldstream Guards in 1884, at age twenty. He served briefly in the Sudan and, then, in 1895, went through the staff college at Camberley. He was made brigade major of the Guards Brigade. In 1899, Maude joined his regiment in South Africa, where he saw considerable action during the Boer War and won the Distinguished Service Order. In 1914, he served in the battles at Mons, the Marne, Aisne, Armentières, and Lys. In October 1914, promoted brigadier general, he was at La Basse and Neuve Chapelle. Soon a major general, he commanded the 13th Division in Gallipoli, conducting the masterful withdrawal from Sulva. In February 1916, he took his division to Mesopotamia.

When the London leadership assumed responsibility for the campaign, their understandable desire was to have their own man in charge. Their kind of officer was Stanley Maude. He was, after all, a Guardsman, and the powerful in London would take one of His Majesty's Guards officers over someone from the Indian Army every time. That reason for choosing Maude may seem fickle. But Indian Army officers—Nixon, Townshend, Aylmer—were proven failures in Mesopotamia. Maude, in contrast, was a veteran of the Western Front who experienced the bitter lessons of trench warfare. Then Gallipoli disabused him of any notions he might have held that the Turks were second raters. Maude also realized that the massive frontal assaults used by Aylmer's relief force failed miserably in an environment that favored the enemy and offered the Anglo-Indian troops little comfort.

The initial phase of an offensive necessarily entailed dislodging the Turks from their well-fortified entrenchments, but for the British to simply walk across open ground into enemy fire was no longer acceptable. Maude's half-trained youngsters needed intense training in small unit tactics, so selected troops were withdrawn from the line to rehearse advancing against replicas of enemy positions. Maude knew that once his men penetrated the Turkish lines, the character of the offense would change from trench warfare to battle in open country, requiring mobility and the rapid extension of supply and communications lines. Thus, not only were Maude's combat troops retrained;

he also enlarged and trained his staff to handle the enormously increased logistical workload.

Unlike Aylmer's battles of 1916, Maude had no intention of leaving anything to chance or allowing the men to suffer from ill-formed and hasty plans. He personally checked and double-checked preparations, rattling his staff, and visiting his frontline troops. His hands-on approach might be perceived as a weakness, a failure to delegate responsibility, and so much meddling in the nuts and bolts of his army. I think it must be understood that Maude's experiences on the Western Front, where generals commanded from afar, and the bloody Mesopotamian battles in which his 13th Division participated, conditioned him to be more of a frontline general. He would make mistakes—but they would be mistakes of judgment, not of ignorance.

That Maude had time to make necessary changes, stockpile supplies, and bring his army to fighting trim was partly the consequence of the beastly weather that made active campaigning impossible. Turkish passivity, as well, was a major contributing factor. Khalil Pasha, the Turkish commander-in-chief, knew he was outnumbered and outgunned. Contemptuous of the British, he believed his troops could hold, but not where they were located. He disengaged, regrouping his force by pulling back from Bait Isa to new positions around the Shatt-al-Hai. A. J. Barker notes in *The Bastard War* that Khalil, having made the adjustments, turned his attentions elsewhere. Sitting in Baghdad, his ego brimming over, he dreamed of a sweeping maneuver into Persia, outflanking the British, cutting off their supply lines, and pushing them from Mesopotamia.

His self-absorbed distraction was a fatal mistake. Elements of the Russian Caucasus Army entered Mesopotamia and threatened Baghdad. Khalil was forced to redeploy many of his men to meet that threat, leaving only three divisions—XVIII Corps commanded by Kiazim Karabekir—to face the British.

The time had come for Maude to strike.

MAUDE'S OFFENSIVE, DECEMBER 1916 TO APRIL 1918

Fortunately, changes in policy coincided with Maude's preparations. The Imperial General Staff telegraphed Maude on 28 September that, if and when possible, British influence should be established in Baghdad. General Sir Beauchamp Duff, visiting Mesopotamia in

October, reported to London that troop conditions were much improved, making a limited offense possible. He suggested advances against the Shatt-al-Hai, and along the Euphrates from Nasiriyeh to Samawa—but not at the risk of high casualties.

The ensuing campaign can be conveniently divided into four phases: Phase I, the retaking of Kut; Phase II, the chase; Phase III, the occupation of Baghdad; Phase IV, consolidation.

Phase I: The Retaking of Kut-al-Amara

By the end of summer, the Turks transformed their positions into formidable obstacles to compensate for their inferior numbers. They dug trenches above Kut and east of Sannaiyat to the marshes. The trench line continued on the other side of the river two miles along the Shatt-al-Hai. In addition to frontal positions, they built strongpoints behind Sannaiyat and trenches extending along the river banks to prevent a British crossing.

But the elaborate defensive system contained flaws. The Turks offered the British a passive, static defense. Their come-and-get-us attitude discounted the impact of increased British artillery—not only the number of guns available but the right kind of guns shooting the right kind of ammunition. The Turks also misaligned their positions. Although Kahlil's calculated withdrawal from Bait Isa made sense at the time, no compensatory repositioning was made on the other side of the river. Thus, the Turkish lines at Sannaiyat were only 120 yards from the British trenches but across the river near the Dujaila Redoubt they were two miles apart, resulting in a twelve-mile misalignment. Next, the Turks lacked reserve troops. With most of their troops committed to the front, the rear areas were vulnerable to British exploitation. Furthermore, the Turks suffered a lack of transport. Without sufficient trucks and an operable railway, the Turks were, as Barker states, "tied to the river," curtailing their ability to move laterally into the desert and around the British flanks.

Kiazim Karabekir, commander of XVIII Corps, tried to convince Khalil Pasha that the British buildup of men and materiel represented a threat that could be countered only by an infusion of troops and artillery. Khalil would not listen, reckoning that Kiazim's three divisions were more than adequate to handle anything the incompetent British could throw at him.

In December 1916, Maude's Tigris force numbered 48,500 combatants and 174 guns, organized into two corps (I and III), and a cavalry division. I Corps (3rd and 7th Divisions) held a long line facing Sannaiyat on the north side of the river (the left bank looking downriver), and from Arab Village on the south side (the right bank) in an arc to the Sinn Banks. III Corps (13th and 14th Divisions) was deployed west of the Sinn Banks to the Dujaila Redoubt and Depression. The Cavalry Division (6th and 7th Brigades) was camped at Arab Village. Three bridging trains with appropriate engineers and sappers were also available. One of the trains could move overland using trucks, and Indian army carts adapted to carry the pontoons.

On 13 December, the British offensive opened as the combined artillery of the two corps struck the Turkish emplacements around Sannaiyat. The artillery cut the enemy barbed wire as the British infantry moved about in obvious preparation for an assault. Maude did not want the Turks observing any of his other troops' movements, so 30 Squadron kept a few B.E. 2s ready to take off in case a Turkish plane should appear. Also, a flight of B.E. 2s bombed the Turkish Shumran boat bridge that was being towed upstream, soon forcing the steam tug to drop its tow lines. Pieces of the bridge floated free with the river current and ran aground. Thus, for the next several days the Turks were without cross-river communications and transport.

Kiazim took Maude's bait and reinforced the Sannaiyat front, not realizing that the bombardment and troop movements were part of an elaborate ruse. The real British attack came on the other side of the river.

During the night of 13 December and into the early hours of the next morning, the Cavalry Division and the 13th Division crossed the open plain, unobserved, to the banks of the Hai. The night march was a complete success. By 6:00 A.M., the leading divisional units were across the Shatt-al-Hai, completely surprising the Turks. The 40th Brigade of the 13th Division marched along the Hai to secure the flank. The 38th and 39th brigades advanced toward Kut. The 38th, commanded by Brigadier General J. W. O'Dowda, was composed of Lancashire battalions. The 39th, T. A. Andrus commanding, was mostly a west country unit, the battalions coming from Staffordshire, Gloucestershire, and Worcestershire. Heavy rifle and machinegun fire from Kut brought their advance to an abrupt halt. Ever conscious of the proscription against high casualty rates, Maude approved the divisions' subsequently cautious approach.

On 20 December, the 40th Brigade, mostly Welsh battalions, swung in an arc to the west. Rendezvousing with the Cavalry Division, commanded by F. S. Crocker, and with the mobile bridge train, they marched toward a loop in the river called the Shumran Bend, where they would cross the river, cut off the Turkish line of withdrawal, and disrupt communications. The plan was feasible because the river was low and only 300 yards wide at that point. But the cavalry patrols, inadvertently alerting the Turks to the British objective, lost the element of surprise. The Turks retaliated with accurate fire from 350 riflemen, two machine guns, and four field guns. A couple of crossings were attempted, but Maude sent a message to Crocker that he should withdraw if the crossing was not already achieved. The withdrawal took place at 2:15 P.M.

Maude decided to consolidate his gains but continued shelling the Turkish positions and bombing selected targets. These actions, according to the *Official History*, made the Turks very nervous. But Maude decided against further immediate advances, awaiting the right moment to achieve three definite objectives. First, he wanted a secure line along the Hai. Second, he wanted to clear the Turks from the right bank of the Tigris. Third, he would attack any developing weak points. These objectives in hand, he would push further north. Such an operation risked heavy losses. Sir William Robertson, imperial chief-of-staff, realizing that dislodging the Turks from Sannaiyat and Kut would be costly, lifted the caution against high casualties. And the price might indeed be high because the operation was against the main strength of the Turkish defenses.

The Turks dug another trench line one and one-half miles long south and west of Kut, between the banks of the Shatt-al-Hai and the Tigris, supported by machine guns and guarded by a broad barbed wire barrier. Swinging north from the Hai, in front of Kut, yet another defensive position extended across a shallow peninsula formed by the so-called Khadairi Bend of the Tigris. Two trench lines extended across the peninsula. The forward line ran in a northerly direction and the second, about 750 yards behind the first, followed the curve of the peninsula around the river bank. The land between the lines was covered with brush and scrub and cut by smaller communications trenches and dry canals.

On 22 December the 1st Manchesters and the Highland Light Infantry moved forward toward the Turks on the Khadairi Bend. This was an important maneuver because this position flanked Kut and covered the line from the Hai back to the Tigris. The two British regiments established themselves 700 yards from the Turkish wire near the river, digging narrow trenches perpendicular to their main trenches, as it were a siege operation. These narrow works, called saps (from sappers who historically dug them) were then linked laterally by another main trench. Saps were projected forward from the new trench, linked, and saps projected again. And so the tedious work continued despite heavy rains. Between 26 December and 6 January, the rains turned the ground into mud flows, stalling transport—even mules and camels. Fighting was reduced to patrols and small raids. The Turks did little to thwart the British digging program, feeling no doubt that their much improved trenches would stop any attack. But the passive defense yielded the no-man's-land to the British, allowing them to move closer and closer.

During 7 and 8 January 1917, British artillery hit the Turks around the Hai and the Khadairi Bend with a violent bombardment, causing, as the commander of the Turkish 45th Division observed, "bloody losses." On the 9th, at 7:30 A.M., fifty-six British guns fired on the Turkish wire and, at 8:45 A.M., the 1/1st Gurkhas, 105th Mahrattas, and the 93rd (Burmese) Infantry, together forming the 9th Brigade, advanced 200 yards against the enemy trenches. Two battalions of the 8th Brigade—the 1st Manchesters and the 59th Rifles—on the right advanced about 400 yards. The Turks, badly mauled by the bombardment, responded slowly. The 9th Brigade managed to occupy some trenches and dry canals but, around 10:00 A.M., a mist covering the field, the Turks counterattacked the Manchesters. Because the mist obscured the targets, British artillery ceased fire for fear of hitting their own men. The infantry had to hold. After intense hand-to-hand fighting, the Turks were repulsed.

British attacks and Turkish counterattacks, a series of small and bitter struggles, continued for the next three weeks. The Turks, a stubborn lot, refused to be pushed from the peninsula. The British attacks continued slowly and deliberately. Between 11 January and 18 January, the Turks were bombarded continuously by artillery as small British infantry detachments edged forward. When close to the Turkish lines, they charged. Gradually, yard by yard, trench by trench, the Turks were forced into a smaller and smaller target area. The British artillery could not miss. The Turks, finally worn down by these attritional tactics, evacuated the peninsula on 19 January.

That single week of small unit combat resulted in 1,639 British casualties. The Turkish losses are unknown.

Full attention now swung to the Shatt-al-Hai front. Despite the marvelously planned December surprise attack, the British withdrew under Turkish counterattacks to a 1,800-yard front that extended to both sides of the Hai. The one advantage they enjoyed was that they no longer could be outflanked.

Preparing for a later full-scale assault on the Hai, Major General W. S. Marshall, commanding III Corps, moved his troops forward 400 yards. Rain made further rapid movement impossible, so trenches and saps were dug until the British front was only 150 yards from the Turkish line. All the while, 103 guns hammered the Turkish positions. According to the *Official History*, the guns included twenty-four 4.5-inch howitzers, three 6-inch howitzers, and seventy-six field guns, including some 60-pounders (the numbers given by Kearsey and Barker vary slightly).

Crocker's cavalry rode to the marshes east of Sannaiyat on 24 January to create a diversion. At 9:40 A.M. the next morning, Marshall's 39th and 40th Brigades went "over the top." Four battalions formed successive assault waves—8th Royal Welsh Fusiliers, 5th Wiltshires, 7th North Staffordshires, and 9th Worcestershires. These battalions penetrated the Turkish lines and, by 10:00 A.M., consolidated their gains. An hour later the Turks mounted a counterattack supported by heavy mortar fire. The British battalions pulled back. They lost 1,135 men during the morning fight. Most of the casualties were from the Staffordshire and Worcestershire battalions that took the brunt of the counterattack. The British repeatedly attacked. The next day, the 26th and 28th Punjabis succeeded in retaking the Turkish line. But half their men lay dead or wounded.

On the opposite bank of the Hai, two Sikh battalions, the 36th and 45th, lost a thousand men on 1 February in a similar attack. Unfortunately, neither reached the Turkish lines. On 2 February, the $\frac{1}{4}$ Devon-shires and the $\frac{1}{2}$ Gurkhas from the 37th Brigade took the trenches.

British artillery fire now ranged freely over the enemy, especially targeting Turkish artillery emplacements as a means of keeping down their own infantry losses. The Turks slowly retreated before the unre-lenting attacks, men on both sides dying for crumbled trenches, dry canals, and grubby ditches. On 4 February, the Turks evacuated their positions around the Shatt-al-Hai and redeployed in a new line from Kut's licorice factory, on the south side of town, westerly to the Dahra Bend.

III Corps attacked this new line on 9 February, beginning with a heavy artillery bombardment. Meanwhile, the 36th Brigade advanced toward the licorice factory in yet another diversion. The main attack came farther west as the King's Own Royal Lancashire Regiment, from O'Dowda's 38th Brigade, crossed a quarter-mile of flat ground. The Turks bombarded them with artillery, and their infantry counter-attacked several times. The King's Own held on and, late in the after-noon, the 6th Prince of Wales advanced as reinforcement. Together, they withstood further counterattacks. On 10 February, the licorice factory, now little more than heaps of churned earth, was taken, and the 36th and 38th Brigades joined in a maneuver that squeezed the Turks into another shrinking perimeter. On 15 February, their will to fight drained by the constant onslaught, 2,000 Turks surrendered.

The successful attacks against the Hai front, however consuming, allowed Maude to refocus on the Sannaiyat defenses. Despite their obvious strength—five trench lines deep and manned by 2,100 men—the Sannaiyat defenses were brittle. Kiazim Karabekir com-manded a total of 10,000 infantry, 500 cavalry, and 91 guns on the Tigris front. The preliminary British attacks, especially their efficiently placed artillery bombardments, reduced his force by at least one-third, and the survivors were getting rather wobbly. In contrast, Maude still possessed a fighting strength of 46,000 men, a number maintained by the constant influx of new drafts, and 174 guns. Kiazim continued to warn Khalil of the seriousness of his situation but was met by silence. Not only did Khalil ignore requests for reinforce-ments, but he also neglected to establish fallback positions for XVIII Corps should they withdraw from Kut and Sannaiyat. In effect, he opened the door to Baghdad.

On 17 February a bombardment by fifty-eight field guns and how-itzers, trench mortars, and by naval gunboats poured down on the Sannaiyat positions. After a two-hour delay caused by muddy condi-tions, two battalions of the 21st Brigade, 7th Division, charged the Turkish lines. The 20th Punjabis and the 1/8th Gurkhas took both the first and second lines in only ten minutes, surprising the Turks with their determination. Then the Turkish artillery opened fire. The captured lines could not be held without serious losses, so the two battalions withdrew at 4:00 P.M.

Even though the attack failed, the Turks shifted their attention to the Sannaiyat front. Maude seized the moment and launched III Corps across the river at the Shumran Bend. Sappers, engineers, and infantry had practiced the crossing in a site model, but the operation remained dangerous. The crossing would take time and could not be kept secret for long. Once discovered, the troops on the river would be completely exposed to enemy fire. To minimize the risks involved, a series of movements were created to convince the Turks the cross-ing would be elsewhere. There was much scurrying about and splash-ing in front of Kut, then a raid mounted across the river and downstream further confused the Turks. The RFC kept patrols in the air to prevent Turkish planes from observing the actual crossing site.

To clinch the deceptions, the 7th Division renewed its attack against Sannaiyat on 22 February. The 1st Seaforth Highlanders and the 92nd Punjabis swept into the Turkish lines. The Turks counterat-tacked, pushing the Punjabis back. But the Highlanders held their position until Colonel T. R. Maclachlan, commanding the 92nd, stopped his men in the middle of the battlefield, restored order, and led them back to the Turkish lines.

At 3:15 P.M., the 51st and 53rd Sikhs attacked the Sannaiyat front lines near the positions held by the 92nd and Seaforths. They were heavily shelled by enemy artillery after entering the trenches. The Turks counterattacked. But, with the steady help of the Seaforths, who laid down enfilading fire on the Turks' flank, and reinforced by other companies from their brigade, the two Sikh battalions with-stood seven counterattacks and consolidated their positions. The 7th Division lost 1,332 men that afternoon.

The first bridging pontoons hit the water at Shumran Bend at 5:15 A.M., on 23 February. Slowly the Turks awakened to what was happening as three separate bridges were established. Their accurate rifle and machine gun fire harried the British, but their artillery was off the mark, and they did not find the range until the first bridge was completed. But British infantry, their supplies, and artillery were already across the river.

All during the afternoon of 23 February, Maude's headquarters received reports from I Corps of a Turkish withdrawal along the Sannaiyat front, and Royal Flying Corps (RFC) observers reported seeing Turkish troops on the Baghdad road. At 3:20 P.M., Cobbe ordered elements of the 7th Division to occupy the Turks' third and fourth lines. More an anticlimax or perhaps an afterthought, the British occupied Kut without meeting any resistance. Maude reported to the Imperial General Staff that "as a result of these operations we now have the whole of the enemy's positions from Sannaiyat to Kut."

Phase II: The Chase

A defeated enemy, hungry and exhausted, their morale battered, retreating across a featureless desert, is prey to a rapidly advancing force that can sweep around their flank and cut their path of withdrawal. The British Cavalry Division had the potential of being such a force but nevertheless failed. Maude's series of orders that sent them hither and thither, wearing out the animals, and Crocker's timid leadership left the division under a pall of indecisiveness. Thus, rather than sweeping anywhere, they became entangled in a series of infantry fights with the Turks' rear guard.

But a new weapon now operated with the cavalry, its proper uses discovered as the campaign progressed. Almost unnoticed in January because winter conditions precluded activation, the 13th Light Armored Motor Battery, known forever more by the acronym LAMB, arrived in Mesopotamia. Listed in the order of battle as artillery, LAMBS were actually Rolls-Royce armored cars, mounting a standard .303 Vickers water-cooled machine gun in a slope-sided revolving turret. With a 4 x 2 wheel drive, they bounced across the desert at 35 mph. A half-dozen cars operated with Crocker's cavalry. On 25 February, they tangled with the Turkish rearguard. The *Official History* notes that they "gave valuable assistance" to the cavalry. Barker increases the praise when he states that the armored cars probably caused the Turks more damage that day than the whole of the Cavalry Division.

British gunboats now steamed north of Shumran Bend. The *Tarantula*, *Mantis*, and *Moth* raced ahead, and *Gadfly* and *Butterfly* followed. At Nahr-al-Kalek Bend, they came upon units of the Turks' rear guard, whose artillery, rifle, and machine gun fire raked the boats. But once around the bend, the gunboats effectively outflanked the enemy and opened fire with every gun they had, causing many casualties in the rear guard and abandonment of several artillery pieces. Sailing farther north, the gunboats came within range of a Turkish flotilla. Under intense fire from the British vessels, one steamer ran aground and another, the *Pioneer*, was abandoned. The *Firefly*, captured from the British at Ctesiphon during Townshend's 1915 advance, was set afire, beached, recaptured, and soon returned to duty again under the British ensign. These naval engagements cost the Turks many dead and 1,500 wounded. The British captured a total of 7,000 Turks in the overall operation.

The Turkish XVIII Corps was grievously damaged. Retreating to Aziziyeh, Kiasim Karakebir expected to find reinforcements and rations. He found nothing.

Crocker's cavalry patrols reconnoitered Aziziyeh on 27 February and reported the Turks occupied the town. The next day they were gone, seeming to have vanished north. Maude's staff persuaded him to occupy Aziziyeh and rest the troops, already on half-rations. The staff needed time to close the supply and communications gap created by the rapid advance. Maude agreed. A week passed.

Ordinarily, such a self-imposed lull might help the enemy, giving them time to strengthen their positions. Yet, little happened on the Turkish side because, for once, Kahlil Pasha, right or wrong, did not know what to do: He could dig in at Lajj or better at Ctesiphon; he could abandon these forward posts and concentrate on holding Baghdad; or, because the flat country around that city left it vulnerable to attack from all sides, he could go sixty miles farther north and prepare a defense at Samarra. Enver Pasha, the Turkish war minister, made the decision for him. Defend Baghdad! Thus, beginning 1 March, the Turks constructed a defensive line along the Diyala River, about 8 miles below Baghdad, and constructed another line three miles southwest at the Umm-at-Tubul sand ridges, extending toward Lake Aqarquf.

Phase III: The Capture of Baghdad

Maude's force, leaving Aziziyeh, marched up the Tigris to Zor (Map 6). On 5 March, an advance patrol from the 7th Cavalry Brigade, accompanied by LAMBs, encountered the enemy at Lajj. A desert storm obscured the Turks' positions, but the *Official History* states there was no reason to believe the defenses were manned by anything but a weak force. What urged that conclusion is not clear. The 13th Hussars launched a mounted charge and ran into concentrated rifle and machine gun fire. Kahlil's 51st Division formed the "weak force." The *Official History* quotes the 13th's regimental history: "The 5th March will always be one of the regiments great days . . . [because it was] a death ride just as brave and devoted as the one which has become immortal," referring to the charge of the Light Brigade during the Crimean War. And just as stupid. In both battles, frontal attacks were ordered against virtually unknown positions. The Light Brigade, unable to see their real target because hills obscured their vision, were misdirected into the wrong valley. The 13th Hussars could barely see 150 yards. The Light Brigade charged into Russian cannon fire, the 13th into massed rapid-fire infantry weapons. The orders to charge were irresponsible, regardless of the romantic gloss that elevated the attacks into high drama. The futility of the 13th's charge was magnified when, after sunset, and under cover of a sandstorm, the Turks withdrew not only from Lajj but as well from Ctesiphon. Indeed, Khalil had opened the door to Baghdad.

British intelligence reports indicated that the Baghdad defenses were thin and hastily built, certainly not the imposing positions encountered at Sannaiyat. Also, Kiazim's XVIII Corps suffered terrible losses in earlier battles. Turkish prisoners were a dispirited crowd, most of them grateful to be out of the fighting. Maude concluded that the coming battle would not be difficult.

By 8 March, the 13th Division led by O'Dowda's indomitable 38th Brigade deployed along the Diyala River near its junction with the Tigris. The Cavalry Division moved north and reported the river guarded for ten miles by the Turk's 14th Division and, beyond that, by a strong cavalry contingent. O'Dowda's brigade tried effecting a crossing just above Diyala village. The river was only 120 yards wide at that point, but a full moon illuminated the water. The moment the British

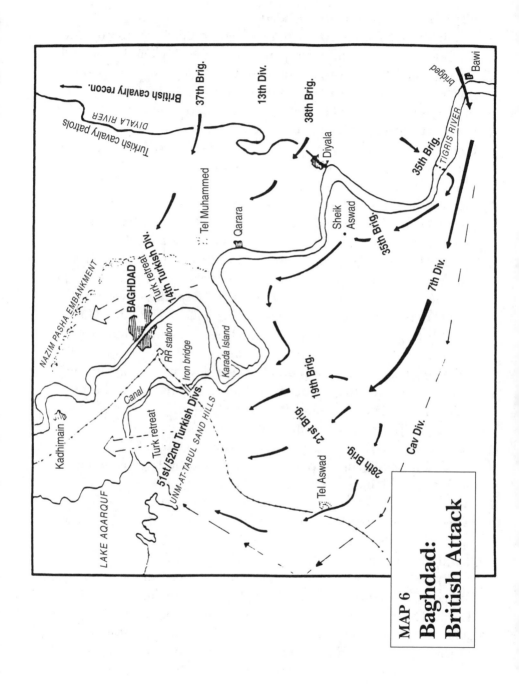

MAP 6
Baghdad:
British Attack

pontoons left the shore, the Turks opened fire. Sixty-four men in three pontoons were immediately hit, and their unwieldy craft, like water-borne coffins, twisted their way down the Diyala currents and into the Tigris.

The next night the Loyal North Lancashires tried crossing the river against heavy rifle and machine gun fire. Only a hundred men made it to the opposite shore where they immediately dug in. The Turks attacked them five times but were repulsed. The little landing party hung on even though whittled down to sixty men and two machine guns. Turkish fire made it impossible to send reinforcements and ammunition across the river. The Lancashires were on their own.

Beginning at 4:00 A.M., 10 March, with O'Dowda's 38th Brigade leading the way, the 13th Division crossed the Diyala in a strong thrust. They built a bridge and, around 10:00 A.M., were one mile north of the river. The Turk's 14th Division abandoned the whole river defense, pulling back to a new line running from Qarara to Tel Muhammed and around to the Nazim Pasha Embankment. But between losses to the 14th along the Diyala and the shifting of some of its units to other positions, only six Turkish regiments defended the line. By late morning, they came under intense artillery fire and could not stop the British advance from the Diyala.

British operations along the Tigris right bank started early on 8 March when a bridge train reached Bawi. The 7th Division, reinforced by the 35th Brigade, crossed the bridge that afternoon and moved toward the Turkish line centered on Tel Aswad. Despite a vigorous defense by his troops, Khalil abandoned the line and withdrew his men to the Umm-at-Tubul sand hills line. The British moved forward in a sandstorm, making slow but steady progress. By midafternoon, Khalil abandoned the sand hills and pulled back to Baghdad. The Cavalry Division, making forays around the flank of the sand hills, occupied Kadhimain to the north, but too late to cut off the retreating Turks. With both his defensive lines collapsed, Khalil issued orders the night of 10 March for a retreat from Baghdad.

Phase IV: Consolidation

Baghdad, according to the *Official History*, was a disappointment to the occupying British troops—a weary anticlimax might be more accurate. A few bazaars remained open and people in the streets smiled, but whether because of the Turks' departure or the British arrival remains ambiguous. Beneath that facade of normality hovered a grim reality. Scrawny dogs scavenged in gutters and alleyways. Atrocious smells from human and animal waste assaulted the air. Wrecked buildings, dynamited by the Turks and their German advisors, etched a jagged skyline. Abandoned and burning military equipment marked the road taken by the fleeing enemy.

Khalil left Baghdad to unite his battered XVIII Corps with XIII Corps facing the still-present Russians. The maneuver involved risk because the slumbering Russians, snowbound throughout the winter, might yet awaken and show some fight. Khalil need not have worried. The Russians were in a deprived state. Moreover, bad news from home sunk their morale. The Germans trounced the Russian Army, fueling mutinies and stirring already volatile civil unrest. In March 1917, mutiny and disorder boiled over in a revolution led by moderate socialists. Tsar Nicholas II stepped aside, his ultimate fate decided by a second but radical revolution in October. The defeat of the army and the subsequent revolutions registered among the troops in Mesopotamia. Their offensive edge rusted in the snow for want of a purpose to fight.

Maude could not let the two Turkish corps unite. He felt confident that his troops could handle them separately, but once joined they represented a strong force.

The British fought a series of engagements designed to push the two Turkish corps further and further apart. Even a selected list of battles, skirmishes, and "actions," however exotic sounding, seems insignificant in the larger context of World War I. There was, for example, an action at Balad, north of Baghdad, on 8 April, followed by a protracted engagement the week of 9 April to force passage of the Khalis Canal. Another engagement took place at Mushalida on 14 April. On 20 April, a battle was fought at Istabulat on the Baghdad-Samarra rail line. The 21st Brigade bore the brunt of this last engagement, losing 2,238 killed and wounded, the Black Watch cut to pieces for about the fourth time since January 1916. The British captured Samara on 23 April, followed by more fighting at Bandi-Adhaim, at Muskaid Ridge, and Ramadi—these last two sites on the Euphrates

River. The list seems endless, even tedious. Attack, outflank, chase. The steady routine of death ground on.

From among all the final engagements, both A. J. Barker and Bryan Perrett focus their historical narratives on the action at Khan Baghdadi, an early demonstration of the potential of desert mobility. As the main British force moved up the Tigris, Major General Sir H. T. Brooking's 15th Division pushed up the Euphrates, reaching Khan Baghdadi on 26 March 1918. The Turks blocked the Aleppo Road near the Euphrates right bank. That night Brooking sent a mobile column comprising the 11th Cavalry Brigade, LAMBs, horse artillery, and Model T Ford vans carrying supporting infantry companies and their machine guns into the desert. They outflanked the Turks at a point five miles above the road defenses. The next morning, Brooking's 42nd and 50th Brigades moved along the Aleppo Road directly at the Turkish defenders. The Turks, squeezed between the oncoming infantry and Cassel's mobile column, surrendered.

The LAMBs then made a 100-mile dash up the Aleppo Road, taking prisoners and rescuing two British officers captured by the Turks from a downed reconnaissance plane. The captives were Major Tennant, commander of 30 Squadron, and Major Percy Hobart of the Bengal Sappers and Miners. Perrett suggests, and I should think him correct, that Hobart was so impressed with the speed and dash of his rescue and the mobility shown by the flanking column at Khan Baghdadi that he later transferred to the Royal Tank Corps. During the 1930s, he led the famous 7th Armored Division, the Desert Rats, through their initial training in Egypt's Western Desert.

The war with the Turks ended in October 1918. Maude did not live to witness the final triumph nor even to see the later phases of the campaign he started. He died of cholera in November 1917. General Marshall of III Corps took command.

ACCOMPLISHMENTS AND POTENTIALS

The early operations in Mesopotamia led by Sir John Nixon and Charles Townshend bogged down in mendacity, faulty assumptions, poor logistics, and bad strategy and tactics. Percy Lake instituted changes when he assumed command in January 1916, but they came too late to save the Poona Division trapped in Kut-al-Amara or preserve Fenton Aylmer's relief force from stupefying casualties. Nothing in their experience or training prepared the Anglo-Indian Army for battle in the Mesopotamian desert, far more vast than anything on the Northwest Frontier, against an enemy as tenacious as the Turks.

Did Stanley Maude know anything more about desert warfare than Nixon, Townshend, or Lake? He served but briefly in the Sudan during his early career, and he did have the later advantage, if it can be called that, of leading his 13th Division for three months as part of Aylmer's relief force. He also enjoyed the confidence of the War Cabinet that gave him the means to create the needed changes. But these advantages did not endow him with any great knowledge of desert warfare. Based on that generalization, I suggest that Maude brought to his command six major perceptions of battle.

1. In early 1916, Maude witnessed the consequence of advancing without ample logistical support: disaster! Even though his London masters did not want to launch a new offensive lest it founder, I doubt that Maude needed that constraint during his first few months as area commander. He required a dependable supply system and communications network by which he could advance and coordinate his units. All that took time to establish. Concomitant to the logistical buildup was the reestablishment of confidence by the troops in their leaders. The filthy barges packed with unattended wounded sent downstream from Ctesiphon in 1915 represented Nixon's neglect, ignorance, and mendacity, encouraging a widespread belief in the ranks that something was very wrong. Morale dropped. Under Maude, conditions changed with the addition of road and rail transport and as river transport increased and became more efficient. Supply depots and hospitals were built, tangible evidence that a new kind of general commanded who cared about his men.

2. Maude did not lead his men at the point of attack, but he did move his headquarters forward with each advance. When preparing for such advances, he bore down on every organizational and tactical detail, annoying several subordinates. Hard cheese. Maude, coming from the Western Front, knew the drawbacks of rear echelon, so-called chateau generals. Thus, Lord Moran tells the story of a senior staff officer who visited

the Passchendaele front in Belgium. His plan called for an attack along a certain road, but he could not reconcile the landscape with his map. "What is that river there?" he asked, looking across the battlefield. "That, sir," an officer replied, pointing to the map, "is this road here." Realizing the disaster he spawned, the staff officer broke down and wept bitter tears. Nixon became the Mesopotamian chateau general, sequestering himself in Basra, seldom visiting the front. Maude would have none of that. His attention to his soldiers' needs and his attitude about command won him their confidence.

3. Maude, as a Guardsman, knew better than most that monotony is a soldier's worst enemy. Although the sorely tested 7th Division remained in the line at Sannaiyat during the summer of 1916, other units were cycled out for rest, recreation, and retraining. Also, the new logistical system kept thousands of men busy loading and unloading, guarding convoys, and building forward depots. The work, a sergeant-major's dream come true, not only overcame lethargy but involved the troops in the improvement of their own conditions. Still, a peculiar monotony did eventually settle in, but from another direction.

4. At a tactical level, Maude knew from experience on three fronts—Belgium-France, Gallipoli, Mesopotamia—that frontal attacks were suicidal. Whole companies, even battalions, were cut down and nothing achieved by the dying. Maude adapted tactics to supposedly minimize losses. Sapping took time, but it shortened the killing zone. How odd to think of battle as monotonous, but when reduced to routine, it very well can be. Maude's system—sapping, artillery bombardment, grenade attack, infantry fighting, only to start all over again with the next trench system—made the battles more impersonal, more mechanical, and even more monotonous. Unfortunately, losses were not lessened by the effort.

5. The Turks' relatively static defense system gave Maude an operational option, what B. H. Liddell Hart, in *Strategy*, termed "attack by indirection," or the end sweep, the ruse, the left hook. The initial attack against Sannaiyat covered the real assault along the Shatt-al-Hai. The attack in the Khadairi Bend, the Tigris crossing at Shumran Bend and, later, the night flank

march at Khan Baghdadi all involved ruses of one kind or another. The Turks did frustrate the British attack along the Hai, ruse or no ruse, but the tactic worked most of the time.

6. Maude enjoyed a superiority of artillery firepower. Both Townshend's Poona Division and Aylmer's relief column suffered artillery shortages, needing howitzers and high explosive shells. Maude made certain his gunners had no cause to complain. He increased the ratio of guns per division, obtained howitzers and trench mortars, and stockpiled a wide variety of ammunition that enabled him to achieve varying objectives. The most dramatic use of British artillery was the massive destruction of XVIII Corps. The British designed bombardments not just to crumple trenches and destroy Turkish batteries. More importantly, they killed a lot of Turks. The survivors, left dazed by the magnitude of the bombardments, willingly surrendered.

Maude was not a gift of the gods. Although the right man at the right time, he made mistakes in two areas. First, he used cavalry ineffectively. The wrong man, Crocker, commanded the division. His flank marches lacked persistence. During the renewed attacks on the Shatt-al-Hai, the cavalry was supposed to take the Turkish left flank between the Tigris and the marshland to the east. They floundered. Ordered to vigorously pursue the Turks following the withdrawal from Kut and Sannaiyat, the cavalry dawdled. Maude should have replaced Crocker earlier. And when a troop or squadron would have done the job and attracted less attention, he had no need to send the entire cavalry division up the Diyala on reconnaissance. The responsibility for that lesson in military overstatement rested wholly with Maude.

Colonel Kearsey, in his study of the Mesopotamian front, identified another problem. The small unit actions Maude launched as he pecked away at Sannaiyat and the Khadairi Bend did finally work. Designed to keep down casualties, the actions were actually rather costly. The Turks usually fell back when the British attacked. But the attacks were carried out by only a battalion or two. The losses they incurred left them open to Turkish counterattacks, causing more casualties. Only renewed artillery fire and another infantry assault carried the enemy trenches. Greater strength in the initial attack might have led to more success. The problem is that these limited attacks had limited tactical objectives, each adding to the whole. At that, Kearsey's evaluation is not too harsh.

Any study of the Mesopotamian campaign creates a nagging question: what made fighting there different than fighting on the Western Front? The sheer size of the Western Front, the magnitude of the slaughter, and the siege mentality that gripped the generals represent some significant differences. Yet, I doubt they had much meaning to a Highlander going over the top into Turkish machine gun fire. Unquestionably, Maude brought to Mesopotamia the battle tactics of the Western Front, inviting the question of what he intended when he began his campaign. Did he want to force a Turkish withdrawal simply to annihilate them? Taken separately these become questions that often force different answers, but I think they are really two parts of the same question. Maude did want the Turks to retreat up the Tigris—and he wanted it to cost them as dearly as possible. Thus, the questions are twin-born elements of the same strategic goal: delivering unremitting punishment to the enemy, allowing the British to dictate the shape of battle and force their goals on the Turks.

The front became more mobile after the breakthroughs along the Hai and at Sannaiyat, the taking of Baghdad merely a brief pause on the way north. But in this context, mobility was vertical rather than lateral. Ford vans and LAMBs increased mobility, but the British could not sweep into the desert at will. There were no roads, and the harsh terrain and heat brought vehicles and logistics to the breaking point. If the British experienced difficulty breaking out laterally into the desert, the Turks, if anything, were less equipped to do so. Consequently, the chase followed the rivers north. There were modest sweeps, such as at Khan Baghdadi, but no one wandered very far. The Mesopotamian front remained a river campaign. Nor could it have been otherwise. Technology gave the armies the means to increase the killing but not to invent strategies of avoidance, necessarily creating a miniature version of the Western Front.

Erwin Rommel, the Desert Fox. NATIONAL ARCHIVES

The Qattara Depression, Egypt. Avoided during World War II, it is now crossed by a modern oil road. RALPH CROSS

The Sinai Desert. A typical desert scene—part sand, part rock, low hills, and scrub. ISRAELI DEFENSE FORCES, SPOKESMAN'S OFFICE

No place to hide: a stereotypical scene of desert warfare. Israeli self-propelled guns deployed near the Suez Canal in 1973. ISRAELI DEFENSE FORCES, SPOKESMAN'S OFFICE

Barren mountains enclosing the Swat Valley. Rough terrain and narrow valleys limited British campaigning. PAKISTAN TOURISM DEVELOPMENT CORPORATION

A British officer and soldier of the 66th Gurkhas. The Gurkhas' fighting prowess, established during Campbell's campaign, was alternately revered and feared through World War II and the Falklands War. FROM C. W. LATHAM, *THE INDIAN MUTINY* (LONDON: OSPREY BOOKS, 1977).

The upper Swat River. This rugged alpine region proved inaccessible to British arms during Campbell's time and always made campaigning very difficult for later commanders. PAKISTAN TOURISM DEVELOPMENT CORPORATION

Battle of the Pyramids. Mameluke warriors charge French infantry squares. BIBLIOTHEQUE NATIONALE PARIS

1914 pattern Rolls-Royce armored cars. The Royal Navy caps worn by two men suggest that this was part of an early troop operating in Mesopotamia. THE TANK MUSEUM

British Matilda Infantry Tank. The tank, part of the 7th Royal Tank Regiment, stands beside an abandoned Italian gun truck near Bardia during Operation Compass. THE TANK MUSEUM

Destroyed Italian M11/39 Medium Tank. One of the many Italian machines destroyed or captured at Beda Fomm. THE TANK MUSEUM

British-built Centurions in the Sinai. The Israelis up-gunned this tank, which was used extensively in the 1973 War, to 105mm and added a powerful drive-train. ISRAELI DEFENSE FORCES, SPOKESMAN'S OFFICE

Israeli infantry resting on a sand ledge. Israeli infantry was subordinated to armored operations, yet they retained a sense of high purpose. ISRAELI DEFENSE FORCES, SPOKESMAN'S OFFICE

Russian-built T-62 tanks. The Russian T-series tanks, although the core of Arab armored strength, were designed for use in Europe, proving unreliable in desert terrain. THE TANK MUSEUM

British Challenger tank (foreground) and a Warrior APC. These machines, part of the 14/20 King's Hussars, 4th Armored Brigade, are maneuvering in the Iraqi desert during Operation Desert Storm. THE TANK MUSEUM

A line of destruction: an Iraqi armored column destroyed in the
Euphrates Valley. U.S. DEPARTMENT OF DEFENSE

CHAPTER 6

Battle in the Western Desert, 1940 to 1941

ITALY'S IMPERIAL AMBITIONS
Predications on a Dirty Little War

The story of World War II desert fighting begins with Italy's imperial ambitions in North Africa. The Italians invaded Libya in 1911 on the pretext that the Turks armed hostile Arabs, thus endangering Italian migrants. The Turks cared less, but the Senussi tribesmen of Cyrenaica, or eastern Libya, resisted. This led to a standoff, the Italians occupying only some coastal enclaves, such as Tripoli, Benghazi, Tobruk, and Bardia. In 1923, Benito Mussolini, leading a Fascist government, impatient with the Senussis' continuing truculence, opted for the complete military subjugation of Libya, igniting the Second Senussi War, a low-intensity conflict but one as brutal as history records. Rodolfo Graziani led the Italian forces. His troops did not do well against the hit-and-run guerrilla tactics of the Senussi. Completely frustrated, Graziani invoked a program of widespread terrorism by burning villages, killing livestock, and mass internment. In 1930, continuing a total war, the Italians built a wire barricade 200 miles along the Egyptian border to keep the Senussi from reaching neutral territory. They finally captured the guerrilla leader Umar al Mukhtar and hanged him before a gathering of 20,000 tribesmen. Senussi resistance collapsed.

In the mid-1930s, bloated by his self-declared Libyan success, Mussolini decided to expand his empire into Albania and link Somalia with Libya. That meant conquering the Sudan and Egypt.

Such blustering confused the new German dictator Adolf Hitler and his generals. Mussolini, uncertain about allying himself with

Nazism, said on different occasions that he did not want war for another two, three, and even five years. The Germans were in a quandary. They wanted a firm Italian alliance to secure their southern flank for an invasion of France. Mussolini continued responding with vague promises, contradictory policy statements, and inflated estimates of Italy's military strength.

Those estimates worried the German army and naval staffs, who knew them to be incorrect, knowing the Italian Army could not sustain a campaign anywhere. In 1936, for example, Mussolini declared he could mobilize 8 million men. In 1939, the figure grew to 12 million. In fact, as Denis Mack Smith points out, the best the Italians could do during all of World War II was to mobilize 3 million. Yet, in June 1939, at a joint naval staff meeting at Friedrichschafen, the Italians airily announced to their German colleagues that they contemplated an invasion of Egypt. But in February 1940, although Mussolini declared Italy war-ready, no plans existed for the proposed invasion. The only constant factor during the long months leading to Italy's involvement in World War II was Mussolini's bombast.

The Italian Army in Libya, 1940

By summer 1940, the German war machine scored a series of quick victories, invading in succession Poland, Denmark, Norway, the Low Countries, Luxembourg, and France. Belatedly, in June, Mussolini cast his lot with the Nazis, invading France at the eleventh hour and forging ahead with the proposed Egyptian campaign. Still, no plan existed. Marshal Italo Balbo, commander in Libya, pleaded for more men and equipment. Then he was accidentally killed when Italian anti-aircraft guns at Tobruk shot down his reconnaissance plane. Rodolfo Graziani, the conqueror of Libya, took his place. Even though the quintessential fascist, Graziani was also a military realist who understood the desert and knew what he needed to invade Egypt, a course of action for which he had no enthusiasm. What he found in Libya appalled him.

Graziani's forces were divided into two armies. The 5th Army was stationed in Tripolitania, or western Libya. The 10th Army occupied Cyrenaica, or eastern Libya. The 10th numbered a quarter-million men organized into nine regular infantry divisions of 13,000 men each, plus three Blackshirt divisions—supposedly an elite force—and two Libyan divisions, each of 8,000 men.

If the numbers were impressive, so too were the problems. As Bryan Perrett states, the army was largely an infantry army and not a very good one at that. Their rifles were based on an 1891 pattern and most artillery dated from World War I. The armored units used light L3 tankettes, a small, flimsy, and unreliable machine, vulnerable to infantry fire, and mounting only a light machine gun. The M11/39 medium tank, weighing eleven tons and with 29mm hull armor, was obsolete the day it went into production. The revolving turret mounted a single light machine gun, but the main gun, only a 37mm, was fixed in the front center of the hull. For air power, the 5th Squadra of the Regia Aeronautica had 282 aircraft in Libya on the day war was declared. The Savio Marchetti S.79 bomber carried a 1,100-pound bomb load, about average for that time. The Riuniti bomber, not as reliable as the S.79, carried a larger 1,750-pound load. The Fiat Cr. 42, probably the best Italian fighter, mounted 12.7mm machine guns and flew at 270 mph.

Graziani appealed to Rome for more tanks, planes, anti-tank guns, anti-aircraft guns, and especially more trucks. In August, he even went to Rome where Mussolini's son-in-law, Count Galeazzo Ciano, received him. Graziani spelled out his army's deficiencies. He concluded, as Ciano recorded in his diary, that "we move toward a defeat which, in the desert, must inevitably develop into a rapid and total disaster." Mussolini, informed by Ciano of this assessment, cabled Graziani on 10 August 1940 that the invasion of Egypt, now encouraged by the Germans, would go forward. But the message ended ambiguously. "I am only asking you to attack the British forces facing you," Mussolini stated. Then what? No invasion plan answered the question. And none ever would.

THE BRITISH IN EGYPT
Leadership: Wavell and O'Connor
General Sir Archibald Wavell was appointed British commander in chief, Middle East, in August 1939. He presided over a vast domain that included Palestine, Trans-Jordan, Iraq, Kuwait, Aden, British Somalia, Kenya, the Sudan, Egypt, Cyprus, and Malta. Only 50,000 men, too few tanks, too few planes, and too little artillery guarded this vast domain. Because of or despite these shortcomings, Wavell was a

good choice to command because he did not feel constrained by military conventions. He would take risks.

Born in 1883 of a military family, Wavell attended prestigious Winchester College and Sandhurst, the Royal Military College. After a six-month course, he entered the Black Watch Regiment in 1901. He joined the 2nd Battalion in India and saw action along the Northwest Frontier. A gifted linguist, he passed army examinations in Urdu, Pushtu, and French. He then took the staff course at Camberley and went to Russia for a year, subsequently passing the examination in Russian. During World War I, he served at Ypres and in the Palestinian campaign where he earned the Military Cross. He was brevetted a lieutenant colonel and then brigadier general. At war's end, he rejoined his regiment, assuming his permanent rank of major. He soon returned to staff duties as his only hope for advancement and was promoted to major general in 1934.

Wavell, more than just another promotion-hungry officer, studied military history with great care and concluded that the purpose of the exercise was to stimulate thinking and imagination, not to reduce warfare to a lot of rules. He also loved poetry, eventually editing a volume of verse and sponsoring a poetry contest among his men. A sensitive man, a man of hard military service, he would need every quality he possessed to juggle the conflicting demands of the Middle East.

Wavell brought Richard O'Connor from Palestine to Egypt and, on 8 June 1940, made him commander of the Western Desert Force, the unit that would defend Egypt and which eventually evolved into the famous 8th Army.

O'Connor is often referred to as a little Irishman but, frankly, I cannot find that he lived a day of his life in that place. Born in India in 1889, educated at Wellington School and Sandhurst, he entered the 2nd Scottish Rifles (the Cameronians) in 1909. Two years later the regiment was in Malta. O'Connor commanded the signals company. With the outbreak of World War I, five of the regiment's twenty-seven officers were transferred to other duties, and O'Connor was sent to England where he served on the staff of the 22nd Brigade. This was fortunate because in 1915, at the Battle of Neuve Chapelle, the Cameronians experienced 70 percent casualties in six days. Of the twenty-two remaining officers from Malta, nine were killed or wounded. Ten more were killed or wounded in subsequent battles. O'Connor served at Neuve Chapelle, but in a staff capacity. He also saw action at the First Battle of Ypres, Loos—earning the Military Cross—and the Somme. At Third Ypres, he commanded an artillery regiment. Sent to the Italian front, he earned the Distinguished Service Order, the Italian Silver Medal for Valor, and received mention in dispatches nine times. After the war he commanded the Peshawar Brigade (the old Peshawar Field Force) on the Northwest Frontier. In 1938, as a major general, he commanded the 7th Division in Palestine and became Jerusalem's military governor. This was a distinguished military career.

Those who knew O'Connor produced a consensus about his character. Small in stature, with quick movements, he exuded an energy that was focused by a considerable intellect. Unassuming and professional, he possessed unwavering integrity. Captured during the desert fighting in Libya and interned in Italy, he escaped to later command XXX Corps in Normandy. But Field Marshal Montgomery sent O'Connor packing to the Far East because he refused to write a negative report about an American officer who served in his command. Even though Wavell is credited (certainly by Churchill) with the campaign about to unfold in Egypt, O'Connor guided its tactics and brought victory. Yet, O'Connor remained intensely loyal to Wavell. In stark contrast to the egos that subsequently surfaced in North Africa, he became, as Correlli Barnett cogently observed, "the forgotten victor."

British Forces in Egypt, Summer 1940

Historians enjoy reproaching the Italian leadership for their pitifully prepared Libyan forces. In truth, the British were not much better prepared, the result of a penurious parliament suspicious of re-arming Britain after the horrors of World War I, and of interservice rivalries that led to confusion over defense priorities. The Western Desert Force numbered 36,000 men, organized into fourteen British battalions, a New Zealand Brigade, and the 4th Indian Division. The 7th Armored Division was composed of two brigades, both short one regiment. Armored cars were the 1924 pattern Rolls-Royce. The car looked superficially like the 1914 model but had view slits in the body, a body door, and a 4 x 4 wheel drive. It still mounted a single water-cooled .303 Vickers machine gun in a revolving turret. The most numerous tracked armor was the Vickers Mark VI light tank. This death trap, its silhouette too high, weighed five tons, had thin 14mm armor, and mounted one 7.62mm machine gun and one 15mm machine gun. The infantry tank Mark II, the famous Matilda, reached Egypt in late 1940. A sturdy machine, it was sheathed in 78mm armor and mounted a 2-pounder (40mm) gun in the turret. But the gun fired only solid shot. The tank also carried a 7.62mm machine gun. Even with a cross-desert speed of only 7 mph, the Matilda was superior to anything the Italians fielded. Cruiser tanks, A9s and A10s, had good speed and 2-pounder guns but were mechanically unreliable.

The Royal Air Force, with a small and motley array of aircraft, could not support a vigorous defense. Could it support a vigorous offense? Machines available in June and July 1940 included Gloster Gladiator fighters, a biwing design from 1934, with a maximum speed of 250 mph and four .303 machine guns. Westland Lysanders proved sturdy but unarmed reconnaissance planes. Hawker Harts, another biwing plane from 1926, Bristol Bombays, part transport, part bomber, and nine squadrons of twin-engined Blenheim medium bombers, capable of delivering 1,000-pound bomb loads, completed the list.

The strongest British arm in the Mediterranean was the Royal Navy, deploying the muscle of seven battleships and two aircraft carriers. But only eight cruisers and thirty-seven destroyers were on station, classes of ships of which the Italian fleet enjoyed superior numbers.

THE DESERT WAR, JUNE 1940 TO FEBRUARY 1941
First Actions by the RAF and the Royal Navy

O'Connor received reinforcements throughout the summer of 1940, but numbers meant little because the troops were not ready for desert battle. That would take time. The RAF and the Royal Navy took the war to the Italians, giving O'Connor the time he needed. Within twenty-four hours of Italy's June declaration of war, RAF squadrons took to the air. Lysanders flew over Italian camps, troop concentrations, and air and naval bases to estimate strengths, especially around Tobruk. Bristol Bombays of 216 Squadron bombed that harbor repeatedly, setting the cruiser *San Giorgio* afire. Blenheims, protected by Gladiators, bombed airfields and supply depots, destroying a large ammunition dump near Bardia on 1 August.

Admiral Sir Andrew Cunningham's naval ships had the primary task of escorting high-risk convoys from Gibraltar to Malta and on to Alexandria. Also, his gunboats and monitors helped contain the Italian Army in Libya by bombarding Bardia twice, striking depots along the coast, and lobbing shells onto the coast road. On 15 August, the RAF attacked the Italian naval base at Bomba, destroying twelve seaplanes. The most famous raid was against the naval base at Taranto in southern Italy, where six Italian battleships rode at anchor. The 813 Squadron, flying twelve Swordfish aircraft commanded by Kenneth Williamson, took off from the carrier HMS *Illustrious*. Armed with bombs and torpedoes, they flew through anti-aircraft fire from a score of 4-inch batteries and 200 machine guns. The Swordfish put three battleships out of action and damaged several other ships and shore installations. The British lost two aircraft. The Italian Navy never seriously challenged the British.

The British Army Learns about the Desert

Wavell and O'Connor realized the impossibility of major action against the Italians during the summer and early fall of 1940. But some ground action was necessary to keep the Italians unsure of British intentions. In the best tradition of British colonial warfare, small units, more or less independent, harassed the enemy. The experience of living and fighting in the desert, and the intelligence they gathered, proved invaluable.

The earliest desert battle unit was the Long Range Desert Group, informally organized in 1932 by Major R. A. Bagnold and a clutch of like-minded officers. The Italians, following the Second Senussi War, established a series of military posts and air strips along the edges of the Libyan sand sea and, farther south, at Kufra Oasis, where the borders of Libya, Egypt, and the Sudan meet. Between 1932 and 1938, Bagnold and his colleagues motored across the Egyptian and Libyan sand seas, trips not thought possible. While stalking the Italian camps, they developed desert navigational techniques and learned how to drive and maintain vehicles in the desert. Most importantly, they learned how to survive.

In June 1940, Bagnold approached Wavell with the idea of establishing long-range patrols to attack Italian posts and keep them anxious about their southern flank. Wavell approved and patrols were formed, each consisting of two officers and thirty men from the New Zealand Brigade. In August and September, after six weeks' training, the patrols raided Italian air strips at Aujila and Jalo, south of Kufra. They also established small supply drops for use by future patrols. In October, they mined the road between Agedabia, on the Gulf of Sidra, and Aujila. The patrols subsequently mined other roads and desert tracks and plotted locations for future British landing strips.

Their value demonstrated, Wavell ordered an increase in the number of Long-range Desert Groups. Volunteers came from the Coldstream Guards and Scots Guards. The longest patrol lasted forty-four days and covered 4,300 miles. In March 1941, the Group moved its headquarters from Cairo to Kufra.

The 11th Hussars were the workhorse of the small units. Among the first cavalry regiments to make the transition from horse to armor, they used 1924 pattern Rolls-Royce armored cars. The regiment arrived in the Middle East in 1934 as part of the fledgling 7th Armored Division. The 11th immediately embarked on a five-year training program, increasing speed and efficiency with each passage into the desert. Navigation improved as they learned to read the desert's natural configurations like so many road markers. Driving through soft sand led to the development of special equipment for dislodging cars. The men ate bullybeef, hardtack, and cheese, calculating rations down to the last portion. Each man learned the job of the other members of his car crew. Each car became a self-sustaining unit. Above all, the 11th learned the oldest and hardest lesson of desert living: everything needed would have to be brought along, because the desert provided nothing.

The Hussars were the first unit to cut through Mussolini's wire fence on 11 June. As the regiment's A Squadron scouted the Italian fort at Capuzzo, a small group was left behind to guard the opening. They ambushed an Italian truck convoy, capturing two officers and their Libyan soldiers. The officers were very upset because no one on their side bothered to tell them that war had been declared. C Squadron went through the wire the next night and again scouted Capuzzo, but Italian artillery drove them away. On 13 June, A Squadron drove to Sidi Omar and found the post abandoned. The Hussars became more aggressive, attacking Maddalena on 14 June and, two days later, mining the coast road between Bardia and Tobruk.

These were only a few of the 11th's adventures. They not only created havoc behind the Italian lines but were O'Connor's on-site eyes.

September 1940 found the Hussars badly worn. The workload had to be shared. The answer was the Jock Columns. Barrie Pitt outlined the logic behind their formation. Italian air and artillery attacks exposed the vulnerability of the British armored cars. Therefore, the light armored force needed some artillery and anti-aircraft guns. Anti-tank guns were needed as protection against Italian armor. The column also required infantry support, some sappers, and a signals unit. Thus, the composite Jock Columns were equipped much like independent small battle groups, taking pressure off the Hussars and creating havoc of their own.

The first column included a troop, that is, a company, of armored cars supported by artillery—a collection of field guns, some 2-pounders, and 40mm Bofors guns mounted on cut-down trucks. Infantry, sappers, and signals were all motorized. The officer in command was Lieutenant Colonel J. C. (Jock)—hence the unit's nickname—Campbell of the Royal Horse Artillery. The daring with which the Jock Columns killed and destroyed every soldier and everything they could find later earned Campbell the Victoria Cross and promotion to major general. Shortly after, in February 1942, he was killed in an auto accident.

The apparent ease with which these independent columns ranged across the desert confounded the Italians. They did not know what to expect down the road, around the next bend, behind a dune, or in the black desert night. They grew hesitant. The small groups indeed helped give O'Connor the time he needed to condition his main force and bring them into position not to defend Egypt but to attack the Italian Army.

THE ITALIANS INVADE EGYPT

At dawn, 13 September 1940, a vast gray column of Italian tankettes, trucks, cars, and motorcycles crossed the Libyan frontier into Egypt. At Sollum, an artillery barrage hit the old and abandoned Egyptian Army barracks. One great column of the Italian 10th Army followed the bombardment into the town; a second column climbed Halfaya Pass, the principal link between Libya and Egypt.

Only the 3rd Battalion of the Coldstream Guards, a company of the King's Royal Rifle Corps, a machine gun company, and three artillery batteries opposed the Italians entering Sollum. British infantry in Halfaya Pass sniped at the leading motorcycles and trucks, causing them to swerve and even plunge off the road. Mines destroyed or crippled other vehicles. British artillery could not miss the packed column, and the 11th Hussars struck again and again, raking them with machine gun fire.

The British plan was strike and withdraw. Back through Buq Buq, Alam Hamid, Alam el Dab they went, covered by the RAF, whose Blenheim bombers loosed fragmentation and high explosive bombs on the crowded coast road, destroying machines and shattering the packed troop columns.

The Royal Navy joined in the death and destruction as the Italians neared Sidi Barrani. Aircraft from *Illustrious* bombed and torpedoed ships in the harbor. Destroyers closed in and shelled the town and port facilities, and the gunboat HMS *Ladybird* fired at traffic still on the coast road.

A despondent Graziani, having engaged the British facing him just as Mussolini ordered, consolidated his gains. The great Italian invasion of Egypt ground to a halt.

Could Graziani have plunged on to Cairo? His logistical support, inefficient from the outset, reached its limit. Furthermore, the vital coast road was in deplorable condition, little more than a dusty rut, made so by British action and the sheer volume of Italian traffic. The retreating British rendered the water wells at Sidi Barrani unusable, so pipelines were laid from Sollum to Bardia. As I. S. O. Playfair's *Official History* notes, German staff officers visiting Sidi Barrani concluded that the Italians could not advance further until mid-December and then only down the road to Mersa Matruh. The invasion of Egypt turned into a fascist fairytale, and a grim one at that.

THE FIVE-DAY RAID: OPERATION COMPASS
Through Enba Gap

Graziani's consolidation plan included establishing fortified camps from Sidi Barrani on the coast south into the desert and from Tummar East to Sofafi. Inexplicably, Graziani left a fifteen-mile-wide gap,

the so-called Enba Gap, between Sofafi and the camp at Nibeiwa.
Wavell and O'Connor saw the consolidation as their opportunity to
attack. A short offensive raid through the Enba Gap would bring
British forces behind the Italian lines. They could destroy the armed
camps, blow up supply depots, and damage communications and
transport facilities. They believed the raid could be sustained for five
days.

Wavell did not reveal the plan to either Anthony Eden, the war
secretary, or even to Winston Churchill. Only after 28 October, the
date on which Mussolini invaded Greece, and after Churchill's
announcement of aid to Greece, did Wavell reveal the plan to London. Churchill was put off at first: he wanted to transfer units from
the Middle East command to Greece and open a Balkans front; he
also thought his general too independent, something he would not
tolerate. But once he understood the raid's implications, Churchill
confessed he "purred like six kittens." The five-day raid was coded
Operation Compass (Map 7).

O'Connor's raiding force included the 7th Armored Division and
the 4th Indian Division reinforced by a British brigade. The 7th had
seventy-five cruiser tanks and forty-eight new Matildas, as well as
squadrons of Vickers light tanks. An independent unit, the so-called
Support Group, consisted of two infantry battalions and batteries of
25-pounder field guns. The 11th Hussars and Selby Force, yet another
independent unit composed of infantry companies with artillery and
armor, lent additional strength. The RAF screened the operation,
using seven bomber squadrons—three Blenheims, three Wellingtons,
and one using the sturdy old Bombays. A squadron of Gladiators and
two of Hawker Hurricanes gave fighter protection. The RAF also
provided O'Connor's headquarters with a special reconnaissance
squadron.

The 4th Indian Division and the 7th Armored assembled southeast of Enba Gap, simulating training exercises. Selby Force moved
along the coast road to a point east of Maktila. Wavell and O'Connor
kept secret the real point of these movements, nothing put on paper
until the very last minute. Life behind the lines remained as normal
as possible to mislead spies in Alexandria and Cairo.

The RAF bombed forward airfields on the night of 7 December
and, on the eighth, struck the fortified camps. On 9 December, after

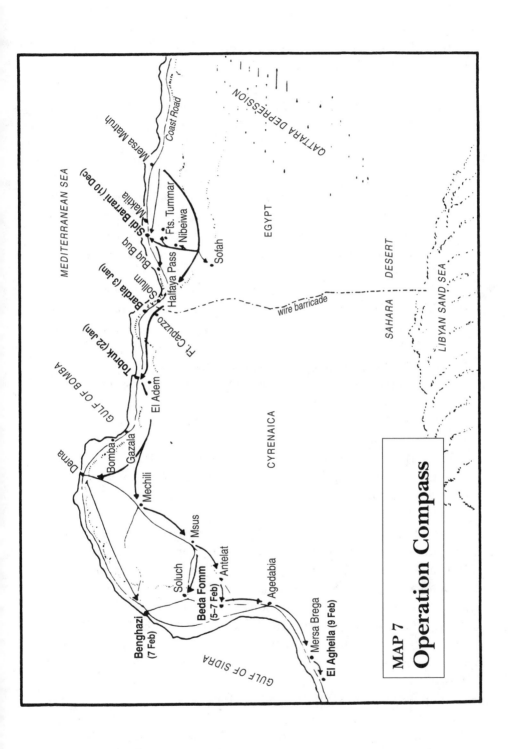

MAP 7
Operation Compass

MEDITERRANEAN SEA

Mersa Matruh

Coast Road

Sidi Barrani (10 Dec)

Fts. Tummar
Nibeiwa
Maktila

Sofah

EGYPT

Bug Bug

Sollum

Bardia (3 Jan)

Halfaya Pass

Ft. Capuzzo

wire barricade

SAHARA   DESERT

LIBYAN SAND SEA

QATTARA DEPRESSION

GULF OF BOMBA

Tobruk (22 Jan)

El Adem

Derna

Bomba

Gazala

Mechili

CYRENAICA

Msus

Soluch

Antelat

Beda Fomm (5–7 Feb)

Agedabia

Benghazi (7 Feb)

GULF OF SIDRA

Mersa Brega

El Agheila (9 Feb)

putting dummy tanks in the desert, Selby Force attacked Maktila, an action supported by naval gunfire. With these distractions established, the main units moved through the Enba Gap. The Support Group, in the meantime, contained the Italian garrison at Sofafi, preventing their assisting the northern camps. O'Connor focused his attention on Nibeiwa.

Nibeiwa was a mile wide, a mile and a half long, and surrounded by a wall, anti-tank ditches, and a minefield. There were 150 artillery emplacements inside. Formidable enough but for one omission: the northwest corner was left unprotected. At 7:15 A.M., 8 December, their approach covered by a haze, seventy-two British guns opened fire. Suddenly inundated by exploding shells, surrounded by burning trucks and destroyed gun emplacements, with smoke rising from everywhere and dust blanketing everything, the Italians, caught completely off guard, did not know how to fight back. Everything happened so quickly. Two squadrons of Matilda tanks, supported by guns of the 31st Field Artillery and Bren gun carriers, smashed through the undefended northwest corner, firing point-blank at enemy trucks, tanks, and gun emplacements. Their machine gun fire decimated the Italian soldiers. As the Matildas spread destruction inside the camp, infantry of the 1/6 Rajputana Rifles and Cameron Highlanders charged through the shattered defenses. By 10:40 A.M., the fight was over. The British captured several guns, even though the Italian artillerymen fought to the last. Two thousand men and twenty-three tanks were also captured. The British lost eight officers and forty-eight enlisted men killed and wounded.

Tummar East and Tummar West were destroyed. The 4th Armored Brigade took Azzisiya on the coast without opposition. With the 4th Indian Division moving northwest through the Gap, the Italians lost all hope of reinforcing Sidi Barrani. By 10 December, British columns ranged inland to the west and along the coast road to Buq Buq. On the eleventh, the 1st Libyan Division and the 4th Blackshirt Division surrendered. Too late, the Italians abandoned Capuzzo and Sollum— the 4th Armored Brigade had just cut the road between Bardia and Tobruk.

Between 14 and 22 December, Bardia and its airfields were bombed; yet many Italian units escaping the disaster engulfing the 10th Army sought refuge there. The garrison swelled to 45,000 and

400 guns. Suddenly, the disintegrating situation looked hopeful. The Bardia defenses included an eighteen-mile perimeter wall, a double barbed wire entanglement, six minefields, and an anti-tank ditch.

O'Connor ordered I. G. MacKay's 6th Australian Division (replacing the 4th Indian) to penetrate the defenses, recommending that the assault, as at Nibeiwa, should be shaped to suit the tanks; however, O'Connor suggested a reversal of tactics. The tanks went in first at Nibeiwa, followed by infantry. At Bardia, sappers and infantry would have to go first, clearing paths through the minefields for the tanks and bridging the ditch. MacKay agreed.

At 5:30 A.M., 3 January 1941, 120 British guns opened fire. The 2/1 Battalion, 16th Australian Brigade, dashed across a thousand yards of desert to the defensive perimeter. Sappers blew gaps in the wire and engineers bridged the ditch. At 7:00 A.M., Matildas of the 7th Royal Tank Regiment, accompanied by light tanks and Bren gun carriers, penetrated the wall. Although much resistance immediately collapsed, some Italian units fought with considerable determination. But, by 8:30 A.M., the leading units of the Australian 16th Brigade were two miles inside the perimeter and captured 8,000 enemy soldiers.

The 17th Australian Brigade, to the 16th's right, crossed the perimeter at 11:30 A.M., accompanied by six Matildas, and moved into the lower defensive pocket. The next morning, the 16th Brigade now supported by the nineteenth, fanned out toward Bardia itself. By 1:00 P.M., the Italians quit.

The 6th Australian Division suffered 456 killed and wounded. But only six of an original twenty-three Matildas remained operational. The Italians lost over 40,000 captured and killed. The British also captured 400 artillery pieces, thirteen M11/39 tanks, 117 tankettes, and 700 trucks and autos.

O'Connor's Left Hook and the Battle at Beda Fomm

Wavell, with the five-day raid now a month old, let O'Connor continue west. Tobruk fell on 22 January after a day-long fight, yielding 25,000 prisoners, 200 artillery pieces, and 90 tanks. The move against Benghazi would not be as easy. True, the fighting reduced the 5th Squadra to thirty-four fighters and forty-six bombers, but the RAF was nearly worn out. Also, the Italians could still field some 100 medium tanks and 200 light tanks, whereas only a score of Matildas and fifty

cruisers remained operational, and most of those needed mainte-
nance. Graziani made the situation more difficult by withdrawing
from Derna and Mechili and concentrating his forces in Benghazi.

O'Connor could attack Benghazi directly, using Derna and
Mechili as marshaling points. Instead, he chose the unexpected route.
The 7th Armored Division, rolling out of Mechili would not attack
Benghazi but cross 150 miles of open desert via Msus to the coast road
at Ghemines, south of Benghazi. Their job was to prevent the Italians
in Benghazi from escaping south into Tripolitania. The Australian 6th
Division, moving rapidly around the shoulder of the Gulf of Sidra,
were to exert pressure directly on Benghazi. As John Strawson wrote in
The Battle for North Africa, O'Connor's maneuver was the first and most
daring of the so-called left hooks in North Africa (Map 8).

The 7th Armored Division neared Msus at dawn on 5 February.
They needed a rest, but O'Connor urged them on because the Italians already showed signs of abandoning Benghazi. In fact, Graziani
decided to abandon all of Cyrenaica and make a stand in Tripolitania.
Michael Creagh, commanding the 7th Armored Division, immediately sent one detachment to cut the road west of Antelat. Another
force, the 7th Armored Brigade (not to be confused with the division) and the remainder of the Support Group, sped west to Soluch
and Ghemines.

Lieutenant Colonel John Combe, 11th Hussars, commanded the
Antelat group. His Hussars were supported by the 2nd Battalion of
the Rifle Brigade and three artillery batteries under Jock Campbell—
he insisted on going along. Using all the skills acquired during
months of desert patrols, the little column reached the coast road just
west of Antelat and below Beda Fomm the afternoon of 5 February.

A long Italian infantry column flanked by tanks, the leading elements of the 10th Army, appeared on the road. Machine-gun fire
from the 11th Hussar's armored cars soon convinced the Italian crews
to abandon their tanks. The entire column surrendered. That
evening another large column came under British artillery fire. These
Italians deployed for action. Combs, meantime, called for assistance
from armored units now at Antelat. Light tanks of the 7th Hussars
and cruisers of the 2nd Royal Tank Regiment sped to Combe's aid,
attacking the rear of the Italian column and destroying many infantry-

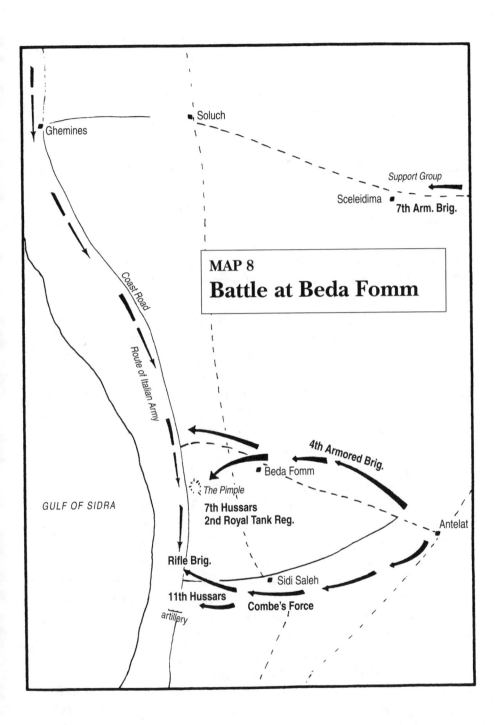

Ghemines

Soluch

Support Group

Sceleidima ●
7th Arm. Brig.

Coast Road

Route of Italian Army

MAP 8
Battle at Beda Fomm

4th Armored Brig.

■ Beda Fomm

The Pimple

**7th Hussars
2nd Royal Tank Reg.**

GULF OF SIDRA

Antelat

Rifle Brig.

■ Sidi Saleh

11th Hussars
artillery

Combe's Force

laden trucks. Five thousand Italians surrendered. Yet another column came down the road. British armor swept its flanks. The Italians again surrendered. The next morning, after a heavy rain, another column lurched into view. They attacked the roadblock but their energy soon withered under artillery fire and the well-aimed shooting of the Rifle Brigade.

Meanwhile, the 2nd Royal Tank Regiment, armed with nineteen cruisers and seven light tanks, occupied a point of high ground dubbed The Pimple, some seven miles southwest of Beda Fomm. They repeatedly attacked Italian units moving past them, destroying forty medium tanks, scores of other vehicles, and creating confusion. But some Italian units did get through.

One of those was a column of thirty tanks and support infantry. They attacked the Rifle Brigade at the roadblock. The British soldiers stayed in place even though sections of their position were overrun. Combs ordered his anti-tank guns to fire into the infantry emplacements at the risk of hitting his own men. The Italian tanks were destroyed. Regrouping, the Rifle Brigade cut down the Italian infantry with rapid fire. The attack collapsed.

With the 4th Armored Brigade and elements of the Support Group keeping a massive column hemmed in at Ghemines, and with the Australians in hot pursuit from the north, the 10th Army surrendered another 25,000 prisoners. Over 100 medium tanks and 100 artillery pieces were captured or destroyed.

From the beginning of the raid in early December to 7 February, British casualties numbered 500 killed, 1,373 wounded, and 55 declared missing. The Italian 10th Army gave up a total of 130,000 prisoners and an uncounted number killed. The British captured a total of 180 medium tanks, some of which they pressed into service, 200 light tanks, and 845 artillery pieces. The 5th Squadra of the Regia Aeronautica was rendered ineffective. The total disaster prophesized by Graziani came to pass. O'Connor sent a message to Wavell: "Fox killed in the open."

British units rushed to El Agheila to contain Italian forces in Tripolitania. O'Connor was eager to press on and take Tripoli, but western Libya was not on the menu. Wavell ordered an end to the campaign on 13 February. He needed men and machines in the

Sudan to mount operations in Somalia and Eritrea. Moreover, Churchill still wanted a Balkan front and looked to Wavell's command for troops. But the prime minister's position carried a contradiction. He stated that holding El Agheila was crucial to maintaining what he called the vital Desert Flank. Yet, stripping what strength remained of the Western Desert Force allowed the Italians to keep their 5th Army intact and maintain Tripoli as a supply base through which Erwin Rommel and his Africa Corps soon entered the arena.

O'Connor's masters, as a practical matter, were not convinced that a march to Tripoli could be sustained. Manpower losses during Operation Compass were negligible, but the cost in armored vehicles was enormous. Many of the surviving tanks went to the scrap heap. Then, no sooner did the Western Desert Force occupy Benghazi than the German Luftwaffe made its first appearance, bombing the port and turning back a convoy. Ammunition and gasoline were in short supply.

For more than fifty years, soldiers, politicians, and historians have debated whether O'Connor should have been allowed to attack Tripoli. Field Marshal Montgomery, in his introduction to Alan Moorehead's *The March to Tunis*, declared that O'Connor's campaign could have been further exploited and, had it succeeded, would have shortened the war. Additionally, according to Montgomery, the decision to intervene in Greece resulted "in disaster on both fronts." Rommel himself added his thoughts to the debate, saying in so many words that a campaign should never be cancelled because of a quartermaster's concerns, for then it is left to history to count the missed opportunities. That is nice for historians and even some of their readers, but the exercise rapidly becomes self-indulgent. The fact is that O'Connor did not advance, the consequences are known, and any subsequent argument becomes so much gamesmanship.

TOWARD A DILEMMA

The Western Desert Force achieved dramatic, even startling, results. The numerical odds, 36,000 versus a quarter-million, were staggering enough. Undeniably, the rapidity and certainty with which the British moved, charging through the Enba Gap and dashing across the desert to Beda Fomm, amply demonstrated that imaginative leadership guided their army into a new kind of battle. Better technology, however primitive by today's standards, made these advances possible. The Gloster Gladiator may be a dinosaur today but it did yeoman service in 1940. The newer Hawker Hurricane, rugged but not on a par with the Spitfire, increased fighter speed a hundred miles an hour and increased armament up to a deadly twelve machine guns. Blenheim bombers, so crucial to the advances, carried a pitifully small thousand-pound bomb load but delivered it with a speed and efficiency unknown in Maude's day only a generation earlier. The Matilda tank, excellent against the Italians, was surprisingly good against the Germans. Although another dinosaur to us, the Matilda was the Queen of Battle in early 1941.

But what did this technology allow O'Connor to do that was so different than Maude's flanking maneuvers or, more significantly, Brooking's flank march at Khan Baghdadi? The Enba Gap and Beda Fomm demonstrated conclusively for the first time in the history of desert battle that a large force—an army corps comprising the 7th Armored Division and the 4th Indian Division—could laterally penetrate the desert over a long distance, survive, and emerge in fighting trim. The lesson was not lost on Rommel nor on generals a half-century later.

Historians of the North African campaign take justifiable satisfaction reviewing all the weapons brought to battle. Technology is real stuff. It can be described, counted, and compared down to the last gun and rivet. But desert battle, indeed any battle, is more than the sum of contending technologies. Again, there is the human side.

The success of O'Connor's Operation Compass must be counted as a tribute both to generalship in the Middle East Command and to the men who did the fighting. Despite the early muddling about and endless experimenting with small units, a mutual confidence emerged among all ranks. Thus, Wavell painted Operation Compass in general strokes, letting O'Connor add the tactical details. O'Connor, in turn, sought the opinions of his officers, quite ready to amend his own ideas. For example, the December attack on the Italian camp at Nibeiwa was originally planned as a frontal assault through the minefield. But, as Major General Eric Dorman-Smith wrote to Liddell Hart, O'Connor invited him to submit an independent appraisal.

What evolved was the assault on the camp's exposed northwest corner. The resulting victory allowed the 7th Armored Division and the 4th Indian Division to push through the Enba Gap and move behind the Italians at Sollum. The flanking maneuver then gave birth to the march across 150 miles of desert to Beda Fomm. Reciprocal confidence nurtured the flexibility and imagination needed in the rapidly changing shape of Operation Compass.

The quality of the units forming the Western Desert Force complimented the generalship. Long-service professional soldiers filled the 4th Indian Division, their basic skills learned in tough Northwest Frontier campaigns. British regiments, such as the Coldstream and Scots Guards, the Camerons, the Argyll and Sutherland Highlanders, and the Rifle Brigade, were among the cream of the British Army. They contained strong cadres of professionals who carried to Egypt long-held regimental traditions and histories. Even new troops distinguished themselves. Barrie Pitt tells us that the 6th Australian Division, filled with green troops, was eager to join the fight and show they were equal to their fathers who had fought so well in France and at Gallipoli. Wavell and O'Connor believed their men would prevail. And so they did.

For all the excellent qualities of the Western Desert Force and their remarkable achievements, there needs be a recognition that not all was perfect. If I may, a friend of mine served as an officer in the desert from near the beginning through to the end in 1943. He has often wondered why the British won because so many things went wrong and because there was so little materiel at hand. Old problems arrived on the battlefield with the British Army and new problems surfaced. Not all the problems found ready solutions, compounding the errors and inefficiencies to follow.

O'Connor moved his forces as freely as he did because his intelligence functions were superior to those of the Italians. The RAF gave him a reconnaissance squadron and the 11th Hussars and Long-range Desert Groups supplied valuable ground-based information. That said, the command and control apparatus were rather primitive. Radios did and did not work, and incompatible frequencies garbled smooth communications; also, most messages were sent by Morse code rather than by voice, slowing the communications process. As Strawson points out,

O'Connor had to be a hands-on front-line general just to keep minimal control over his units. That is why, for instance, he could be found at Antelat following the left hook maneuver. Fortunately, his energy and quick intelligence were equal to the task.

Independent columns created an area of concern. Nearly a century before Operation Compass, Colin Campbell led British forces to quell the Great Indian Mutiny. One of the first situations he encountered was a cloud of officers, from generals to captains, all wanting their own independent commands, their own flying columns, so that they could race about, all dash, doing whatever they wanted. Campbell flatly rejected their pleas. Neither Wavell nor O'Connor was inundated by a cloud of officers, although many submitted proposals, but the tradition of independent columns was an old one in the British Army, and it begged for attention in the Western Desert. British resources were slim, and time was needed to sort things out. The various groups—the Long Range Desert Group, 11th Hussars, Jock Columns, Selby Force, and the Support Group—bought that time.

These groups made tactical sense in their time and place. In 1940, the British struck the Italians anywhere possible, to keep them guessing. Later, the tactical picture changed, but the reliance on independent groups did not, leading to stagnation when the British faced the challenges presented by Rommel. P. G. Griffith notes what must be the supreme irony of the North African battles. After the lateral penetration into the desert was demonstrated, first by the independent groups and then by the 7th Armored and 4th Indian divisions, it took the slugfest of Montgomery's El Alamein offensive, really a World War I battle of attrition, to bring down Rommel.

Could the British have done better? I think not. The draining away of experienced troops remained a constant. The 4th Indian Division was abruptly taken out of battle and replaced with the inexperienced 6th Australians. After Beda Foram, practically the entire Western Desert Force was cycled away from the front, leaving only green troops to face Rommel's battle-seasoned veterans. The British 7th Armored Division was returned to the front but, as Griffith clearly indicates, it was not the veteran unit that left. Eventually seventeen different battalions were cycled through its organization. Thus, the division that battled the Italians was not the division that fought at El Alamein.

O'Connor shaped tactics to fit the best use of tanks. That is why specific tactics varied between the battles at Nibeiwa and Bardia. That pragmatic approach fortunately did not match British tank theory that evolved between the two world wars. Masses of tanks, so the theory went, were supposed to battle masses of tanks. Not until Beresford-Preise tried to draw out Rommel's armor with a tank fleet in Operation Battleaxe in June 1941 did the British theory come close to being battle tested. But rather than meeting Rommel's armor, the British tanks ran onto his anti-tank guns, a situation the British did not anticipate. Whether the British were too driven by dogma or Rommel too clever is a judgment I shall avoid for the moment. Later, in November 1941 during Operation Crusader, tanks of the British 4th Armored Brigade finally met German tanks in open battle. A total of 230 machines were involved. Only forty-five were damaged, and over half those were later repaired. Rommel was right in the context of North African battles: tanks did not routinely destroy tanks. The means by which the British adjusted to Rommel's tactics did not arrive until the summer of 1942, when the 6-pounder gun provided some parity with German anti-tank gun capabilities. Yet, the British, completely ignoring the pragmatics of O'Connor and the need for a more powerful anti-tank weapon than even the 6-pounder, did not produce a coherent, much less consistent, theory of tank battle from their North African experiences. The result was an inability to develop a first-rate main battle tank. Instead, beginning about mid-1942, they placed increasing reliance on the American M-4 Sherman tank.

The most significant problems revealed by Operation Compass were logistical. The further and faster O'Connor's force advanced, the more exhausted were his men and machines, and the more vulnerable the supply lines. The dilemma between mobility and vulnerability was the inescapable consequence of desert battle. The broad desert table invited rapid movement. But the support services needed to keep pace. Soon, British supply lines stretched from Cairo and Alexandria to the Gulf of Sidra. Once there, they were bombed by the German Luftwaffe flying in from Sicily. The worn RAF could not stop them. The British inevitably withdrew from Cyrenaica.

Of course, the British contributed significantly to their own design for disaster; then Rommel added the element of surprise. He attacked a month earlier than anyone, including his own superiors, thought possible. The pattern of attack and counterattack ranged back and forth along the coastal strip until even the great Rommel ran out of gas, both literally and figuratively, an equal victim of the mobility-vulnerability dilemma. The desert does not play favorites, even with legends. Indeed, to twist an idea by F. Spencer Chapman, the desert is neutral.

CHAPTER 7

The Arab-Israeli War, 1973

WAR UNTO WAR

From the founding of the Jewish state shortly after World War II to 1967, two wars, state-sponsored terrorism, and random violence between Israel and its Arab neighbors surfaced, then recurred with biblical certainty. Nothing short of total destruction of one side by the other seemed to offer any hope of peace. The Arab states also inaugurated propaganda campaigns in which each tried to convince the others that it was the most anti-Israeli. But, in early 1967, the Arab states stopped flaying each other long enough to gang up on Egypt, whose president, Gamel Abdel Nasser, offered policies that might lead to regional stabilization. Nasser, not wanting to be perceived as the one Arab leader who compromised with Israel, escalated his own anti-Israeli rhetoric and, through the verbal barrage, put himself forward as the leader of Arab nationalism. To strengthen his rhetorical stand, he mobilized troops near the Israeli frontier. Nasser, "one of the most charismatic leaders who ever lived," according to Conor O'Brien in *The Siege*, lifted himself from whipping dog to hero in a very short time.

The Arabs demanded the annihilation of the Jews. Many Israelis, survivors of the Nazi Holocaust and all too familiar with such a call, worried that the Arabs might repeat the Nazi extermination program and recoiled at their own government's tepid response. Levi Eshkol, combined prime minister and defense minister, suddenly seemed too old, too fumbling, too mild. The political hawks in the Israeli parliament forced a change with the appointment of Moshe Dayan, an esteemed former army officer, to the post of defense minister. Political doves suddenly became hawks. Nasser's threats sounded very real as Israel moved toward war—in fact, toward a preemptive strike—as the means to prevent an Arab first attack. At the end of May 1967, the United States, a dominant player in the byzantine dynamics of Middle Eastern politics, and ally of Israel, subtly waived any objections to Israel's provoking another war.

On 5 June 1967, Israeli Air Force squadrons crossed the Egyptian coast and at one stroke destroyed 300 Soviet-made fighters and bombers, most of them on the ground. Cairo radio erroneously announced that 75 percent of the Israeli planes were shot down. In Amman, the capital of Jordan, King Hussein joyously received the news and immediately declared war on Israel. That same afternoon, a supposedly crushed Israeli Air Force pounced on Hussein's airfields, wiping out his combat aircraft. The Israelis also bombed Syrian airfields and some in Iraq. By dusk, Arab air power ceased to exist. The Israeli Air Force could now focus attention on tactical support for ground forces.

The Israeli Army used large amounts of U.S. World War II surplus equipment—Jeeps mounting recoilless rifles, durable and versatile M-3 half-tracks, Sherman tanks with guns upgraded from 75mm to 105mm—and newer U.S. M-48 Patton and British Centurion tanks. They burst into the Sinai Peninsula, savaging Egyptian resistance. At Mitla Pass, a small Israeli force held off continued Egyptian counterattacks until the Israeli Air Force screamed down, creating a three-mile trail of death and destruction along the narrow passage.

In four days, as Bryan Perrett notes, the Israelis lost 275 killed and 800 wounded. Most of their damaged armor was repaired. But seven Egyptian divisions lay shredded, their casualties totaling 10,000 killed and wounded, with another 5,500 captured. They lost between 600 and 700 tanks, thousands of other vehicles, and 450 artillery pieces. The Syrians also lost heavily and yielded the Golan Heights. The Jordanians withdrew from Jerusalem, unable to stop a powerful Israeli attack.

The Arab states quarreled among one another, seeking to fix blame for the defeat. The Soviet Union became the common scapegoat, accused of providing obsolete equipment and second-rate advice. The Arabs swallowed their poor performance, put the best face on a propaganda campaign to minimize their collective humiliation, and plotted brutal revenge. Thus, the short battles of 1967 guaranteed only that there would be another war.

The new war had to wait as diplomatic efforts, vacillating though they were, offered a chance for a Middle East peace. The Israelis agreed with some Arab positions, but Syria and Egypt demanded that Israel give up the newly conquered lands on the Golan Heights, the east bank of the Suez Canal, and the west bank of the Jordan River. Israel adamantly refused.

Arab groups unleashed terrorism, uncoordinated and widespread, against Israel and upon its citizens wherever they could be found. Guerrillas crossing into Israel from Lebanon repeatedly attacked small truck convoys, military outposts, civilian buses, collective farms; they killed anyone in their way. Mines, letter and car bombs, skyjacking, sniping, and outright assassination spread the terror. The most dramatic episode was the killing of members of the 1972 Israeli Olympic team at the Munich games by Black September, a radical subgroup of the Syrian-backed paramilitary Fatah.

The Israeli response was intense. Special commando units assassinated terrorists. The government detained without trial captured terrorists and their alleged sympathizers. At least eleven air and ground raids were made into Lebanon against camps of the Palestine Liberation Organization and other Arab groups. The Israeli Air Force also made several deep penetration bombing raids into Egypt during 1970.

Most impressively, the Israelis established the hundred-mile-long Bar-Lev Line along the Suez Canal's east bank. Donald Neff, in his *Warriors against Israel,* declared the Bar-Lev the world's second Maginot Line, referring to French defenses established before World War II to thwart a German invasion. But a major difference separated the two. The French planned the Maginot Line from the beginning to be an interconnected fortress system with heavy artillery in bunkers and turrets, all connected by an elaborate tunnel system that included a small railway. The Bar-Lev Line had no such grand design. Like Topsy, "it just grow'd." The line began life as an early warning system of electronic sensors placed every ten miles along the canal. Next, small garrisons, up to a half-company, were posted to operate and protect the sensor stations. But the troops needed protection, too, so the army added bunkers, minefields, and barbed wire entanglements. Artillery emplacements protected the miniforts. Finally, the bunkers were made bomb and artillery proof. The Israelis built thirty such forts. Most intimidating of all, a continuous sand berm, as high as seventy feet and sloped 45 to 65 degrees, stretched the canal's length. The base merged with the canal to deny the Egyptians any landing space. Oil vats positioned along the berm could let flaming oil into the canal, incinerating any Egyptians foolish enough to try a crossing.

On 28 September 1970, Nasser died and was replaced by Anwar Sadat. Five months later, Sadat announced a desire to extend the 1967 cease-fire and open the Suez Canal in return for a partial Israeli withdrawal from the Sinai. He even agreed to a United Nations peacekeeping force along common frontiers. The Israelis found several of Sadat's ideas acceptable yet refused to withdraw to pre-1967 borders. As the Insight Team of the London *Sunday Times* concluded, the refusal ended Sadat's hopes for a diplomatic settlement, leaving him with the tragic perception that war was inevitable. He realized Egypt needed conspicuous success—not a repeat of the 1967 debacle—to force the Soviet Union and the United States into brokering a peace settlement with some meaning.

To buy some time within which to establish the basis for success, Sadat purposely projected an attitude of uncertainty toward Israel. The *Washington Post* commented on 4 May 1972 that "Sadat's continuing vacillation on a no peace-no war policy appears to be slowly eroding his authority, both among the civilian population and among his own government." Thus, earlier in March, having flooded the canal's west bank with artillery and infantry preparatory to a crossing, Sadat pulled them back. The Soviets, never trusting him, sponsored an abortive coup. Even members of his government openly opposed him. Sadat arrested the most vocal. Then civilian riots convulsed Cairo. The Arab world shuddered at the man's visible weakness. However, appearance disguised reality as Sadat prepared for war. He met secretly in April 1972 with Syrian president Hafiz Assad. Egyptian chief of staff General Abdel Ghani Gamasy, attending the two leaders, suggested the three months he considered optimum for attacking Israel—May, September, and October. They chose October 1973.

PREPARATIONS FOR A NEW WAR

With the Egyptian Air Force in shambles after the 1967 War, Sadat purchased 210 MiG 21 fighters from the Soviet Union in Early 1972, boosting total combat aircraft to 620. The purchase was cosmetic; for Egyptian pilots were ill trained, and none had combat experience.

Reluctantly, the Egyptian high command conceded air superiority to the Israelis. According to the conventional wisdom of desert battle developed from World War II, that concession paved the way for disaster.

The Egyptians, in a creative response, developed a new airground strategy to compensate for their lack of air strength. They networked older surface-to-air missile batteries, SAM-2s and SAM-3s, from the Suez Canal to Cairo. The SAM-2, with a range of twenty-eight miles and a ceiling of 70,000 feet, was considered ineffective against high-speed aircraft flying at low altitudes. The SAM-3 had a ceiling variation between 500 feet and 40,000 feet and carried electronic cloaking devices. Both models were large, heavy, and immobile. The newer and more mobile SAM-6 batteries were effective over a twenty-five-mile range with a ceiling variance between 100 feet and 100,000 feet. Altogether, the Egyptians deployed about a thousand SAM batteries. Deadly Soviet ZSU-25 multiple-barreled, radar-directed anti-aircraft guns supplemented the SAMs. With four barrels, the gun churned out 4,000 rounds a minute. Other anti-aircraft batteries included 37mm, 85mm, and 100mm guns that ranged to 45,000 feet. The Israeli Air Force could not penetrate Egyptian air space with the impunity of the 1967 War.

Sadat revamped the Egyptian Army. Thousands of new artillery pieces rolled into Egypt, and the number of tanks increased to nearly 2,000, mostly T-54s and T-55s. The T-54, mounting a 100mm gun and with a low silhouette, was a true successor to the World War II T-34. But its gun could be depressed only four degrees, a disadvantage in desert war in which tanks often fired from dug-in positions. The T-55 had an infrared light system for night firing. Both models fired only solid armor-piercing shot and gave a rough ride on the burnt surfaces of Middle Eastern deserts. The Russians also supplied a few T-62s. Even that latest model came with flaws. The low-slung transmission housing gave scant ground clearance, and its 115mm gun lost accuracy at ranges exceeding 1,000 yards.

The Egyptian Army's real strength was its infantry. Sadat weeded out incompetent officers, stopped rampant nepotism, and promoted better-educated soldiers. He appointed General Ahmed Ismail, a seasoned officer, commander in chief, and Lieutenant General Saad el Shazli, trained in both the Soviet Union and the United States, was appointed chief of staff. The front line force swelled to 260,000 with another half-million in reserve. Although they had new artillery and armor, the army needed something more to counter the strong Israeli tank formations. Rather than rolling out their armor, playing the big tank battle scenario so dear to the Israelis, the Egyptians equipped their infantry with thousands of hand-held anti-tank missiles and rockets. They would advance first and destroy Israeli armor, after which Egyptian tanks would exploit gaps in the Israeli offensive line.

The Egyptians formed the southern flank of the proposed war. The Syrians were the northern flank, attacking along the Golan Heights. Their highly professional army numbered 120,000 men, with a reserve of 200,000, and a thousand tanks—again, Russian T-series machines. The Syrian Air Force numbered 326 aircraft. The Jordanians, if they entered the war, added a small but well-trained army of 68,000 regulars and 20,000 reservists, together with 420 tanks, and 52 aircraft.

Despite obvious Arab strength, the Israelis felt invincible. The 1967 victory left little doubt among the civilian population, politicians, and army leaders that they possessed the ability to defeat the Arabs. The permanent army numbered 95,000, with another 180,000 in reserve. When compared to any one of the Arab armies, the Israelis were proportionally tank-heavy, having 1,900 machines. Their two main battle tanks were the U.S. M-48 Patton and the British Centurion. Both carried a British designed 105mm gun. The Israelis added more powerful engines and transmissions to the Centurions, making them very reliable weapons. The army also had 1,450 other armored vehicles, including upgraded M-4 Sherman tanks and M-113 armored personnel carriers. The M-113 was armed with a 12.7mm machine gun and could speed eleven men to the battlefield at 55 mph.

The Israeli Air Force flew 488 combat aircraft. Among those were the French Dassault-Breguet Mirage F-1. A design from 1966 and considered outdated in 1973, the Mirage remained useful in a tactical role as it carried two 30mm cannon and an external bomb load of 8,800 pounds. Older still, from a 1954 U.S. design, was the Douglas A-4 Skyhawk, originally made as a carrier plane. The E series was especially modified for the Israelis, adding a 30mm cannon and new electronic equipment. The F-4 Phantom was at the leading edge of jet design and proved very reliable for the Israelis. They rebuilt the plane to their own specifications, adding newer electronic equipment. The Phantom carried a four-barreled rotating 30mm cannon, four air-to-air missiles, and a 16,000-pound bomb load.

To disguise military preparations along a desert front is nearly impossible. The Egyptians, in order to cloak their preparations, wanting to effect complete surprise, created an atmosphere of normality along the Suez Canal. They routinely maintained a strong force facing the canal, making sudden and massive movements to the front unnecessary. To bring that force to full strength, the Egyptians held twenty-two mock mobilizations between January and September 1973, their maneuvers becoming familiar to Israeli spotters. With each maneuver, supplies, fuel, guns, tanks, and men were filtered into advanced staging areas. The equipment included fire-fighting water pumps, capable of discharging a thousand gallons a minute, purchased from a German firm under the guise of improving domestic fire brigades. In actuality, they would be used to cut through the great sand berm of the Bar-Lev Line.

Egyptian ruses notwithstanding, the Israelis were too distracted by other events to pay much attention to military movements across inviolable borders. In July 1973, to everyone's surprise, Sadat ordered all Soviet personnel out of Egypt. The Soviets seemed to control the Egyptian military, having 200 pilots and their ground crews on station and 20,000 personnel in various support functions, including the manning of the SAM sites. But the Soviets rankled Sadat by refusing to support another war and blatantly attempting to control Egypt's interior policies with a coup that failed. The Soviets started pulling out on 17 July, creating a perceived breach that, to outsiders, weakened Egypt's military establishment.

Another Israeli distraction and a source of immediate concern was terrorist activity. In late September, a group called Eagles of the Palestine Revolution took several hostages off a train carrying migrating Jews from Moscow to Vienna. The group demanded that Schonau Castle, the Austrian center for these Jews, be closed. The Austrian government complied. The London *Sunday Times* Insight Team questioned whether the Schonau affair was actually planned by Egypt as a purposeful distraction. Planned or not, Schonau consumed the Israelis, provoking demonstrations, rallies, petitions, and broad mass media coverage.

Sadat himself contributed to the air of distraction. He leaked information that he intended to participate in the October UN debate on Arab-Israeli relations. The Israelis, believing Egypt would do anything to avoid war, thought Sadat might develop another peace initiative. Sadat added more smoke to the atmosphere by going on a Middle East tour in August.

Were these distractions enough, the Israelis lulled themselves into a rather smug and, from the Arab standpoint, arrogant view of Egyptian and Syrian intentions about war. The Syrians, according to Israeli thinking, could not go to war without Egypt. And "everyone" knew the Egyptians were helpless without Soviet assistance—and the Soviets were gone. Furthermore, the Egyptians no longer possessed a viable air force. Thus, the Israeli tank wall could repel any Egyptian ground attack. Israeli defense minister Moshe Dayan continually dismissed reports of Egyptian and Syrian preparations. The U.S. State Department's Intelligence and Research Bureau, analyzing reports from other intelligence agencies, calculated in May 1973 that a 45 percent chance existed for another Arab-Israeli war within six months. The U.S. Central Intelligence Agency agreed. Yet, Israeli military intelligence chief Eliahu Zeira confidently told the general staff on 24 September that Egyptian and Syrian movements were unrelated. Even as late as 3 October, Dayan reported to the cabinet that neither Egypt nor Syria could go to war. Mohamed Heikal, Egyptian newspaper editor, confidant of Sadat, and sometime minister of information, wrote in *Road to Ramadan*: "It is strange to see how completely Israeli thinking . . . was obsessed by the conviction that Egypt was not going to fight. . . . [and how] arrogance made the Israeli Army blind to what was happening in front of its nose" (27 and 44).

THE 1973 WAR
Opening Moves, 6 to 10 October
Saturday, 6 October, the day the Jews celebrated Yom Kippur, the Day of Atonement, was the date selected by the Egyptians and Syrians to begin the war. The Egyptians would cross the Suez Canal and move into the Sinai peninsula. Appropriately, this was called the Sinai Front. The Syrians would attack along the Golan Heights—the Golan Front.

No one really believed the Egyptians competent enough to cross the Suez Canal; besides, the Bar-Lev Line was too intimidating. The

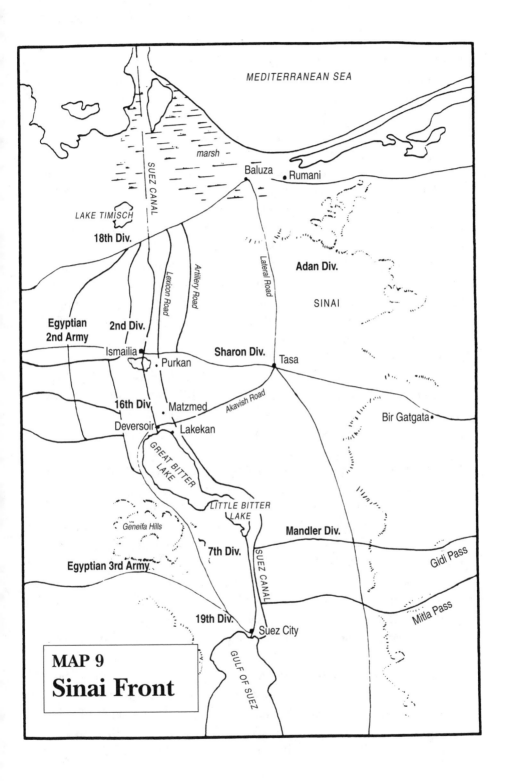

MEDITERRANEAN SEA

marsh

Baluza • Rumani

SUEZ CANAL

LAKE TIMISCH

18th Div.

Adan Div.

Lateral Road

SINAI

Lexicon Road

Artillery Road

Egyptian
2nd Army

2nd Div.

Ismailia •

• Purkan

Sharon Div.

Tasa •

16th Div.

• Matzmed

Akavish Road

Deversoir •

• Lakekan

Bir Gatgata •

GREAT BITTER
LAKE

LITTLE BITTER
LAKE

Geneifa Hills

Mandler Div.

7th Div.

SUEZ CANAL

Gidi Pass

Egyptian 3rd Army

19th Div.

Mitla Pass

• Suez City

GULF OF SUEZ

MAP 9
Sinai Front

Egyptians proved everyone wrong. On the night of 5 October, frogmen swam to the east bank, stuffed the oil discharge outlets with wet cement and cut the feeder lines. There would be no inferno. At 2:00 P.M. on the sixth, a terrible, unexpected roar burst from the canal's west bank as the Egyptians opened a bombardment by 2,000 tank guns, artillery pieces, mortars, and missile batteries (Map 9). Rubber boats, nearly a thousand of them, were launched into the canal, delivering the first wave of 4,000 troops to the east bank against little or no resistance. Only 450 Israeli reservists manned the forts of the great Bar-Lev Line. By 3:00 P.M., another 4,000 Egyptians lunged up the sand berm, surrounded some forts, pummeled them with mortar fire, and bypassed others. Special teams crossed with the water pumps and, by 6:30 P.M., cut sixty pathways through the berm. The Egyptians now had 32,000 men on the east bank. At 8:30 P.M., the first of ten bridges spanned the canal and armored units moved east. The Egyptian high command expected 25,000 casualties during the assault. By midnight, they lost only 208 killed and wounded.

In the north, Israel defenses on the Golan Heights included three armored brigades, totaling 12,000 men, 177 tanks, and 70 guns arrayed behind anti-tank ditches and berms with wire entanglements and minefields. Seventeen strongpoints or miniforts, each manned by ten to thirty men supported by three tanks, added defensive depth. Against these defenses the Syrians brought three infantry and two armored divisions equipped with 1,300 tanks and 600 guns.

The Syrians also attacked at 2:00 P.M. on 6 October. They planned to overwhelm the Golan defenses, move down the west slopes, take the bridges across the Jordan River, and spill onto the plains of Israel. Tel Aviv would soon be theirs. The assault opened with an hour-long artillery barrage. Then tanks with flails mounted on the front of the hulls moved forward, clearing paths through the mines. Bulldozers needed to fill the anti-tank ditches were delayed on crowded roads, so that infantrymen had to fill in using shovels. The work was hazardous. The Syrian 7th Division moved along the Kuneitra Road toward Mt. Hermon. The Israeli 7th Armored Brigade counterattacked, knocking out sixty-five tanks, some at ranges up to 2,000 yards.

Despite heavy losses, the Syrian 7th continued working toward Mt. Hermon. Their 9th Division closed on Kushneiya, and the 5th Division in the south made significant progress toward Tel Saki and Tel

Juhadar. Meantime, 500 Syrian commandos helicoptered to Mt. Hermon, overpowering the Israeli stronghold that held some of the most sophisticated intelligence and communications equipment in the Middle East. The Israelis staggered under the massive attacks, the Barak Brigade losing seventy-five of ninety tanks. The miniforts were evacuated. The Israeli Air Force streaked to the rescue but lost thirty planes to missile fire. The situation was growing desperate.

The Syrians fought through the night. Their 5th Division crossed the Tapline Road—an oil road running the length of the Golan (Map 10)—and, by dawn on Sunday, pushed southwest toward Rumat Magghamin. They lost 250 tanks. Israeli reinforcements arrived but, committed to battle in twos and threes, they were easily killed. Like the Egyptians, Syrian infantry carrying rockets and missiles completely surprised the Israeli commanders. Some Israeli tank losses can also be attributed to lack of coordination caused by a brave but foolish armored corps tradition. Tank commanders were trained to stand up in their turret hatches, ostensibly for better vision, more often as a badge of courage. For instance, Colonel Ben Shoham was standing in his turret when a burst of fire from a disabled Syrian tank killed him. That same burst also killed Major Ben Katzin, Shoham's executive officer, as he rode exposed in his turret. Too many key personnel were lost.

On 7 October, the Syrian 7th Division and the 81st Tank Brigade attacked the Israeli 7th Armored Brigade. The Syrians brought forward 500 tanks and infantry armed with Sagger and RPG anti-tank missiles. They attacked behind a massive 400-gun artillery bombardment. The Israeli brigade fielded only forty Centurions, five of them located near an abandoned bunker. Their commander, Colonel Nair Nofshe, let the Syrians close to within 500 yards, then ordered all his guns to open fire. They crippled twenty-five T-62s. The confusing battle continued into the night, tanks battling at only a few yards' distance from each other. Morning revealed 130 destroyed Syrian tanks and hundreds of dead infantry scattered across the battlefield. The Israelis called the area the Valley of Tears.

The Egyptians on the canal front enjoyed great success. By 8:00 A.M., Sunday, 7 October, 90,000 men stood on the east bank, together with 800 tanks and 11,000 other vehicles. They penetrated five miles into the Sinai, but twenty miles short of their goal. The Egyptian 2nd

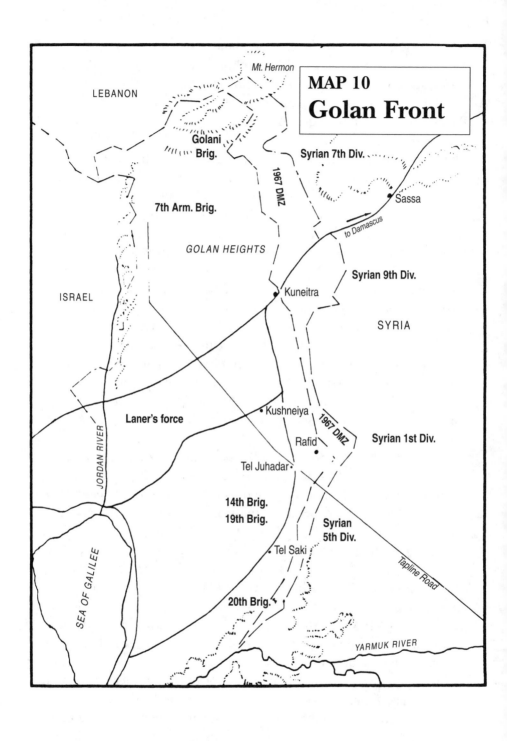

MAP 10
Golan Front

LEBANON

Mt. Hermon

Golani Brig.

Syrian 7th Div.

1967 DMZ

Sassa

to Damascus

7th Arm. Brig.

GOLAN HEIGHTS

Syrian 9th Div.

Kuneitra

ISRAEL

SYRIA

Laner's force

Kushneiya

1967 DMZ

Rafid

Syrian 1st Div.

JORDAN RIVER

Tel Juhadar

14th Brig.
19th Brig.

Syrian 5th Div.

Tel Saki

Tapline Road

SEA OF GALILEE

20th Brig.

YARMUK RIVER

Army—the 2nd, 16th and 18th Divisions—deployed north of Great
Bitter Lake from Deversoir to Qantara. The 3rd Army—the 7th and
19th divisions—held a line between the south end of Little Bitter
Lake and Suez City. A gap of twenty-five miles existed between the two
armies.

The Israeli southern command placed their forces in three
groups: the Adan Division in the north, the Sharon Division in the
center, and the Mandler Division in the south. Their response to the
Egyptian attack was confused. Egyptian air strikes destroyed 40 percent of their guns and what was firing did not hit targets with any con-
sistency because artillery spotting posts in the Bar-Lev Line no longer
existed. Israeli tanks charged forward like so much cavalry and without support. Suddenly, Egyptian infantry from seemingly everywhere
fired their RPG and Sagger missiles, grinding up the Israeli counterattacks. But Israeli reinforcements arrived on Sunday afternoon, sta-
bilizing the front. Then something strange happened. The Egyptian
advance shuddered to a halt.

Major General Gorodish Gonen, Israeli commander of the Sinai
front, counterattacked on Monday, 8 October. Avraham Adan's division assaulted the Egyptians around Purkan, charging in with 183
tanks, but with only 10 artillery pieces and no infantry support. As
they approached a line of sand dunes, they could see dark specks scattered about. One officer said they looked like tree stumps. They were
actually Egyptian infantry holding anti-tank missile launchers. Fire
and smoke consumed the Israeli attack. Adan lost eighty-three tanks
and could barely fight his way out of the debacle. Ariel Sharon, who
had asked Gonen that he be allowed to lead the attack with his division, and was refused, moved his men south, whether following his
own agenda, or out of spite, is difficult to know. The move exposed
Adan's flank. Gonen ordered Sharon to turn around. According to
the Insight Team, Sharon did so with great reluctance, placing the
attack's failure squarely on Gonen, the opening shot of the subsequent infighting between the two men.

Gonen then ordered Sharon to relieve some forts still holding out
on the Bar-Lev Line. Sharon exceeded his orders. He advanced
toward the Egyptian bridgehead with the idea of crossing the canal
and wreaking havoc in the Egyptian rear area. Gonen, he believed,

would surely send reinforcements. He was wrong. Gonen did not have any reinforcements. Colonel Assaf Yagouri's 190th Armored Battalion led Sharon's unauthorized attack and immediately met strong resistance. Yagouri committed his remaining tanks, unsupported, in small clusters. Egyptian missile infantry allowed the tanks to pass over their positions. They then rose up and attacked the Israelis from the rear, destroying the 190th in a few minutes. Yagouri was captured and was the last Israeli officer released after the war.

Egyptian chief of staff Saad el Shazli wrote in his diary that the Israelis wasted men and machines by attacking in small and unsupported tank groups, allowing Shazli to shape the battlefield to suit his army's fighting capabilities. He concluded, a note of astonishment lingering in his words, "We never expected [the Israelis] to cooperate."

Time for Decision: 11–13 October

On Thursday, 11 October, with reinforcements moving onto the Golan, the Israelis attacked the batted remnants of the Syrian 7th Division that still held several key points. The Syrians, although pushed back, did not collapse. Their infantry hid among the rocks and lava beds, striking the advancing Israelis with their missile fire. The Syrian Air Force bombed and strafed the Israelis, helping their comrades on the ground. Slowly, the battle's initiative turned in the Israelis' favor as the attack against the 7th received assistance when two Israeli divisions in the southern Golan broke through Syrian lines and moved down the Damascus Road to a point six miles inside Syria.

A problem surfaced. The Israelis could not endure very much longer the losses of this two-front war. Moreover, the Israeli public still did not know what was happening, the bleak reality replaced by glowing affirmations of government support of the army. Something different was necessary.

Moshe Dayan wrote a memorandum outlining a war plan. Syria had to be resoundingly defeated, not only punishing them for going to war but, as well, discouraging entry by Jordan and Iraq. He was less certain about the Sinai front, believing the Egyptians could not be easily pushed back across the canal. Before any counteroffensive, Dayan wanted to establish a strong defensive line between Mitla Pass and the canal. Dayan's memo, suppressed by the government until after the war, contradicted Israeli beliefs in their military superiority.

That national conceit, ideologically and psychologically comfortable in their hostile world, fostered an unwillingness to deal with reality. The cabinet reached consensus about taking Syria out of the war first, but the proposal to establish a defensive line in the Sinai did not receive enthusiastic support. Yet, one idea to bring the war to the Egyptians was rejected as too impractical. Sharon wanted to cross the canal and let loose his armor on the west bank's open land. Gonen not only rejected Sharon's plan; he wanted him sacked for disobeying orders. The enmity between the two was so great that chief of staff David Elazar brought Haim Bar-Lev, after whom the line was named, out of retirement and sent him to the Sinai. He became the unofficial commander. Bar-Lev, Gonen, and Dayan finally agreed to establish a line beyond the range of Egyptian missiles. Israeli tanks were dug in under artillery and air support. The apparently static defense was meant to draw the Egyptians further into the Sinai, away from their protective missile screen, where they could be destroyed.

General Ahmed Ismail, Egyptian commander in chief, was well pleased with his army's performance. They had crossed the canal, breached the Bar-Lev Line, tenaciously held what territory they gained, and confused the Israelis. But Ismail was cautious, not wanting his forces racing into the Sinai simply for the sake of more land. He ordered his positions consolidated within a narrow five- to ten-mile strip beyond the canal's east bank. That is why the Egyptian attack stopped. What the Egyptian Army did next would depend on Israeli actions. Ismail, by that fateful if not fatal decision, gave the Israelis battlefield initiative.

Yet, Ismail's reasons for consolidation appeared reasonable at the time. His army needed resupplies of food, fuel, and munitions. Without that resupply, further advance into the barren Sinai seemed too risky. His men would be subjected to air attacks, and he worried that an Israeli counteroffensive might break through to the canal, threatening Egypt itself. As a safeguard, he kept 700 tanks on the west bank.

Ismail's consolidation did not meet with enthusiastic approval. His *bête noire* was Saad el Shazli. The two men were longtime colleagues who developed an intense mutual dislike. Thus, it was no surprise that Shazli, undermining Ismail's position, wanted to attack, maintaining the momentum of the initial assault. Shazli thought consolidation would encourage an Israeli counterattack. The narrow strip held along the east bank gave the Egyptians little room to maneuver and, correspondingly, gave an Israeli attack every chance to succeed. Shazli's view was widely shared. Mohamed Heikal thought Ismail's plan too timid, rooted in his fear that a continued attack would fail. Like Shazli, Heikal wanted to maintain the momentum. He believed seizure of the Mitla and Gidi passes would open the Sinai to Egyptian conquest. The Soviets worried that consolidation invited Israeli air attacks and the possibility of high casualty rates. Ismail stood firm, fended off his critics, and rejected Shazli's urgings to attack. Events quickly eroded his position.

The Last Battles: 14 to 27 October

The Syrians paid heavily for their involvement in the war. Their casualty rates were high, and they lost great numbers of tanks and other equipment to the stubborn Israeli resistance. As if to heap indignity on tragedy, the Syrians now faced Israeli air raids on Damascus and the possibility of a ground attack on the capital. The Syrian Army, despite its losses, pulled back from the Golan in good order and, reinforced by its 3rd Armored Division, awaited the assault. Supplies airlifted by the Soviets gave renewed confidence, but Hafiz Assad wanted more. Syria, he told Sadat, was prepared to continue the fight, but only if Egypt renewed the Sinai offensive. Sadat agreed.

Ismail gave in under pressure from Cairo and ordered an attack against Gidi Pass and Mitla Pass by armored units of the 3rd Army. The 2nd Army was to move against Tasa Pass. Both armies would then strike Bir Gifgala, a major Israeli operations center. A third movement toward Baluza, a few miles from the coast where Israeli artillery and supply roads intersected, would cut the main route from the Gaza.

At 6:30 A.M., Sunday, 14 October, Egyptian armored units moved forward *en brigade*. The troops were confident. Ismail and Shazli were not. Ismail transferred 500 of his reserve tanks to the east bank to give the attack more punch. But the protective missile screen was left far behind. That tactical change was at once a reflection of inadequate planning and a challenge to the Israelis to fight a set-piece tank battle.

The Israelis accepted the challenge, having been resupplied by airlifted American munitions and equipment, but in their own time and in their own way. Dug in amongst the dunes and gullies along the defensive line, Israeli tanks enjoyed considerable advantage over the oncoming Egyptian armor. Able to depress their guns 10 degrees below horizon, the Patton and Centurion tanks could fire from hull-down positions without rolling forward to the crest of the dune, as did the Russian T series, to obtain an angle of fire, thus revealing their positions. In addition to solid shot, the Pattons and Centurions also fired APDS and HEAT projectiles. The armor piercing discarding sabot (APDS) is a dartlike projectile within a soft metal case. On discharge, the casing strips away, and the dart accelerates to high velocity, penetrating the armor. The high explosive anti-tank (HEAT) round is a low-velocity projectile with a shaped warhead that, on penetrating the armor, directs a molten stream forward.

The main Egyptian attack was against Gidi Pass. The armored brigades charged forward, blind and deaf to exact Israeli deployments and uncertain of the extent to which the Israelis recovered from the initial assault a week earlier. They soon found out. Israeli tanks and artillery opened fire at ranges up to 1,500 yards, setting afire a score of Egyptian tanks. According to Heikal, the attack was piecemeal and uncoordinated. Some Egyptian tanks returned fire at a range of a thousand yards. Firing solid shot, their rounds merely bounced off the sides of the Pattons and Centurions. Israeli fighterbombers swooped in and blasted the advancing Egyptians. The Egyptian commanders realized that the unsupported tanks needed help. Armored personnel carriers and missile carrying trucks sped forward but came under air attack and gunfire from Israeli tanks that now maneuvered easily across the desert. Added to the Israeli battle order were their own armored personnel carriers carrying squads of missile infantry together with mobile artillery that closely supported the tank groups. The Egyptian reinforcements were cut to pieces.

The Egyptians attacking Tasa lost eighty tanks when they ran into Sharon's division. Farther north at Baluza, an Israeli mechanized infantry brigade, armed with up-gunned Sherman tanks, let the Egyptians close on their positions. Then they opened fire, destroying thirty-four of sixty T-62s.

Estimates vary of Egyptian tank losses—264, 250, 175, 100 are common figures. The larger number was probably Israeli hyperbole, the smallest the Egyptians' attempt to disguise the magnitude of their defeat. The remaining two figures bracket an acceptable range. These numbers, however, do not include armored personnel carriers, trucks, mobile artillery, and other vehicles. As many as 1,000 Egyptians were killed. Israeli losses included 50 tanks, half of which were repaired.

The Egyptians withdrew to their original east bank positions amidst an argument between Ismail and Shazli about pulling back to the west bank. Sadat waived the argument aside: Egypt would stay on the east bank.

The Israelis prepared a counteroffensive, cheered by news from the Golan that a combined Jordanian-Iraqi attack was completely destroyed. The Sinai offensive, coded Operation Gazelle, called for Sharon to lead a paratroop brigade, reinforced by tanks, across the canal. Adan's division would cross to the west bank, then sweep south, destroying missile batteries and troop concentrations. Sharon's troops remaining on the east bank would keep open a wide corridor west of the Artillery Road area, securing the bridgehead.

At dawn, Monday, 15 October, Sharon's division moved forward. To make better time, he divided his force, sending Colonel Amnon Reshef's brigade in a wide arc across the desert to capture the stronghold at Matzmed at the top of Great Bitter Lake. Simultaneously, some of Reshef's units continued north toward Titur Road. The action that followed Reshef's maneuver lifted the phrase "all hell broke loose" beyond a cliche of military history. The Israelis blundered into the administrative and communications center of the Egyptian 16th Division. Remnants of the 21st Armored Brigade were also in the area, recouping from the battering it took during Sunday's abortive attack. The Egyptians opened fire in all directions, often at ranges of less than fifty yards. Israeli tanks scattered for cover. The point-blank fighting continued through the night, each side mauling the other. Tanks lurched about, turrets rotating, stopping, firing, lurching on, finding another target, stopping, firing, all the while hoping that an enemy tank did not get a blind-side shot or that a friend was not confused for a foe. Every time the Israelis broke through a strongpoint, the Egyptians regrouped and closed the gap. First light revealed a battlefield that looked like a smoking junkyard, the weapons of war scattered in grotesque twisted piles. Bodies were everywhere, grim evidence that the battle was more than a contest between machines. Reshef disengaged and withdrew to Lakekan on the shoulder of Great Bitter Lake.

While Rashef's force battled for survival, Colonel Danny Matt led his paratroop brigade from Mitla Pass toward a staging area commonly known as The Yard. The site was constructed when Sharon commanded the area before the war. Planned as a strongpoint for a canal crossing, a sand berm enclosed an area 700 yards by 150 yards. Gun emplacements covered the west bank. Matt's progress toward The Yard was slow as Egyptian artillery hammered the column, but they made it through. Early in the morning, 16 October, Matt's artillery blanketed the west bank opposite The Yard. By 5:00 A.M., all his infantry was across the canal. The arrival of Adan's division secured the corridor through the Egyptian east bank positions.

Shazli believed that Matt's paratroops were only the beginning of a larger Israeli push across the canal, so he requested that tanks be redeployed to the west bank. Both Sadat and Ismail rejected the idea, favoring instead attacks on the Israeli bridgehead by the 4th Armored Division and the 25th Armored Brigade. A telltale dust cloud signaled the Israelis that the 25th was coming their way. Armored units from Adan's division adroitly boxed in the Egyptian brigade on three sides against Great Bitter Lake. The 25th could not escape. They lost eighty-six of ninety-six T-62s, all their armored personnel carriers, and the supporting supply column. The 4th Armored Division was stalled by Israeli armor and artillery before their attack developed.

The Israelis slowly brought forward a preconstructed 570-foot steel bridge. Movement was slowed by Egyptian artillery fire, but tanks finally hauled it into place shortly after midnight, 18 October. Adan's division streamed across the bridge and turned south, taking the Geneifa Hills and advancing toward Suez City. At the same time, Brigadier General Kalem Magen's division (formerly Mandler's until he was killed on the thirteenth), also crossing the canal, headed south on a course parallel to the west of Adan's force. By noon, 19 October, units of Magen's division cut the Cairo–Suez City Road just seventeen miles east of the capital. Adan, meantime, attacked a series of fortified camps north of Suez City. By noon, 21 October, the Egyptian 3rd Army was cut off, isolated in the lower Sinai.

Lacking coordination, their command and control apparatus a shambles, the 3rd Army edged toward disintegration. Even though a cease-fire was declared on the 22nd, many Egyptian 3rd Army units, unable to contact their headquarters, tried fighting through the closing Israeli ring. Gonen regarded the small unit actions as violations of the cease-fire. He ordered Aden and Magen to strike farther south in a hammer blow to end all armored resistance and deny the 3rd Army the port facilities at Suez City. Israeli units entered Suez City but could not hold it. On 24 October, the Israeli Air Force attacked and destroyed the 3rd Army's bridging equipment, trapping substantial numbers on the east bank. Only the movement through the United Nations of another cease-fire averted more fighting and the 3rd Army's possible annihilation. With the cease-fire holding in the northern sector and on the Golan Heights, the war was over.

SO MANY IRONIES

The 1973 War brought a new wrinkle to the face of battle. As Chaim Herzog points out, the war introduced the widespread use of rockets and guided missiles. Mohamed Heikal called it an electronic war. The conclusions are correct. The irony is that all the new equipment and weaponry, for all its destructive potential, did not create battlefield dominance of sufficient duration that the outcome of the war was tilted in one direction or another. There are two reasons for that lack of impact.

First, all three major combatants were client states of superpowers: Israel of the United States; Egypt and Syria of the Soviet Union. The superpowers, because they provided the military equipment, implicitly limited the combatants' war resources and eventually determined the war's scope and duration.

Second, neither side revised its battle tactics enough to take full advantage of the new weapons. The Egyptians, true enough, assaulted the Bar-Lev Line and penetrated the Sinai with remarkable success by using missile-equipped infantry. The Syrians also made good use of missile infantry during their assault on the Golan Heights. The Israelis on both fronts were unable to immediately overcome the new manner of fighting. Locked into an all-tank theory of desert battle, the unsupported Israeli armor was swept aside. Unfortunately for the Egyptians and Syrians, the initial attacks consumed their reservoirs of tactical imagination. The Egyptian attack on 14 October rapidly degenerated into a desperate and failed affair without definitive military goals, more a quick response to Syrian pressure. Egyptian armor, moving forward beyond the protective missile screen, with only belated artillery and infantry support, ran into concealed Israeli tank fire. The Israelis made the necessary adjustments to defeat the Egyptians with very limited time and with the weapons at their disposal. Their tanks attacked, supported by missile infantry in armored personnel carriers and some self-propelled artillery. How ironic that the Egyptians' Sunday attack was a reverse image of the position into which they had initially forced the Israelis.

The Israelis already dominated the battlefield when their counteroffensive unfolded in full fury, enabling them to cross the canal onto the west bank where they fought the tank battles for which they were trained—almost. Caution must be exercised at this point. The sweep down the west bank did not fully vindicate Israeli tank theory. Rather, the theory worked precisely because Israel owned the battlefield, a consequence of the inherent superiority of its weapons and tactical adaptability. Both the Pattons and Centurions outshot their opponents at long ranges and with great accuracy, leading tank historian Kenneth Macksey to argue in his book *Tank versus Tank* that most Egyptian tanks were destroyed by Israeli tank gunfire, not by missiles. That conclusion may be too enthusiastic. The Egyptian and Syrian missile infantry was very effective early in the war. Although Israeli tanks did have great success, that came later in the war as they broke through the narrow east bank belt into which the Egyptians squeezed themselves. Furthermore, not having saturated their army with missile infantry as had Arab forces, the Israeli tanks would naturally kill a proportionately higher number of enemy tanks.

But the war ended before the Syrian and Egyptian armies could be annihilated. The roads to Damascus and Cairo were open, but the Israeli Army did not travel down either one. Instead, much as Anwar Sadat hoped from the beginning, the United States and the Soviet Union negotiated a U.N. cease-fire that included rules for disengagement and the posting of U.N. observers along common frontiers. In effect, a stalemate was created.

Sadat's hopes notwithstanding, the war could not end unless the Israelis became participants in the process. That they did so resulted from uncomfortable realities thrust upon them. The Israelis were so confident of their military prowess, amply demonstrated in 1967, that they convinced themselves the Egyptians were incapable of attacking in 1973. Israeli intelligence even put before the general staff an accurate assessment of the forthcoming Egyptian attack, but no one thought them skilled enough to cross the canal, much less puncture the Bar-Lev Line. Their bold and successful attack and the strong Syrian offensive nonetheless shook the Israelis. True, their enemies lost 16,000 men, 2,000 tanks, and 450 aircraft. But the loss of 2,523 of their own soldiers stunned the Israeli public.

A gloom settled over the land. Fingers were pointed in all directions. Ariel Sharon, who was blistered for not obeying orders, heaped scorn on David Elazar and Gonen for their timidity. The Israeli high command looked a little foolish as endless bickering, posturing, and political maneuvering obscured reasoned analysis. Moshe Dayan was excoriated in the press and parliament for not foreseeing the danger, for not ordering preemptive strikes, and for responding too slowly to the first attacks. Menachem Begin accused Golda Meir of criminal negligence.

The accusatory atmosphere within Israel expressed the war's ultimate irony. The Egyptian Army came close to annihilation on the battlefield, forcing Sadat to seek a cease-fire. Yet the courage and determination with which the Egyptians fought, even after the Israelis took the initiative, earned them the respect of other Arab states, and Sadat's prestige soared. Israel, the triumphant battlefield force, was wracked by self-doubt as the nation's vulnerabilities lay exposed to the world. The familiar panacea of war as a means of resolving regional conflicts suddenly looked less attractive. A long and convoluted path to peaceful negotiations lay ahead.

CHAPTER 8

The Gulf War, 1991

BLUNDERING TOWARD WAR

Despite a peace accord with Egypt, problems continued to plague Israel's relations with its other Arab neighbors and the indigenous Palestinian population. Were that not enough for the troubled Middle East, an Iranian revolution erupted in 1979. Islamic fundamentalists, led by the Ayatollah Khomeini, overthrew the ruling shah and executed many of his followers. As if to confirm the movement's fervor, several revolutionary fundamentalist leaders were executed for being too compromising with the West or too Western in their lifestyles. The United States Senate condemned the executions. Iranians staged anti-American demonstrations, overran the U.S. embassy in Teheran, and held the staff hostage for over a year. Efforts to rescue or negotiate release of the hostages, efforts both frustrating and humiliating in their failure, helped bring down the presidency of Jimmy Carter.

Arab states applauded the humiliation because they resented continuing U.S. support for Israel. But the victory by the Iranian fundamentalists also bothered those same Arab states. Many Arabs, especially in the ruling families and the growing middle class, enjoyed the lifestyle purchased with petro-dollars—especially away from home—and feared fallout from Iran's return to arbitrary medieval morality and violence. Moreover, as Persians, the Iranians were not real Arabs. Suspicion fed fear.

September 1980: Saddam Hussein, Iraq's leader, thinking he might be the next fundamentalist target, used a long-standing border dispute along the Shatt-al-Arab to start a war with Iran. The morality was completely Machiavellian—do unto others before they do unto you. The ensuing war, really the First Gulf War, ground on for eight long years. The Iraqis dug in after their initial offensive failed to gain

161

the support of Arabs around the Shatt-al-Arab. The Iranian Army, using waves of unarmed true believers as shock troops, bled to death against Iraq's static defenses. Artillery, machine guns, barbed wire, and poison gas reproduced the battle conditions of the World War I Western Front. Finally, late in the war, the Iraqis launched a fairly effective offensive, but it fell short of clear victory. The war collapsed from sheer exhaustion on both sides.

Saddam Hussein emerged from the war with the fourth largest army in the world. Even though he received financial aid from many Arab nations, and material aid from China and the West, Saddam was not taken seriously as a major player in the international political and military scene. What an insult to a man who, by self-proclamation, was leader of the Arab World! Saddam needed another war. He needed a clear victory. The war had to be a short and tidy affair because the Iran slugfest took a great toll. Kuwait loomed as a likely prospect. The little emirate at the top of the Persian Gulf had been a sore spot with Iraq since World War I. Saddam could revive old territorial claims and have history on his side.

The Kuwaitis also managed to put Saddam personally on the boil. He thought the country's ruling family were a pampered lot, their oil-generated wealth making them insufferable, especially since they greedily stored all their riches in foreign banks, mostly in England, a nation whose relations with Iraq were long storm ridden. Kuwait also lent Iraq great sums of money to fight Iran and then demanded payment. This affront angered Saddam. He accused the Kuwaitis of slant drilling into Iraqi oil fields and of manipulating oil prices to deny Iraq its fair market share.

In early 1990, Saddam secured agreements with Kuwait and the United Arab Emirates to lower their oil production, thus elevating market prices. The scheme did not work because world oil prices generally declined. Unable to control such complex developments, he vented his frustrations on Kuwait. As if to seal his intentions, he strengthened his troop concentrations along the common Kuwaiti-Iraqi border. United States Ambassador April Glaspie met with Iraq's deputy foreign minister in March and with Saddam himself in July, on both occasions indicating the United States would not take sides in Arab border disputes but insisting such disputes should be settled peacefully. Saddam assured Glaspie that he did not really want to invade Kuwait. That assurance not only placated the United States but, by telephoning Egyptian President Hosni Mubarak and saying essentially the same thing, Saddam calmed his Arab neighbors. How much more convenient to view him as a moderating regional influence and as the front line against Iranian fundamentalism than as a potential aggressor who could upset the delicate Middle Eastern power balance, setting Arab against Arab. Thus, Saddam's lie, coupled with the acquiescence of the United States and the Arab states to that lie, distorted perceptions of reality.

THE INVASION OF KUWAIT AND ITS CONSEQUENCES
A Short Fight

The U.S. declaration of noninterest in border disputes, ambiguous if not dissembling, led Saddam Hussein to believe he could invade Kuwait without interference from the United States. Consequently, over the summer of 1990, he increased his troop strength along the Kuwaiti border. Tensions escalated. The Saudis tried, unsuccessfully, to negotiate a settlement. An evaluation by the U.S. Central Intelligence Agency, dated 1 August, pointed to an imminent invasion by Iraq. They were right. At 2:00 A.M., 2 August, the Iraqis invaded Kuwait.

Three divisions of Saddam's elite Republican Guard—two armored and one mechanized infantry—spearheaded the invasion. One division moved against Kuwait City, another fanned out into the inland oil fields, and the third drove to the Iraq-Kuwait border.

The suddenness of the attack quickly overwhelmed the Kuwaiti Army, catching several capital garrison units still in their barracks. Other Kuwaiti units managed a stubborn defense. Armed with British Chieftan tanks, Kuwaiti armored battalions fought the invaders until they ran out of ammunition. Flights of the Kuwaiti Air Force, operating from a base north of Kuwait City, kept flying despite Iraqi artillery fire until they had only enough fuel to reach Saudi bases. An estimated 3,000 soldiers from an army of 20,000 also escaped south. Many of those left behind were either killed or captured. Some, eluding the Iraqis, formed a resistance force in Kuwait City.

The conquest complete, the Republican Guard divisions withdrew to the north, replaced by regular units of the Iraqi Army that took position along the Kuwait-Saudi border. The Saudis looked upon this movement as a provocative gesture. Would or could the Iraqis invade

Saudi Arabia, overrun the Gulf emirates, and link with allies in Yemen? Did the Kuwait invasion signal the beginnings of a militant Iraqi pan-Arabian movement?

Operation Desert Shield

Saddam did not order an invasion of Saudi Arabia, regardless of what he intended. Norman Friedman, in *Desert Victory*, and James Blackwell, in *Thunder in the Desert*, suggest that Saddam's army in Kuwait reached the end of its logistical tail at the Saudi border, not having the fuel, food, munitions and, most importantly, the transport to go further. Roads crossed the vast Arabian Desert but the main north-south highways paralleled the Gulf coast, routes easily blockaded and vulnerable to artillery fire and air attacks. An inland trek across the desert by several divisions without sufficient transport entailed great risk. The Iraqi Army waited at the border.

The United Nations reacted quickly to the Kuwaiti invasion. On 6 August, they imposed an embargo against Iraq that included a prohibition on oil purchases from Iraq. Even though representing only 5 percent of world production, Iraq's oil was its major revenue source. Four days later, twelve members of the twenty-one Arab League nations voted to send troops to defend Saudi Arabia. On 16 August, the United States, Great Britain, and France sent combat air squadrons to Saudi Arabia and sent more warships to the Persian Gulf, reinforcing naval inspection zones for all ships going to or leaving Iraq.

The U.S. Air Force dispatched 400 combat aircraft to the Gulf within a month. The first U.S. ground troops in the region were the Marine Expeditionary Force. When later reinforced, the unit was designated the 1st Marine Expeditionary Force. The British soon deployed the 7th Armored Brigade (Royal Scots Dragoon Guards, the Royal Irish Hussars, and the 1st Battalion, the Staffordshire Regiment). Then the United States sent the 82nd Airborne Division, the 101st Air Assault Division, the 24th Mechanized Infantry Division, and the 3rd Armored Cavalry Regiment. The 2nd Marine Expeditionary Force soon arrived, expanding the Marine Corps presence to 45,000 men and women. Operation Desert Shield, the protection of Saudi Arabia, was born.

Through the auspices of the United Nations and the deft political maneuvering of U.S. President George Bush, a coalition of twenty-nine nations emerged to guard the Saudi frontier and represent the military strength behind efforts to make Saddam withdraw from Kuwait. Arab states included Egypt, Morocco, Saudi Arabia, Syria, Pakistan, and the United Arab Emirates. In addition to the United States, Britain, and France, Western nations included Canada, Belgium, Italy, Denmark, Greece, Poland, Portugal, Spain, and Argentina. The United States, Britain, and France contributed the largest forces from among the Western nations. By September, 72,000 coalition troops were in or near the Persian Gulf. In January 1991, 172 cargo ships supplied the coalition. These were supplemented each day by 125 planes. By the end of January, coalition strength grew to 700,000 men, 1,700 combat aircraft, and 174 naval vessels. The overall commander of coalition forces, some fine points notwithstanding regarding who commanded which Arab units, was U.S. General Norman Schwarzkopf. A battalion commander in Vietnam, he later led the 24th Mechanized Infantry Division. Allegedly mercurial in temperament, he nonetheless held the coalition together and garnered much public support with his alternately brash and jolly approach to the war.

The Iraqi Response to Desert Shield

Saddam shifted his Kuwait forces into a defensive alignment. To diminish a threat on his east flank, Saddam gave territory along the Shatt-al-Arab back to Iran. That released substantial Iraqi forces for redeployment to Kuwait. By early October 1990, he sent an alleged 400,000 more troops to Kuwait supported by 3,500 tanks and 1,700 artillery pieces. Those numbers escalated during the next few months. A debate developed about the exact size of the Iraqi Army in Kuwait, the U.S. House of Representatives Armed Forces Research Office considerably downsizing the estimations. The confusion is explained by Norman Friedman in *Desert Victory*, where he notes that counting large numbers of troops and their equipment when they are already scattered about in the field is very difficult, even with modern satellite probes. Accounting for units—brigades and regiments—is much easier. By counting units, the coalition made the assumption that the Iraqi were at full strength when they may not have been.

The Iraqi Army fortified the Saudi-Kuwait border. They built huge sand berms to slow coalition armored attacks and dug in tanks to provide covering fire for infantry positions. Mortars, machine guns, and hand-held missiles strengthened the defensive line. Heavy artillery, 122mm and 155mm guns, gave added support. These front-line positions stretched down the Gulf coast from Kuwait City to the Saudi border, then extended inland along the Saudi border to a point just beyond the joint border with Iraq.

As late as January 1991, Saddam seemed convinced that the United States, the catalyst of the coalition, did not have the fortitude to commit its troops to a major battle that risked high casualties, a legacy of the Vietnam era. To capitalize on that supposed weakness, he flaunted his army's desert battle experience, boasted of his deadly arsenal, including poison gas already used on the Kurds, and dangled the possibility of biological warfare. Believing that the United States was gutless, Saddam threatened that if attacked, he would unleash the "mother of all battles."

Trying to influence world opinion, he took hostages from among Americans and Europeans living in Iraq and launched a massive propaganda campaign. Although soon released, the hostages, including children, were paraded across Iraqi television, their plight beamed to the rest of the world. Saddam portrayed himself as a rather avuncular fellow put upon by the evil forces of American and British imperialism.

On the diplomatic front, the Soviet Union tried to stop further conflict. But the United Nations, urged on by George Bush, who was increasingly impatient and disenchanted with the embargo, gave Saddam an ultimatum: withdraw from Kuwait by midnight, 15 January 1991, or risk war. Saddam, propped up by his advisers, so many yes-men and fawning relatives, ignored the ultimatum, convinced the coalition would not risk the "mother of all battles."

DESERT STORM: THE AIR WAR

The Iraqi Air Force, 550 aircraft strong, formed Saddam's first defensive line. That number included nonoperational planes and some obsolete craft like the Soviet Tu-16 and Tu-22 medium bombers. But the Soviet Su-25 Frogfoot, mounting a 30mm cannon and carrying conventional or laser-guided bombs, remained a capable plane. The MiG-21 formed the core of the force. Mounting two 23mm cannon, it carried just over a ton of missiles and bombs. A few Su-24 Fencers, with moveable wings were, however, the only really long-range fighter-bombers in Saddam's arsenal.

A complex ground-air defensive system, supposedly supporting the air force, included SAM-2 and SAM-3 missile batteries. Handheld missile launchers supplemented these older weapons. A variety of Soviet anti-aircraft artillery backed the missile component. These included 23mm and 57mm rapid fire weapons, and 130mm high altitude guns. Long- and short-range radar, a mix of Soviet and French hardware, screened Iraq's borders and the city of Baghdad. The defensive weapons systems were linked by a communications complex centered in Baghdad.

The coalition carried out a four dimensional air attack against the Iraqis, according to James Blackwell in *Thunder in the Desert*. First, a general attack destroyed the Iraqi command and control apparatus and crippled Iraq's war production and transport facilities. Second, the coalition established absolute superiority over Iraqi air space. That included destroying the Iraqi Air Force and the ground-air defense system. Third, the air attack isolated the Iraqi Army in Kuwait away from all sources of supply and transportation. Last, the Iraqi Army was heavily bombed.

The list of aircraft used was prodigious. Nine hundred U.S. Air Force planes were finally sent to the Gulf. Squadrons of F-14 4D interceptors roamed the skies looking for Iraqi planes. F-15E and 249 F-16 fighter-bombers swept down on tactical targets. Only around forty F-117A Stealth fighters went to the Gulf, used as tactical bombers, and even though they flew 1 percent of the sorties, they did 40 percent of the damage. Eighty B-52s, each carrying a 40,000-pound bomb load, and escorted by F-15C fighters, carpet bombed Iraqi troop concentrations and supply centers. F-4G Wild Weasles hit radar installations with their HARM missiles. A-10 Warthogs flew missions against tanks, firing a seven-barreled rotating 30mm cannon that disintegrated armor with depleted uranium bullets. A-64A Apache and AU-1W SuperCobra helicopters added to the tactical ground support arsenal. Additionally, U.S. aircraft carriers provided more than 400 combat planes for bombing missions and direct ground support. Planes from the carriers *Saratoga* and *John F. Kennedy*, positioned in the Red Sea, literally outflanking the Iraqi defenses, made important bombing raids on Baghdad.

The British Royal Air Force contributed forty-two Tornado GR-1s and eighteen Tornado F-3s for ground attacks, especially against airfields where they scattered bomblettes and mines across landing strips. The British and French provided squadrons of Jaguar fighters. Not on a technological par with the U.S. F-16s, the Jaguar proved a rugged machine when used in close ground support missions. The Saudi Air Force had seventy Tornados and sixty-three F-15Cs. The Canadians, Italians, Dutch, and Kuwaitis also contributed aircraft. Midnight, 15 January: Not a word from Baghdad.

2:30 A.M., 16 January: F-117A Stealth fighters swooped across Baghdad, dropping laser-guided Paveway bombs on selected targets. Simultaneously, U.S. fighter-bombers and British Tornados raided Iraqi airfields, and other raids hit radio and central telecommunications installations, Scud missile sites, command and control apparatus, oil refineries, nuclear, chemical, biological war facilities, and even Saddam's palace. In twenty-four hours, the coalition flew 2,000 sorties. Off the coast, the battleships *Wisconsin* and *Missouri* sent a barrage of 100 Tomahawk missiles streaking to targets in Iraq. The bombings were accompanied by the enthusiastic applause of those who believed the time had come to demonstrate that an air campaign, by itself, could win a war. Perhaps the ground troops would be spared the mother of all battles.

Coalition aircraft flew an impressive 12,000 sorties by 23 January. The confirmed results were less impressive. According to a postwar Pentagon briefing, only 60 percent of all guided bombs hit their targets, possibly the result of incorrect targeting information being fed into the guidance systems. So-called dumb, or free-fall, bombs missed targets with predictable certainty, just as they had since World War I. Further, bomb damage to many installations could not be verified for lack of on-site intelligence. Half the Scud missile batteries, used to bombard bases in northern Saudi Arabia and to harass Israel, were destroyed by 3 February. The remaining batteries, moved about and camouflaged, proved embarrassingly elusive through the end of the war.

Beginning 10 February, with 41,000 sorties flown, the air campaign shifted from strategic targets to tactical targets along the Saudi-Kuwaiti border. Using high-intensity concussion bombs and 15,000 conventional bombs, the raids destroyed bunkers, tanks, and artillery emplacements. Minefields exploded and front-line supply depots burned. Road and bridges leading to the border were cut. Some Iraqi divisions lost 40 percent of their personnel. The bombing continued without relief, a constant torrent of destruction, noise, flame, dust, and smoke. Life along Saddam's defensive line became a struggle for day-to-day survival.

By 23 February, coalition aircraft flew 94,000 sorties, an average of 1,200 each day. U.S. Defense Department estimates claimed 135 Iraqi aircraft destroyed together with 1,685 tanks, and 1,485 guns. Further estimates put Iraqi dead at 30,000, with another 88,000 wounded. Perhaps as a legacy of the Vietnam War, when the military measured success by numbers of enemy dead, the Gulf estimations of destruction and death were alternately encouraged as demonstrations of the efficient new high-technology weapons and discouraged as bloody and bloated distractions from the alleged high moral purposes of the war.

Whatever doubts and criticism were or continue to be directed at the air campaign's efficiency, four conclusions are incontrovertible. First, Saddam did not, could not, mount a counter air campaign. The Iraqi Air Force, not seriously damaged, never got off the ground for fear of being blown out of the sky. Saddam even moved some of his best aircraft out of harm's way, sending them to Iran of all places with the understanding they would be returned at the end of the war. Second, the air campaign severely disrupted the defensive line, the psychological impact of the bombings ultimately more valuable than any physical damage. Third, exponents of a victory by air power alone were quickly silenced. Fourth, the campaign established total aerial domination by coalition aircraft over Iraq and Kuwait.

DESERT STORM: THE GROUND WAR
Preliminary Operations
General Schwarzkopf concentrated his ground forces along the Saudi-Kuwait border as the air campaign continued to deliver its daily ration of death and destruction. As Schwarzkopf later told television interviewer David Frost, Saddam reacted to the concentration by stuffing more troops in the "bag called Kuwait." Saddam must have envisioned coalition forces being hurled against his defensive line, the ensuing slaughter a reprise of Iraqi battles of annihilation against Iran. To further convince Saddam that the mother of all battles would be along the border, and to complement the shift of the air war to tactical targets, U.S. Army, Marine Corps, and British artillery joined

the aerial destruction by racing to the border at night and, using special night targeting equipment, firing a specific number of rounds at specific targets. Digitalized, computerized fire control and communications technology, much of it unavailable twenty years before, enabled the artillerymen to coordinate the fire of several guns or several artillery battalions, all spatially separated, onto a single target. The gunners worked with such speed and precision that they slipped away before Iraqi guns could return fire.

Any Iraqi artillery that did open fire was quickly located and hit by an air strike or other artillery. Alas, finding targets was not easy for the Iraqi gunners. They lacked night vision equipment and were bewildered by so many rounds hitting from so many different directions. Another problem limited the Iraqi artillery. Their heavier guns, 122mm and larger, were pre-sighted on fixed targets or killing zones in expectation of a coalition ground attack. The rapidly moving coalition gunners did not give the Iraqis time to alter their fields of fire. Bombed, strafed, and pounded by guns and rockets, Iraqi artillery, like their air force, was rendered ineffective.

Over the Top

More Iraqi troops poured into Kuwait to repel a border attack and Marine amphibious assaults. But the Iraqi defenses, running along the coast and the Saudi-Kuwaiti border, extended only twenty miles into Iraq, leaving the western approach to Iraq across the Arabian Desert completely undefended. Perhaps Saddam naively assumed the coalition would never attack Iraqi territory. Perhaps he believed the desert formed an impenetrable barrier (Map 11).

Schwarzkopf and his planners decided to exploit the western flank. Early in the air campaign, the French 6th Armored Division moved to a point near Rafha, 200 miles west of the bend in the Saudi-Kuwaiti border. They were joined by the 82nd Airborne Division and, just to the east, the 101st Air Assault Division. Together, these units formed XVIII Corps. A large supply depot was established in the area to support a sixty-day campaign. Then the U.S. 24th Mechanized Infantry moved to Ash Shubah, just east of the 101st. Quickly, VII Corps took position between the 24th and the units remaining on the Saudi-Kuwaiti border. Principal units of VII Corps included the U.S. 1st and 3rd Armored Divisions, the U.S. 1st Infantry Division, and the

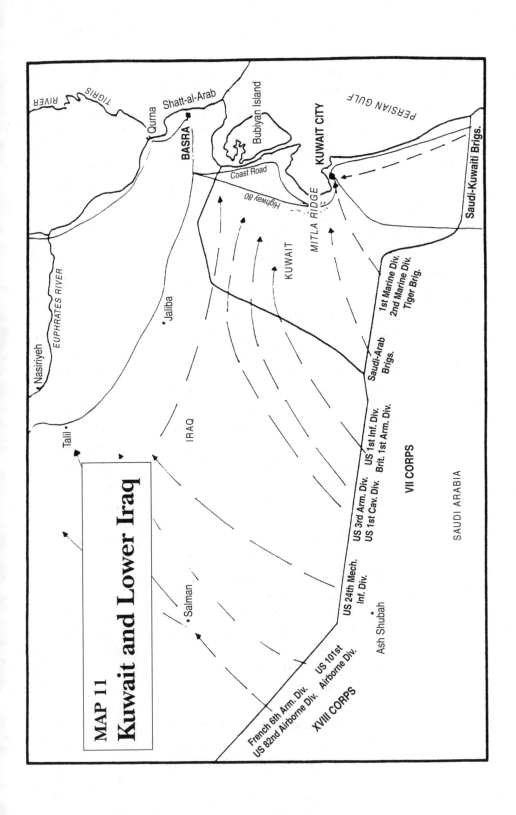

MAP 11
Kuwait and Lower Iraq

British 1st Armored Division. Egyptian, Kuwaiti, Syrian, and Pakistani units still faced the Kuwaiti border. A combined Arab force of five brigades from Saudi Arabia and the Gulf Emirates deployed near the coast. The U.S. 1st and 2nd Marine Divisions, supported by the Army Tiger Brigade (armored), flanked the inland road to Kuwait City.

On 22 February, U.S. Army and British artillery fire intensified. On 24 February, the coalition ground forces moved through the Iraqi defensive line. As I pointed out in my book *Sieges: A Comparative Study,* the attack reflected all the elements of a classic siege operation, involving ruse, breaching, and escalation of the defenses. As part of a ruse to rivet Iraqi attention on the coast, the *Wisconsin* and *Missouri* fired salvoes from their 16-inch guns at coastal defenses. Smaller vessels maneuvered offshore, firing their guns and missiles into entrenchments, minefields, and barbed wire. The ruse worked for, three hours later, the French 6th Armored Division far to the west, supported by a brigade from the 82nd Airborne, dashed unopposed across the Iraqi border toward Salman. There, seventy miles inside Iraq, they encountered the Iraqi 45th Division, crushed it, and took Salman and its airfield. The remaining units of the 82nd flew in by helicopter. With the French protecting the west flank, the 82nd headed north toward the Euphrates Valley to cut roads, bridges, and block any reinforcements coming down from Baghdad. Meantime, units of the 101st flew inland by helicopter and established an operational base. The rest of the division followed by truck convoy. The division then moved to points lower in the Euphrates Valley to cut Iraqi paths of withdrawal from the battle zones. At noon, fifteen hours ahead of schedule, the 24th Mechanized Infantry charged across the border toward Talil and Jalibah.

The Saudi and Gulf Arab brigades moved into Kuwait along the coast road, having fended off an abortive attack by the Iraqis around Khafji just inside the Saudi border. Farther inland, the two Marine divisions and the Tiger Brigade cut across detonated minefields and oil-filled ditches. They exploded the mines by firing linked charges into the fields. Some electronic triggers did not work, so they had to be fired manually. The ditches were covered with bulldozed sand. Then M-60 tanks equipped with bulldozer blades swept the pathways to make certain that there were no more mines. The Marines drove forward toward El Jabr airport south of Kuwait City. They were met by a large Iraqi armored force. The Marines attacked using their own M-60s and borrowed Abrams tanks. The M-60 armor was reinforced by British-designed chobham blocks, consisting of an epoxy core in a ceramic shell encased in aluminum and a layer of steel. The block was appliqued to existing armor. The chobham blocks increased resistance to rocket and missile projectiles, especially HEAT rounds. The Marines also used TOW missiles, artillery, and tactical air support from their British designed Harrier jump-jets. The Iraqis lost 320 T-62s and T-72s, and many armored personnel carriers and guns, a portent of future battles. El Jabr belonged to the Marines.

Monday morning, 25 February, VII Corps breached the defenses. Artillery from the British 1st Armored Division and the U.S. 1st Infantry Division fired a massive bombardment. The 1st Infantry's divisional armor, some tanks equipped with bulldozer blades, slashed through the sand berms. The British 1st Armored moved through the openings on the right side of the attack, defeating the 12th, 17th, and 52nd Iraqi Armored Divisions. The British main battle tank was the Challenger, protected by chobham armor and mounting a 120mm gun with rifled bore. Some doubts existed about the gun's reliability but, to cite an example from Friedman's *Desert Victory*, a Challenger gunner of the Scots Dragoon Guards hit an Iraqi tank with his first shot at 5,100 yards. That was far in excess of anything the Iraqis could do. The Challenger's gun passed its battlefield test.

The U.S. 1st and 3rd Armored Divisions used the untried Abrams 1A1, mounting a 120mm smooth bore gun and protected by depleted uranium armor. With a big gas turbine engine, the Abrams was not fuel efficient, but it glided effortlessly over the desert at 45 mph. Ballistic computer target devices and thermal imagery, as in the Challenger, gave the Abrams superior accuracy and range over the Russian built tanks. The Abrams could stand off beyond the range of the T-72s and, even in dust storms, destroy their targets.

The VII Corps turned east, completely outflanking the Iraqi Army in Kuwait. An early morning broadcast from Baghdad reported that coalition forces were thrown back. In fact, Iraqi troops were looking for ways out of Kuwait, perhaps wondering what had happened to the vaunted Iraqi Army and the "mother of all battles."

Coalition air attacks pounded many Iraqi units into insensibility. Already suffering hunger and thirst because of cut supply lines, some units decimated by the bombings, officers abandoning them, the regular Iraqi troops were shocked, exhausted, and ready to surrender. But some Iraqi units, such as those at El Jabr airport, and the Hammurabi and Medina divisions of the Republican Guard, did stand and fight, only to be wiped out. Overall, however, the process of disintegration was nearing a fait accompli.

On 25 February, the Iraqi Army received formal orders to withdraw from Kuwait City. The pullout quickly degenerated into a panicked flight from coalition forces. Tanks, armored personnel carriers, gasoline and ammunition trucks, and stolen civilian vehicles jammed the six lanes of Highway 80 leading north. Occupation loot—television sets, furniture, carpeting, and personal effects such as perfume—was greedily stuffed into the vehicles. Twenty miles northwest of Kuwait City at Mitla Ridge (not to be confused with the Sinai pass), planes from the carrier USS *Ranger* spotted the crawling, packed column and immediately attacked the front and rear. The column could not move. Waves of fighter-bombers darted over the stalled vehicles, dropping cluster bombs, then returned to the carrier to load any ordnance they could find and took off to hit the column again and again and again. The sky filled with aircraft awaiting their turn to bomb the column, as Martin Yant wrote, "like sharks in a feeding frenzy" (*Desert Mirage*, 145). The 2nd Marine Division and the Tiger Brigade received orders to attack the column. After forty hours, nothing was left but miles and miles of carnage. Bodies and parts of bodies littered the blood red ground. Incinerated vehicles trapped their passengers, in rictus, teeth like broken pebbles in slag. Tanks were blown apart, their turrets often catapulted from the hulls, gun barrels twisted into strange configurations.

On 28 February, the Iraqis shifted their withdrawal to the coast highway where hundreds of tanks, ammunition trucks, artillery, armored personnel carriers, and an assortment of stolen civilian vehicles were bombed and strafed by fighter-bombers and helicopters. The slow-moving column soon bumped into the 24th Mechanized Infantry. The ensuing slaughter repeated the scenario on Highway 80.

What motivated such destruction? Of course, Saddam's 25 February order put his army into motion, but he had no idea of their desperation. Not much of an army, more a crowd, they tried to flee the "Kuwait bag." But General Schwarzkopf issued two orders: the first to block all forces withdrawing into Iraq and the second to let nothing or no one escape from Kuwait City. General Colin Powell, chairman of the U.S. joint chiefs-of-staff, announced at an early Pentagon press briefing, "We're going to cut off the Iraqi Army in Kuwait; then we're going to kill it." Schwarzkopf's orders represented the operational equivalents of Powell's seemingly rhetorical remark.

By 28 February—the Arab forces and U.S. Marines in Kuwait City, VII Corps pushing against the coast road to the north, and XVIII Corps operating in the Euphrates Valley, blocking the retreat of the Republican Guard around Basra—the Iraqi army was ready to be annihilated. That did not happen. The Iraqis had already lost 82,500 killed, a figure developed by Dilip Hiro from various sources. According to the Manchester *Guardian*, 1 March 1991, they also lost 3,500 tanks and 2,000 armored personnel carriers. The pictures of the two Kuwaiti death highways televised around the world made the coalition look like butchers. President Bush, acting on Powell's recommendations, unilaterally stopped the ground war after 100 hours.

SOME PROBLEMS AND MATTERS OF DEFINITION

Saddam's war emerged from several monumental political and military blunders. The political side has been discussed at length by Norman Friedman and Dilip Hiro, to mention but two authors; so I shall emphasize those errors more directly related to desert warfare.

Saddam's most egregious blunders were in underestimating the skill and determination of Western forces, especially the Americans, and in overestimating his own army's capabilities based on its battle experience and modern equipment. Four problems hid behind the facade of Iraqi strength.

First, having the latest equipment did not equate with a widespread knowledge of how to use and maintain it. The regular Iraqi Army was a peasant force of low educational background and perfunctory training. They had proven quite capable in the Iran war, but Iranian soldiers, responding to the call of fundamentalism, were less trained than the Iraqis. The armies of the United States, Britain, and France were better educated, as Friedman significantly notes; thus their cultural milieu, more technologically sophisticated than that of Iraq, better prepared the men to receive military training in high technology weaponry. The Western armies also underwent extensive training in Europe to combat Soviet weapons technology and were consequently well prepared to battle anything the Iraqis threw against them. Nor were U.S. units, especially the armored divisions, strangers to deserts. They regularly took part in tactical exercises at the National Training Center in California's Mojave Desert.

Second, Saddam boasted that his army had greater battle experience than the Western armies. He was not entirely wrong. Among U.S. forces, according to retired Colonel David Hackworth (*Newsweek*, 21 January 1991), no one from private to battalion commander could boast any battle experience. But Saddam could not see, or chose to overlook, the reality of his army. Indeed, the Iraqi Army fought an eight-year war, but at great cost to the soldiers. The waves of Iraqis who surrendered to coalition forces suggest a war weariness among the men even as they marched into Kuwait. The coalition air campaign and artillery barrages brought them rapidly to their last gasp. The massive coalition ground attack ended whatever will to combat may have survived. That exhaustion helps explain why the Iraqis, for all their hardware, could not match the coalition's firepower nor manage very well what they did get to use. Moreover, the Iraqi Army was tightly controlled from Baghdad, a system that worked in the Iran war. In 1991, however, once Saddam's communications system fell apart under aerial bombardment, and coupled with incompetent officers, many of whom deserted their troops, the army lost direction when it was most needed.

Third, Saddam's army was a stratified organization. The Republican Guard brigades were the strongest units, typically having a battalion or two more than those in the regular army. The men were generally better educated because, when Saddam closed the universities, he made certain the dispossessed students were pressed into his elite corps. The regular army used Soviet T-55 and T-62 tanks, but the Guards received all the T-72s. The regular army, less educated, tired, using older equipment and less of it, took over the front-line positions in Kuwait. The Guards withdrew to the north, sealing the Iraqi border lest the coalition break through, and acting as battlefield police to keep the regular troops in the forward positions.

Fourth, Saddam made a major strategic blunder, thinking he could replicate in Kuwait the static, defensive war he fought against Iran. The Iranians had less armor and a limited air force, made more so by withdrawal of U.S. military aid following the Islamic revolution. They did have manpower, and they were sent forward in great crowds to die on the sand. Did Saddam and his generals really believe the same conditions existed against the coalition? If not, then the defensive line around Kuwait was nothing more than a failed bluff.

The coalition also had problems. Much debate during and after the war focused on the real effectiveness of the air campaign. One problem was that the U.S. military fed inflated damage figures to the press, a purposeful policy of disinformation, mostly to confuse and frighten the Iraqis. But the military leaders, cognizant of the Viet Nam legacy of despair over a lost cause, and doubtlessly giving the press full credit for it, also limited their access to the front and to personnel. Feeling used and bruised, the U.S. press wrote increasingly critical if not cynical evaluations. Were the smart bombs really so smart? What did the B-52 carpet bombing really accomplish? These and similar questions asked by the press did not clarify the situation, nor could they in the restrictive atmosphere created by the military. Surveying the print news, television coverage, and press briefings, it is obvious the military created an aura of high expectations, if not infallibility, around the new high technology weapons. The visual evidence of unparalleled accuracy could hardly be disputed as a hundred million television viewers watched the hinges blown from a bunker door. The military later admitted that 40 percent of the smart bombs missed their targets. Free-fall or dumb bombs sometimes missed targets by as much as a mile. But that was well within the off-target range of ten miles common in World War II. Winston Churchill, in 1943, acidly described RAF Bomber Command as a "ramshackle air-freight service delivering packages to the wrong address" (Thornton, 25).

Collateral damage, that done to persons and property near a target, seemed extensive in the Gulf War. Three thousand civilians were supposedly killed. When an alleged civilian bomb shelter in Baghdad was hit, the Iraqis cried foul. Many private residences were bombed, but whether as a result of bad bombing or because Saddam chose to hide weapons in civilian neighborhoods remains vague. Yet, considering that the amount of ordnance dropped during the first two weeks of the Gulf air campaign was greater than that delivered by the U.S. Army Air Corps over Europe during all of World War II, Baghdad could never be compared to London, Dresden, Hamburg, or Berlin.

My comment is not that of a military apologist. Rather, I do think an important element of the air campaign has been overlooked in many evaluations. What the Gulf air campaign attempted to do was unlike bombing in any other war. Time and again, coalition aircraft went after very specific, single targets. That was vastly different than sending a thousand B-17s or Halifax bombers over a Ruhr Valley city and hoping for the best.

The traditional standard by which bombing has been measured is physical damage. That may be all wrong in the context of desert battle. There is not that much to blow up. A more appropriate measure for desert battle might be the psychological pressures imposed by bombing. Thus, even though the news media received standard reports of physical damage, the air campaign planners recognized the importance of psychological dislodgement. A B-52 raid was a terrible thing. The bombers flew so high that they could not be seen or heard by anyone standing below. Suddenly the whole world erupted as each plane dropped a 40,000-pound bomb load in a tight area, the concussive impact so great that it was felt a hundred miles away. Adding to the on-ground horror was the question of who would be next. The air command dropped leaflets giving the place and time of the next bomb run, intentionally spreading the terror.

But bombing alone will not necessarily psychologically destroy those in the target area. Other conditions must be present upon which disaffection grows. The ordinary Iraqi soldiers commonly suffered from hunger and thirst, the result of inadequate logistical support, compounded by coalition air attacks against those support services. The raids also cut bridges and roads, forestalling escape. The Iraqi leadership consistently lied to the soldiers. Saddam and his generals said the army would not be fighting other Arabs, but they were. The soldiers were told they were miles from the Saudi border; in fact, the frontier was only a few hundred yards from their positions. Their officers treated them like trash at the same time the Republican Guard received the best. These conditions led to a state of *anomie*, a loss of legitimate meaning, purpose, and direction to action. The soldiers doubtless felt trapped, their only way out to break the military norms and desert or surrender. And they did just that by the thousands, walking into the desert looking for someone, anyone, anything to whom they could surrender, including an auto filled with newsmen and an intelligence drone that came down in the battle zone. Those who sought escape from Kuwait City along the two highways were cut off and killed.

The violence heaped on the two escaping columns, at first by air strikes and then by land forces, was a critical point in the war, creating an unanticipated problem. The destruction produced a surprising reversal of expectations—was all that lethality necessary? The question followed hard upon the news pictures. That the question could be asked at all reflected a perception that the American population, at least, would no longer accept wholesale destruction as a matter of course, the inevitable consequence of battle. Yet, if the statements and orders of Powell and Schwarzkopf are taken at face value, this was meant to be a war of annihilation.

The war against an impersonal enemy executed with surgical precision by weapons that, on television, looked like images from a video game, suddenly assumed a horrible reality. The dazed prisoners feebly wandering the desert waving their white shirts and towels were a wretched lot, hardly the murderous hands of the Hitler of the Middle East. The chilling pictures of the "highways of doom," the burned bodies looking like bloated overcooked sausages, showed that real people were getting killed. They would not get up and plug another quarter into the game machine. This was battle, real battle, close-up and terrifying in its aftermath, and human after all. Abruptly, the fun went out of the war. Bush ordered a cease-fire. Enough was enough.

Schwarzkopf, of course, obeyed orders and stopped all hostilities—but not before advising Bush and Powell that with another forty-eight hours he could completely wipe out the Republican Guard. General Sir Peter de la Billiere, British ground commander, was taken aback by Bush's decision because the Iraqi Army was still a viable fighting force. That viability received unwitting reinforcement because U.S. Army divisions—the 101st and 24th in particular—were not able to reach their proper blocking positions in time, allowing many Iraqi soldiers to escape north from Nasiriyeh and letting Republican Guard units escape from the Basra area to Qurna north along the Tigris River road. Colonel Hackworth wrote in *Newsweek* (20 January 1992) that victory in the Gulf War, as in Korea and Vietnam, was never clearly defined, denying the army the fulfillment of its role. That role, it would seem, was annihilation of the enemy.

Clear definition or not, many Westerners were dumbfounded by Saddam's later announcement that Iraq had won the war and had established its rightful place as the leader of the whole Arab world. From Saddam's perspective, the declaration of an Iraqi victory made a kind of sense. The Iraqi Army never formally surrendered. The cease-fire was Bush's idea, not Saddam's. The capital of Baghdad was never occupied. Saddam remained in power. The numbers of Iraqi soldiers who died were of little relevance because they were Islamic martyrs against the forces of Western imperialism. Therefore, Iraq won, if nothing else, a spiritual victory over Western imperialism—just as Sadat's Egyptians declared spiritual victory over the Israelis in 1973. These essentially Islamic definitions of victory, reflecting a basic culture clash, lay beyond the parameters of Western warfare.

At a more mundane level, the coalition was constrained by U.N. resolutions. The capture of Baghdad and the killing or arrest of Saddam were not on the program. Also, only a delicate political thread held the coalition together, that in itself a moderating force on what the United States and Britain, the traditional Middle Eastern prime movers, could and could not do. Thus, a march on Baghdad was militarily possible, but that would have left the Americans and British alone on the field, having incrementally and, for all intents and purposes, unilaterally expanded the war. The Arab states and France were among the nations that resisted any thought of such a maneuver and would have abandoned the coalition if necessary to mark their objections. The Gulf War was open season against land piracy, not national leaders, however reprehensible.

But Colonel Hackworth warned that, once launched, war must be total—meaning annihilation. There is no such thing as a nice war, a clean war, or an antiseptic war. That, Hackworth quickly added, is the reason to avoid war, especially one in which the political objectives were ill defined and the overall military strategy did not adequately consider possible contingencies. Anything less, he declared, is not victory. Or is it?

CHAPTER 9

Desert Battle: Trends and Perspectives

The Gulf War apotheosized high technology weapons. Laser-guided bombs, Stealth fighters, and satellite communications created a new and deadly configuration of battle. The Global Positioning System led armored commanders to their quarry with navigational precision. Challenger and Abrams gunners, using thermal imaging targeting instruments, destroyed enemy tanks at ranges of five miles, the Iraqi crews often unaware of the danger lurking across the desert. When the Iraqis fought back, their tank gun projectiles frequently fell short or bounced off the reactive armor of the British and American tanks. Only eight Abrams sustained damage, and four of these were repairable. Thus, General Schwarzkopf's "Hail Mary"—his version of the World War II North African left hooks—swept across the Mesopotamian desert, crushing all resistance with deadly efficiency.

The war was announced in the West as a moral crusade to liberate Kuwait, bring democracy to the abused little nation, and punish the abuser Saddam Hussein for his transgressions. Little was said about restoring the Middle East power balance or protecting oil deposits. Dissembling or not, the war's leaders received overwhelming public support. On 13 January 1991, the London *Sunday Times* reported that twenty-one national newspapers believed the war was justified and, on 20 January, the same paper published poll results indicating 80 percent public support for the war. In the United States, similar public support boosted President Bush's approval ratings. In the end, even the Soviet Union voted in the U.N. Security Council for military intervention in Kuwait.

Perhaps—and here I turn speculative—another motive for the war existed, not in the dark corridors of power but in the shadows of our minds. I suggest the vast public support was a xenophobic outpouring through which Saddam Hussein became the symbolic target of long impotent outrage against Middle Eastern extremists who for years emasculated the Great Western Powers. During the 1970s and 1980s, for example, Arab groups in Lebanon took American and European hostages with impunity. Iranian fundamentalists overran the U.S. embassy in Teheran, took the staff hostage, and contributed to the downfall of an American president. In 1983, an Arab terrorist murdered more than 200 U.S. Marines by driving an explosives-laden truck into their barracks at Beirut airport. The Libyan leader Muammar Qadaffi spawned terrorist acts around the world. These unanswered humiliations begged for revenge. The level of frustration found expression in the disproportional support for three unrelated acts of military adventurism: the British Falklands War; the U.S. invasion of Grenada; and the U.S. incursion in Panama City to arrest one man. Whatever other motivations provoked these incidents, the need to win something, anything, anywhere, cannot be ignored. But those actions were not really grand enough, and none were directed toward the Middle East. Then along came Saddam Hussein, too self-important by half. A just war, comfortably wrapped in moral clichés and historical stereotypes, could at last be fought on the West's terms. The time had come to annihilate an army.

Going to war in the Gulf was neither cheap nor easy. None of the major Western powers had fought a major desert battle since World War II. An entire army needed transportation to the Gulf. Supply lines were stretched and, despite all the electronic gadgets, intelligence gathering and analysis nearly overloaded the computer systems designed to handle it all.

How the coalition met the challenges of desert battle has been told and retold, but the narratives generally lack historical perspective. The campaigns selected for review in this study provide that context by demonstrating the different ways different armies fought in deserts and how changing technologies influenced desert war. But I want to take the narrative process one step further. Closer examination of the campaigns, at the risk of some redundancy, yields six major trends of desert battle. The leaders of the Gulf War—coalition and Iraqi alike—inherited those trends. Whether they were true beneficiaries remains to be seen.

1. The Water Factor. Every major desert battle in modern history took place near water. Bonaparte never strayed far from the Mediterranean, and Desaix's march was a river campaign. The Swat and Kabul Rivers bracketed Campbell's operations. Maude, the Persian Gulf at his back, battled up the Tigris. O'Connor and then Rommel fought along the North African coast's narrow shelf. The Egyptians in 1973 used the Suez Canal as their front line; the Syrians battled for the Golan, overlooking the Jordan River. The coalition operated near the Persian Gulf.

Rivers and coasts had relative significance. They were often the only barriers between desert states and regions, the only visible lines in the sand. At a practical level, rivers and coasts also provided convenient but uncertain supply routes. The British navy made Bonaparte's sea route unsafe, forcing him, albeit willingly, to depend on what Egypt supplied. Campbell's reluctance to operate above the Swat River was partly based on the lack of a navigable river for supply. Maude created a river fleet and rebuilt the Basra port facilities to meet his growing logistical needs. Between 1940 and 1943, many British convoys headed for Alexandria eschewed the dangerous Mediterranean route for the longer but safer journey around the Cape of Good Hope. By 1943, with the Royal Navy and RAF growing stronger, Rommel discovered just how dangerous the Mediterranean could be as the British played havoc with his supply convoys. The massive 1991 Gulf War buildup necessitated a sea-lift that delivered six million pounds of materiel. However, the United States, its merchant fleet gutted following World War II, leased ships, revealing a major vulnerability.

Early campaigns went forward under the naive assumption that desert rivers provided fresh water. The Nile nearly brought Bonaparte's army to its knees, and the British discovered the Tigris to be a running sewer. Only Campbell's forces enjoyed potable river water. Modern armies depend on fresh water being piped or trucked to forward areas. The Saudis supplied the coalition with desalinated water from Gulf coast stations, the war unthinkable without that steady source.

Rivers and coasts also gave armies added firepower from gunboats. Bonaparte's vessels battled the Mameluke flotillas for control of the Lower Nile. Maude's Tigris gunboats provided valuable flanking fire that helped dislodge Turkish defenses. In 1940, Royal Navy gunboats and monitors bombarded Italian supply depots, harbors, and the coast road. During the Gulf War, navy gunfire convinced Saddam that an amphibious assault was imminent. Thus, water provided a functional and steady flank for many desert campaigns.

2. Mobility. For most of history, rivers and seas defined one flank of desert battlefields. Because river vessels were often scarce and unsuitable, the only way to outflank and surprise an enemy was to sweep the other flank—the open desert, a maneuver involving high risk. Bonaparte's march across the desert directly to Embaba nearly cost him his army. Campbell resisted plans to penetrate the arid Frontier mountains, wanting to keep his operations on the plain. Maude did execute several flanking maneuvers but always well within a clearly defined battle zone.

Then in 1918, at Khan Baghdadi, the future rolled out for all to see. Brooking's flanking maneuver, using motorized infantry, cavalry, and LAMBs, demonstrated the efficacy of desert penetration. Mobility had arrived on the barren battlefields. O'Connor used essentially the same maneuver as Brooking when dashing through the Enba Gap and then later marching to Beda Fomm across the desert. In April 1941, Rommel reversed the trek as he sent four columns cross country to converge on Tobruk. But for sheer weight of attack, speed, and destructiveness nothing matched the coalition's left hook in the Gulf War, doubtless a remarkable achievement but not a unique maneuver.

Machines, using the internal combustion engine, made desert penetration possible. But increasing mobility meant constant refinement of those machines. Tanks, for example, underwent many transformations. Speed increased from the World War 14 mph, to the Matilda's 7 mph across desert terrain, to the Centurion's 21 mph under optimum conditions. The Challenger and Abrams both rolled across the desert at better than 40 mph. Gun size increased from the 2-pounders common in early World War II models—Matildas, the A-series cruisers, and the German Pz Mark III—to the 120mm guns of the Gulf War. More speed meant larger engines, bigger guns meant more armor, and all these meant more weight. The Matilda weighed twenty-six tons, but the Abrams grossed fifty-five tons and the Challenger sixty-two tons. Speed and weight produced a clear equation, some would say a dilemma: The greater the weight of attack, both in tonnage and number of machines, the greater the needed logistical support. During the Gulf War, one U.S. armored division needed double the gasoline used by George Patton's entire 3rd Army in its dash from the French coast into Germany during World War II. Fortunately, all the coalition's attacks began in Saudi Arabia, the biggest gasoline station in the world. The equation continues: the deeper the desert penetration and the greater the logistical support, the greater the vulnerability of the support columns to enemy artillery fire and air strikes. The possibility also grows that the entire attack, front and rear echelons alike, might collapse of its own weight. Graziani, O'Connor and all the subsequent British commanders, Rommel, and Ismail found out about vulnerability in their campaigns.

3. Battlefield Size. The third trend of desert battle is drawn from John Keegan's observation in *The Face of Battle* that battlefields have spatially enlarged. Certainly this is true in desert warfare, the enlargement made possible by increased mobility and efficiency of machines. Black powder battlefields, by comparison, were small stuff. Bonaparte's Egyptian force, marching in squares, probably did not extend for more than two miles. The Battle of the Pyramids, requiring the squares to close on one another for mutual support, occupied even less space. On the Northwest Frontier, at Iskakote, the fully deployed Peshawar Field Force presented a front 300 yards wide. The entire battlefield was only 800 yards wide and a thousand yards deep.

The massive armies of World War I inaugurated the larger desert battlefields of modern times. During the Mesopotamian campaign, the Turkish front at Sannaiyat extended sixteen miles. The 1940 Egyptian front, once Graziani stopped his advance, stretched from the Mediterranean coast inland for fifty miles to Nibeiwa and Sofafi. The 1973 Bar-Lev Line followed the Suez Canal for ninety miles from the Mediterranean to the Gulf of Suez. The Gulf War encompassed one large battlefield that included all of Kuwait, the Iraqi desert to the Euphrates Valley, and back to the Shatt-al-Arab, an area 300 miles square.

4. Combined Arms. Some armies are trained for desert fighting; others must adapt. But our historical selection indicates that training or lack of it did not mark the parameters of victory or defeat. Rommel and his men, fresh off their transport ships, lacking any desert preparations, launched an extremely effective campaign in April 1941. The

Israelis, trained for desert combat, confident in their abilities, nearly lost the 1973 War. The Iraqis, likewise, thought they knew all about desert battle, yet performed miserably. But even Rommel eventually lost because victory and defeat were not just matters of training, leadership, logistics, or how many tanks an army put into the field. Victory usually went to the army that discovered what combinations of armaments worked best against a given enemy in a given battle.

That scramble—often a quick if not panicked reaction to enemy tactics—for the right combination of arms constitutes the fourth trend of desert battle. The scramble, I will hazard to say, did not start in desert warfare until after 1917. Before that time, Bonaparte and Campbell, certainly, but even Maude, were constrained by their limited technology. In their armies, most men walked most of the time. The weapons they carried—swords, knives, muskets or rifles, and cannons—allowed little flexibility for maneuvering. The arrival in World War I of rapid-fire weapons such as machine guns, if anything, further limited infantry movements. Not surprisingly, a predictable and repetitious offensive pattern emerged. Artillery battered enemy defenses or troop formations, allowing the infantry to advance and puncture the enemy positions. Ideally, the cavalry charged through the openings to exploit the enemy rear echelons.

In 1918, after actions such as Khan Baghdadi, and after development of more reliable, powerful, faster, and more heavily gunned machines, the possibilities of combining different armaments multiplied. So too did the debates over which combination of arms was best. Should artillery open the way for the tanks, to be followed by infantry who would hold the gains and exploit the advance? Or should artillery hammer the enemy, enabling mechanized infantry to penetrate the defenses and hold their openings for tanks to burst through and exploit the gains? Or should tanks go in first, fighting enemy tank formations and penetrating the enemy defenses, the mobile artillery and infantry following?

O'Connor and Rommel supplied strong answers to these questions. O'Connor, short of everything, adapted his tactics to the situations facing him, never opting for a single formula. At Nibeiwa, his artillery shelled the fort, tanks crushed the outer defenses and shot up the interior, followed by motorized infantry that exploited the confusion already created. At Bardia, O'Connor reversed tactics, first sending infantry and sappers to penetrate the layered defenses. Then the tanks followed, and all under an artillery umbrella. The two British left hooks at Enba Gap and Beda Foram completely dislocated the Italians, rendering their numerical superiority irrelevant to the campaign's outcome. Rommel's march on Tobruk was five days faster than O'Connor's dash to Beda Fomm. Speed and surprise, not power and weight, keyed the advance. The British counterattack, Operation Battleaxe, featured Beresford-Preise's left hook—but with unsupported armor. Rommel's antitank guns, not his tanks, made the weight of the British attack irrelevant as the Matildas were picked off without getting close to the German line.

The British recoiled in confusion, trying to discover the right combination of infantry, machines, and weapons to stop Rommel. The results were uneven, for the reliance on independent columns, used by O'Connor when so many shortages made such action necessary, continued without interruption. As P. G. Griffith commented, brigadiers, colonels, and several junior officers wanted their own little armies, independent brigades, flying columns, desert groups—all reflecting the romance and myth of desert fighting (could the ghost of T. E. Lawrence ever be far away?). The groups dissipated British strength. Even though new British commanders, particularly Claude Auchenleck, planned sound campaigns, it was not until Montgomery's massive and punishing combined arms assault at El Alamein that the Desert Fox was finally put in a box.

Post–World War II military thinking must have absorbed the lessons of desert battle played out in North Africa. Would it were so, the Arab-Israeli wars might have been different. Instead, Israeli military theorists re-invented the old arguments about the proper role of armor, settling on the solution—read dogma—that tanks should be the main battlefield weapon, charging like cavalry, their weight and firepower creating battlefield havoc. The 1967 War convinced them that since tanks dominated the battlefields of that war, they would do so in future wars.

The decision left artillery and infantry choking in tank exhaust. The Israelis did purchase U.S. M-113 armored personnel carriers and self-propelled artillery, but not in sufficient numbers to redress a growing imbalance of arms. As John English points out in *On Infantry*, the Israeli Army's basic infantry skills suffered from benign neglect. Thus, when the Egyptians and Syrian missile infantry attacked in October 1973, the Israelis reacted in confusion, allowing their tanks to attack in splendid isolation. For example, when the 190th Tank Battalion charged, Egyptian missile infantry and dug-in tanks wiped them out in three minutes. Only after the Israelis recovered from what F. H. Toase calls Sagger missile shock, quickly integrating tanks, artillery, and infantry, were they able to reshape the battlefield, seize initiative and, at least on the canal's west bank, utilize tanks as they wished.

The integration of tanks and infantry, only one dimension of the combined army debate but arguably the most important, seemed resolved in the Gulf War. The U.S. Army deployed 2,000 Bradley armored personnel carriers, or infantry fighting vehicles, and the British armored division used 135 Warriors. The Bradley mounted a 25mm gun and a TOW anti-tank missile launcher. Designed as an offensive weapon, not just another battlefield taxi, the infantry inside could fire their weapons without dismounting. According to Norman Friedman, "It does not matter too much that [the infantry] cannot aim and fire terribly accurately" (393). What mattered was the total firepower delivered—"sprayed"—against enemy positions. The British Warrior, mounting a 30mm gun, and its infantry complement were meant to dismount, using their Milan anti-tank missile. A typical action occurred when the Scots Dragoon Guards breached Saddam's defensive line, mounting a night attack on an Iraqi communications center protected by tanks, APCs, and infantry in bunkers. The Scots Challenger tanks quickly destroyed much of the Iraqi armor and shelled the bunkers. A company of the 1st Staffordshire Regiment arrived in Warriors, dismounted, cleared the remaining bunkers, and fired Milan missiles at escaping APCs. As one British infantryman said, "Of course, everyone inside the APCs were immediately killed." This engagement represented the typical Gulf War subordination of infantry movements to tank movements.

Armor stresses weight of attack. Infantry, as John English argues, emphasizes disruption, dislodgement, and dislocation of enemy forces. The differences between the two roles, as O'Connor and Rommel demonstrated, are not antithetical. Only by dogmatically forcing a choice do they become so. The alternative to dislocation is annihilation, a battle concept introduced into desert warfare by Western armies. Bonaparte always, Campbell at Iskakote, Maude, Montgomery, and Schwarzkopf were all determined to annihilate their enemies by weight of attack. In the twentieth century, the tank perforce became the queen of battlefields, replacing the power of massed infantry typical of the nineteenth century.

5. Lethality. Weapons and more weapons, mass destruction, viciousness—how much more can the mind and body of man endure? For, as Keegan notes in *The Face of Battle*, battlefields are increasingly lethal environments. More soldiers, equipped with a "superabundance" of enormously destructive weapons, occupy larger battlefields for longer time periods.

Immediate qualification is needed for desert battles. A case can be made that they are shorter in duration than battles in more normal environments. In World War I, for instance, the Battle of the Somme, in all its phases, lasted just over four months. The World War II siege of Leningrad lasted 900 days. But Maude's battle for Kut and the breakthrough at Sannaiyat took two months. O'Connor's Operation Compass lasted an overall two months; within that time, however, Sidi Barrani fell in three days, Bardia collapsed after a two-day fight, and Beda Fomm was two days' work. The entire Arab-Israel 1956 War lasted two weeks, the 1967 War six days, and the 1973 War eighteen days. The Gulf War ground campaign lasted 100 hours.

Brevity does not mitigate lethality. Alan Moorehead characterized the Battle of the Pyramids as "more tumultuous than most, quicker in action, more savage in character and more concentrated in time" (*Blue Nile*, 111). The French killed 3,000 Mamelukes in about an hour. Campbell's fight at Iskakote lasted an hour, after which he reported that "Great slaughter had been committed on the enemy."

We usually associate the slaughter of World War I with the Western Front. The Mesopotamian desert provided another arena. During the ill-fated attempt to relieve the Kut garrison, battalion after battalion of Aylmer's force were butchered crossing open desert against Turkish rifle and machine gun fire. The Black Watch, for example, normally fielded 800 men. In two attacks, one at Sheikh Sa'ad and the other at Hanna, the battalion lost 1,500 men. On 8 April 1916, the Turks opened fire on the British 7th Division, killing 1,200 in twenty-five minutes. But the British killed the Turks with equal certainty. On 17 April, at Bait Isa, Aylmer's force lost 1,600 men; the Turks lost 4,000 of 10,000 in their counterattack. The defending riflemen of the

British 8th Brigade, using the Lee Enfield Mark III rifle, could fire between eighteen and twenty-five shots a minute. At twenty rounds a minute, a battalion of 850 might discharge 17,000 rounds, an increase of 750 percent over the black powder battalions of Campbell's time. Even though that rate, the so-called mad minute, was not sustained, the 8th Brigade averaged 400 rounds per man on the day, or an overall expenditure of 1,200,000 rounds.

But it was Maude's artillery that really created battlefield domination. At Khadairi Bend, for example, British infantry squeezed the Turks into a concentrated killing zone. Artillery pounded them into insensibility. The Turkish division commander bemoaned his 'bloody losses." The Turks managed to evacuate their positions. But 2,000 surrendered after a heavy bombardment on Kut's licorice factory. Five thousand more surrendered during the next two weeks. The remnants of the Turkish XVIII Corps reeled under the continuing lethality of the British advance.

The 1973 Arab-Israeli War ostensibly continued battles of annihilation. Burned out tanks, heaps of torn and charred bodies littering the battlefields, trails of devastation from air attacks—these are the war's received pictures. On Sunday, 14 October, to restate one example, Egyptian tanks charged the newly established Israeli defensive line. The Egyptians soon realized their mistake and tried to reinforce their tanks, now under heavy fire, by sending out infantry and missile-carrying trucks. Israeli tanks bolted from cover, destroyed about 200 Egyptian tanks, all their APCs and missile trucks, and killed a thousand soldiers. The middle of the battle was not the time for the Egyptians to change tactics from an all tank attack to a combined arms attack. Mohamed Heikal was right: the attack was completely uncoordinated, and they paid for it.

Maximum lethality was central to planning the Gulf War ground attack. The coalition fielded 443,000 men, about 3,000 tanks, as many APCs, and hundreds of artillery pieces, all calculated to deliver the greatest lethality possible. The 24th Mechanized Infantry Division's artillery, for example, simultaneously poured twenty-four tons of explosives onto a single target. Just four 30mm rotating cannons delivered the same one minute fusillade as an entire World War I British infantry battalion, and the 30mm depleted uranium projectiles penetrated armor. A Milan missile fired by a British infantryman hit a T-62 tank at the base of the turret, separating it from the hull, the commander still in the hatch, and pitched it the length of a football field. A flight of Apache helicopters firing Hellfire missiles destroyed an Iraqi APC column at two miles' range in less than two minutes. Just two A-10 Warthog tank-buster jets destroyed twenty-three Iraqi tanks in one day. A 3rd Armored Division tank company outflanked dug-in Iraqi tanks. The Iraqis awakened to the attack as their tanks exploded, most hit by single shots at ranges of 2,300 yards to 3,500 yards. The destruction of the two Iraqi columns escaping Kuwait City was an unanswered display of concentrated lethality. The litany of Iraqi disasters seems endless, but the point is clear. The Gulf War did not repeat the grinding stop-shoot-go armored battles of past wars; it was military surgery.

6. Desert Battle Zones. The final trend of desert battle is suggested by John Keegan, this time from his work *A History of Warfare*. Most wars, he observed, occur within relatively narrow zones of the world, the same battlefields used over and over. Thus we find that all the major desert battlegrounds, and many smaller ones, were located in a band extending along the North African coast, through the Middle East, to Afghanistan and the Northwest Frontier. The connection between these battlefields is not merely geographical. First, the wars all exemplified a category called "little wars" or "small wars." Second, with only a couple of exceptions, these deserts were the context for culture clashes between peoples of the West and of Islam.

The phrases "small" and "little" attained popularity with the publication at the turn of the century of Captain C. E. Calwell's provocative study *Small Wars*, defined by the author as operations of regular armies against irregular forces. In the historical long view, only the campaigns of Bonaparte and Campbell seem to fit that definition. But A. P. Thornton would argue that the other campaigns were also small wars because, just like Bonaparte's Egyptian campaign and Campbell's Frontier operations, they were faraway noises, second-rate war theaters compared to really big events in Europe. For example, troops uprooted from the Western Front and sent to Mesopotamia during World War I complained they had taken a step down to a minor fight; moreover, wounded men sent back to England for convalescence felt the sting of public apathy when they revealed their wound was received in a backwater campaign. And North Africa during World

War II? Certainly the theater received high marks for public interest, the British press closely following events—albeit U.S. news magazines such as *Time* and *Life* barely recorded O'Connor's victory. In truth, the British and Germans used the Western Desert much like a rented arena where they could hammer each other until something better came along. Although they were the only show in town, P. G. Griffith concludes that the North Africa theater was a sideshow compared to European developments.

The Arab-Israeli wars were fought for national survival and cultural integrity; yet, they were small wars in the context of the titanic political struggle between their patron states, the Soviet Union and the United States. They were also wars between Islamic people and an essentially Western state; for, whatever its biblical justifications for existence, Israel is a Western nation both politically and economically. The Israeli population was built on migration from Western nations. The newcomers not only brought with them a religious orientation but, as well, Western business, educational, technological, and cultural attitudes. New generations, born and bred in Israel, to whom deserts were a natural part of their world, absorbed that Western culture, using it in whatever means applicable to defend their homeland.

That the Israelis generally won battlefield victories against the Arab states is partially a testimony to superior weaponry and a collective drive for national survival. In the end, however, the Israelis had the facility to organize, deploy, and maintain their army, and fight within the framework of Western-oriented annihilating wars. The Arab states, manifesting all the trappings of Western military might, found it more difficult to organize, deploy, and maintain their armies, and fight protracted battles of annihilation. The great bulk of Arab armies, drafted from farms, bazaars, and the streets of Middle Eastern cities, with high illiteracy rates, did not have sufficient manpower with the cultural background and familiarity with high technology instruments to do the job expected of them. This in no way questions their bravery, only their leaders' waste of it.

In his conclusions about the Gulf War, Norman Friedman recognized the cultural differences between the Western powers and the Arab states, differences really between fully developed high technology industrial powers and emerging nations, some rich in natural resources, but none really industrialized. Friedman believed that if a state—Islamic by strong implication—wishes to challenge Western power in the future, it must first undergo profound changes to bring it up to a comparable level of Western technocultural development. I think Friedman has it wrong on two counts.

First, many Arab states have tried to Westernize and some have paid a terrible price. Egypt, modern in many ways, blithely accepted the Western way of war—and went bankrupt arming and re-arming. Lebanon—Beirut dubbed the Paris of the Middle East—exploded in gang warfare between religious groups and even between anti-Israeli groups, resulting in Syrian and Israeli incursions. The late Shah of Iran tried to pull his nation into the twentieth century, often by autocratic and brutal means, and was met by the Islamic fundamentalist revolution, a retrograde movement that, amid the cheers of the multitudes, restored medievalism thought long forgotten. Some Arab states actively resisted change beyond those carefully controlled conveniences bought with petrodollars. The Saudis, for instance, were torn over accepting U.S. military intervention to forestall an Iraqi invasion and the moral and social dangers they thought accompanied U.S. forces into their closed society. For example, they expressed deep concerns that the young American troops, the relations between servicemen and women far too casual by Saudi standards, might have corrupting influences. Higher education in some Arab states is much circumscribed. Saddam Hussein, for example, shut down Iraqi universities, and those in Iran and among the Palestinians became academies for religious zealots and political indoctrination. The broad liberal arts education that is the basis of Western nations is often missing, making the possibility of developing something comparable to the West rather remote and, from the Muslim viewpoint, not always necessary.

The second problem with Friedman's conclusion is the assumption that Islamic states can only challenge Western powers by fighting on terms dictated by the West, that is, by fighting battles of annihilation. Indeed, Calwell states that small wars are not about taking territory; they are rather about killing the restless natives—in short, annihilating the enemy, a conclusion seemingly confirmed by the campaigns reviewed in this study. Yet, we must realize, as A. P. Thornton candidly noted, that there are limitations on any small war, the military goal of which is to bring the enemy to annihilating battles.

Battles of annihilation in desert campaigns have brought more than one general to the realization of an uncomfortable irony: despite all the rhetoric of mass destruction, the real purpose of battle has been to severely punish the enemy, convincing them in incontrovertible terms to back away, alter their offensive behavior, and accept the will of the Great Power doing the punishing. As Gordon Martel points out, punitive battles become the means by which to stabilize a region, for it is only within a fairly predictable social, economic, and military environment that Great Powers can rationally exercise their influences. Stabilization therefore becomes a constraint on military action. Most Western generals were not trained in a philosophy of constraint, and that establishes the basic conflict between military and political goals in war, one that will never be resolved so long as annihilation remains the dominant battle philosophy of military leaders. This helps explain Schwarzkopf's plea for another forty-eight hours in which to obliterate the Republican Guard and Colonel Hackworth's disenchantment with the manner in which the Gulf War ended. But punishment was the inherent goal of the Gulf War and, moreover, in reverse chronology, the goal as well of the Arab-Israeli wars, the Mesopotamian campaign, and the campaigns of Campbell and Desaix.

Annihilation is a frequently unattainable military goal for four additional reasons. First, as Calwell himself admitted, an enemy often avoids annihilation by refusing battles requiring the commitment of large formations that can be decisively defeated. This situation was demonstrated during Bonaparte's campaign and in Campbell's forays against the Mohmands. There were no formal armies to defeat, only clouds of tribesmen who came and went. A more modern example was the Algerian guerrilla war of independence against the French. Second, as in the Gulf War, public perceptions of the enemy may change as they become aware of what annihilation really entails. When scenes of the destruction leading from Kuwait City appeared on television and in mass-circulated newspapers and news magazines, the definition of good guys-bad guys blurred. Viktor Filatov, a Soviet newsman (forgetting the Soviet record in Afghanistan) called U.S. forces twentieth-century barbarians, and asked "How much blood do they want?" (Hiro, 391). Kenneth Roth, of Human Rights Watch, saw the two destroyed Iraqi columns as the desperate flight of lowly soldiers. Any further action would look like senseless violence visited on a defenseless mob. Thus, the Iraqi soldier underwent a sudden mutation from the avaricious beast sent to rape Kuwait to the innocent tool of an uncaring dictator. Third, annihilation is never complete. Survivors, hate-filled by the endless slaughter of their comrades, may live to fight another day or, worse, transmit that hate to another generation, perpetuating the fighting and instability. Doubtless, that condition contributed to the endless bloodletting on the Northwest Frontier and colored the entire Israeli-Arab situation. Fourth, the unthinkable might happen. The army of the Great Power might lose to the tribal forces, contradicting the cliché that a small disciplined force will always defeat a larger undisciplined force. Even though the Great Power armies that have marched across these pages won handily, the memory of the lost British column during the First Afghan War and of the killing in 1880 of nearly a thousand British troops at Maiwand, again in Afghanistan, should have caused military thinkers to reassess their' options. That seldom happened, as each new generation of soldiers was exposed to the same old dangers often in the same old way. Thus, a comparison of the 1852 reports of the Peshawar Field Force with the reminiscences of a young Winston Churchill at the Malakand Pass nearly fifty years later finds the tactical problems and solutions disturbingly the same.

If constraints exist on annihilation, the costs of stabilization can also be limiting. Again, the Northwest Frontier provides a classic example. Peace occasionally surfaced along the Frontier, but the baleful tribal presence, their raiding habits never subjugated, formed a constant reminder to the British what a relaxed vigil might unleash. Let me be clear: the British did not suffer an intergenerational paranoia. The tribes, doing what they had done for uncounted years, did threaten stability. The British invested fortunes to fortify and garrison the Frontier against raids and to mount reprisal campaigns as constant reminders to the tribes of British military might. The tribes either paid no attention to these lessons or had short memories because generations of British troops, grandfathers to grandsons, marched against the same tribes over the same ground to the same tunes of glory. Careers, both political and military, instantly brightened along the Frontier and just as quickly smashed against the barren landscape. The Frontier fur-

thermore shaped the military thinking of many British officers—of all
the principal British generals mentioned in this study, only Stanley
Maude did not serve on the Frontier—and considerably shaped the
tactics of two world wars. As a result of their warlike habits and their
persistent if elusive existence, the Frontier tribes influenced British
affairs far beyond their numbers and military capabilities.

The Mesopotamian campaign in World War I superficially
appeared to be a contest between two regular armies; but, going back
to the origins of the campaign, we find a situation akin to the Northwest Frontier. If the Indian government, charged with providing the
military forces for the operation, adhered to the incursion's original
intent—the protection of the oil facilities around Abadan—the Tigris
campaign would not have developed. However, Beauchamp Duff,
commander in chief in India, and his advisers viewed the Turks lurking upriver as a menacing force, more like a horde of Mohmand
tribesmen than a regular army, causing an incremental military
expansion that ballooned into a march on Baghdad. In 1915, had the
Indian authorities avoided imposing onto the Mesopotamian situation their Frontier-conditioned perceptions of stability, and had the
London War Cabinet possessed the fortitude to restrict the operation's continual growth, scarce resources would not have been dissipated in another sideshow under the spurious excuse that taking
Baghdad would impress the Arabs.

Stabilization, not annihilation, always hovered around the Arab-
Israeli wars. In 1973, for all the rhetoric and all the terrible fighting,
Sadat harbored no illusions about obliterating Israel. A political realist, he knew the United States would never allow that to happen and,
most likely, neither would the Soviet Union. The continued existence
of Israel was essential to the ongoing propaganda war between the two
superpowers, a convenient excuse for any failures in intra-Arab diplo-
macy, and a perpetual *raison d'être* for those on all sides who loved
their guns more than peace. From the start, Sadat wanted a negotiated peace but realized only superpower intervention in the process
could bring that about. Therefore, a war in which Egypt showed its
mettle, win or lose, became essential to future stabilization of Middle
Eastern frontiers. Sadat's wishes were fulfilled, as the United States
and the Soviet Union effectively shut down the war. In the long term,

Egypt became the first Arab state to sign peace accords with Israel, paving the way, ultimately, for the 1993 Norwegian-hosted agreements between Israel and the Palestinians.

Given these historical antecedents, the limits placed on the coalition forces at the end of the Gulf War were not surprising. Annihilating the Iraqi Army and, following the desired scenario, bringing down Saddam Hussein were popular and traditional signs of military victory that were denied. Hackworth is quite correct when he implied that goals toward the end of the war, muddled by contradictory messages coming out of Washington, D.C., confused rather than clarified the military situation. But disappointing as it might be to Hackworth, one lesson emerged clearly from the confusion: very seldom are generals allowed to define victory.

Unfortunately, the lesson that power alone cannot achieve all goals has yet to be learned. The Somalia incursion ordered by President Bush in 1992 is an example. U.S. Marines, fresh from the Gulf War, landed on Somalian beaches amid a news media carnival, quickly moved inland, and secured the airport at Mogadishu, the capital. Units of the U.S. Army and Air Force followed. The stated goal was humanitarian—to secure food supplies in a desert nation dying of starvation. For Somalia's dictatorial political regime collapsed in 1991, amid a drought that devastated the country's agriculture, to be replaced by rival clans fighting each other over relief supplies. Shortly after their arrival, U.S. troops were ordered to disarm the clans. Mohamed Aidid, a clan chief or warlord, refused. Fighting erupted. The United States sent more men, tanks, helicopter gunships, fighter-bombers, and special forces units with orders to arrest Aidid, now branded an outlaw. More men and more equipment only led to frustration because the clans fought as urban guerrillas, melting into the population. All the firepower possessed by the U.S. forces could not subdue the clans' activities. And for all the sophisticated equipment and green berets employed, Aidid could not be found. The bloodletting continued. During 3–4 December 1993, eighteen U.S. troops were killed in street fighting. The Somalis lost 300. A new U.S. president, Bill Clinton, decided to withdraw American units and let a twenty-four nation U.N. peacekeeping force take over. A peace agreement was signed between Aidid and his major rivals, but Somalia nonetheless remained dominated by the clans, now legitimized, whose fighting brought tragedy to the nation in the first place. Force of arms achieved nothing.

From the historical perspectives developed in this study, there is reason to wonder why the United States sent all those men and all that equipment, signaling great lethality, to an impoverished and starving desert country where some marginally armed clans offered the only threat. Nothing in Somalia even hinted at another mother of all battles. The rationale provided was familiar enough: the weapons were needed to protect the ground troops, creating a certain invitation to incremental escalation of forces and goals. The real answer must be, to borrow an argument from Keegan's *History of Warfare*, that the level of response was sheer force of habit. But, as often happens in wars between regular and irregular forces, the United States ended its Somalia tenure sequestered in a wire-wrapped, heavily guarded compound at Mogadishu airport, much like the compound Campbell established outside Peshawar in 1849, where, with each passing month the troops became less a punitive force against the clans and more the captives of a distorted mission and an enforced military overstatement.

I have no doubt Somalia was, along with the Gulf War, a prelude to similar desert small wars to be fought during the next several decades. If the geopolitics are correct, battles will occur in the desert band across North Africa, through the Middle East, and into Afghanistan to the edges of the old Northwest Frontier. Future desert fighting will spring from late twentieth-century strains—border disputes, internal security concerns, treaty disagreements, conflicts over finite natural resources, and civil wars (such as that in Yemen in 1994)—some within states reluctant to join the modern world, and some within states rushing too fast toward the modern world, others motivated by ethnic-tribal conflicts, and still others generated by religious sectarianism. These conflicts will often involve third-party referees or peacekeeping forces, perhaps deployed under the aegis of the United Nations. With all that glibly stated, I should hasten to add that at least four problems are associated with involvement by external agents.

First, the United Nations must find a workable and permanent structure for the management of military forces. The Gulf War, the enthusiasms for a New World Order subsiding beneath fresh tides of regional conflict, failed to establish any precedents. The coalition formed to fight Iraq now seems less the road to a future world order than an aberration born of special circumstances. Thus, the United Nations subsequently stood aloof from intervening between battling ethnic groups in a disintegrating Yugoslavia, offered only a glacial silence to the factionalisms and renascent ethnic conflicts in the former Soviet Union and, despite efforts by the U.N. secretary general to do something, chose a slow response to the intertribal genocide in Rwanda.

Second, to create a viable U.N. peacekeeping force, Great Powers—Western powers—must concede to the United Nations a measure of their own military sovereignty. That is a new direction for nations whose shared philosophy is that warfare is a natural extension of politics and who, I should think, will be reluctant to forgo their traditional and self-declared right to exercise force wherever and whenever they choose in defense of their national interests.

Third, given the geopolitics of desert battle, future conflicts involving Western intervention at whatever level inherit the legacy of a culture-clash between their own industrialized and materialistic social organization and Islamic societies. Western attitudes toward Islamic states, seeing them as not quite the equal of the West, are carryovers from the colonial past. These have been reinforced by a recent history of what seemed generic Arab terrorism coupled with a Western resentment that these strange people with strange ideas sit on a natural resource vital to the industrial West. Likewise, Islamic states often wallow in their own self-declared spiritual superiority over the materialistic West, contemptuous of the pragmatic relations necessitated by oil markets. Yet, they can also be tantalized by what profits from those markets can purchase. That inconsistency between overt cultural values and covert wish lists places unreconciled internal strains on Islam that could seek resolution through war.

Fourth, the traditional Western military response—lethal weight of attack and victory defined as annihilating the enemy on the field of battle—will not be appropriate in future desert small wars. A major consideration is that such a massive response simply involves too many men and too much equipment transported over great distances at great cost. The Gulf War cost an estimated $61 billion. An Abrams tank cost $7 million and a Tomahawk cruise missile is another $1 million—300 were launched in the Gulf War. How many times can that be done? The British and the French, having fought several small desert wars since World War II—for example, Aden, Yemen, Egypt, Algiers, the Chad—have an understanding of limited response. Thus, the British continue to develop vehicles for long-range desert work. Their Pink Panther dune buggies were used by the SAS (Special Air Services) in Desert Storm and, in 1992, Land Rover developed a new special operations desert vehicle with a range of 450 miles. Even though the United States deployed its own dune buggies in the Gulf and ordered some fifty of the Land Rovers, the manifest military response by the United States to crises of any magnitude is weight of attack, demonstrating little inclination to alter traditional concepts of engagement. Why, for instance, station an aircraft carrier off troubled and tiny Haiti? Who was going to be bombed or shot down? Or was the carrier a symbol of power to come?

Keegan, again in his *History of Warfare*, suggests that habitual over-stated, and overheated, responses can be avoided by studying the intellectual restraints, the means of avoiding sustained conflict, and the symbolic war rituals of alternative, even primitive, military systems. I would add to Keegan's list a study of Victorian small wars, less exotic but more familiar ground, for these contain many examples of what not to do and also some shining examples of military restraint and outright avoidance of war.

The problem is that such study involves a reorientation of West-ern political and military thinking, including at a base level the restructuring of military academy curricula. That will not happen in the foreseeable future. In the United States, at least, too many resi-dents of the Pentagon and Capitol Hill have too much invested in the philosophy of annihilation. Political perspectives and commitments, devotion to developing various weapons systems—workable or not—and the power politics of the military budget are too entrenched to concede that alternative military viewpoints might have value. Until the suggested changes become a reality, we may have to search for a field commander with the fortitude to tell his masters that, no, power alone will not work in small wars, urging them to face responsible alternatives to battles of annihilation. I think such a commander, serv-ing honor, can impose on future desert war its most intellectual and moral restraints.

Selected Bibliography

MANUSCRIPT SOURCES

Edinburgh, Scottish National Library, MS. 351/82, Colin Campbell, Fugitive Letters and Notes, 1814–1857.

Edinburgh, Scottish Records Office, GD45/6/344, Papers concerning the Peshawar Field Force; GD45/6/345, Correspondence between Colin Campbell and Lord Dalhousie, 1851–1852.

Kew, Richmond, Public Records Office, PRO 30/64, Letters between Colin Campbell and Sir Charles Napier, 1849–1850.

London, India Office Library and Records, MSS. Eur. F. 85, Sir Henry Lawrence, Papers; MSS. Eur. F. 90/3, Sir John Lawrence, Papers.

NEWSPAPERS

Bombay:	*Times and Courier*, 1852
Lahore:	*Chronicle*, 1852
London:	*Illustrated London News*, 1850–1852, 1940–1942, 1990–1991
	Sunday Times, 1990–1992
	Times 1850–1852, 1916–1917, 1940–1942, 1990–1991
Manchester:	*Guardian*, 1990–1991
New York:	*Times*, 1990–1991
Washington, D.C.:	*Post*, 1990–1991

NEWS MAGAZINES

Life, 1940–1942
Newsweek, 1990–1992
Time, 1940–1942, 1990–1991

BOOKS AND PERIODICALS

Asher, J., and E. Hammel. *Duel for the Golan.* New York: Morrow, 1987.

Bagnold, R. *Libyan Sands.* London: Hodder, 1935.

Barclay, C. *Against Great Odds: The Story of the First Offensive in Libya in 1940–1941.* London: Sifton, 1955.

Barker, A. J. *The Bastard War.* New York: Dial, 1967.

Barnett, C. *The Desert Generals.* London: Kimber, 1960.

Baynes, J. *Morale.* Garden City Park, NY: Avery, 1988.

Bertaud, J-P. *The Army of the French Revolution.* Tr. R. Palmer. Princeton: Princeton University Press, 1988.

Blackwell, J. *Thunder in the Desert.* New York: Bantam, 1991.

Brégeon, J-J. *L'Égypte français au jour le jour, 1798–1801.* Paris: Perrin, 1991.

Calwell, C. *Small Wars.* 3rd ed. London: HMSO, 1906.

————. *Life of Sir Stanley Maude.* London: Constable, 1920.

Chapman, F. *The Jungle Is Neutral.* New York: Norton, 1949.

Churchill, W. *Their Finest Hour.* Vol. 2, *The Second World War.* Boston: Houghton-Mifflin, 1949.

————. *The Story of the Malakand Field Force.* New York: Norton, reissue, 1990.

Ciano, G. *Diaries, 1936–1943.* Ed. H. Gibson. Garden City, NY: Doubleday, 1946.

Cloudsley-Thompson, J. *The Desert.* New York: Putnam's Sons, 1977.

Connell, J. *Wavell, Scholar and Soldier.* London: Collins, 1964.

Connelly, O. *Blundering to Glory: Napoleon's Military Campaigns.* Wilmington, DE: Scholarly Resources, 1987.

Cook, H. *The Sikh Wars.* London: Leo Cooper, 1975.

Crow, D., ed. *British AFVs, 1919–40.* Windsor, England: Profile, 1970.

Dalhousie, Marquess of. *Private Letters.* Ed. J. Baird. London: Blackwell and Sons, 1910.

Davies, C. *The Problem of the Northwest Frontier.* 2nd ed., rev. London: Curzon, 1975.

Elliott, J. *The Frontier, 1839–1947.* London: Cassell, 1968.

English, J. *On Infantry.* New York: Praeger, 1984.

d'Este, C. *Decision in Normandy.* New York: Dutton, 1983.

Farwell, B. *Queen Victoria's Little Wars.* New York: Norton, 1985.

Federal Research Division. *Iraq: A Country Study*. Washington, DC: Library of Congress, 1975.

————. *Libya: A Country Study*. Washington, DC: Library of Congress, 1989.

Fortescue, J. *History of the British Army*. Vol. 13. New York: Macmillan, 1930.

Friedman, N. *Desert Victory: The War for Kuwait*. Annapolis, MD: U.S. Naval Institute, 1991.

Graziani, R. *Cirenaica Pacificata*. Milan: Modadori, 1932.

Griffith, P. C. "British Armoured Warfare in the Desert, 1940–1943," in *Armoured Warfare*. Ed. J. Harris and F. Toase, pp. 70–87. London: Batsford, 1990.

Hall, L. *The Inland Water Transport in Mesopotamia*. London: Constable, 1921.

Harris, J. "British Armour, 1918–1940: Doctrine and Development," in *Armoured Warfare*. Ed. J. Harris and F. Toase, pp. 27–50. London: Batsford, 1990.

Harris, J., and F. Toase, eds. *Armoured Warfare*. London: Batsford, 1990.

Heikal, M. *The Road to Ramadan*. New York: New York Times Books, 1975.

Herold, J. *Bonaparte in Egypt*. New York: Harper and Row, 1962.

Herzog, C. *The War of Atonement: October 1973*. Boston: Little, Brown, 1975.

————. *The Arab-Israeli Wars*. New York: Random House, 1982.

Hiro, D. *Desert Shield to Desert Storm*. New York: Routledge, 1992.

Ingram, E. "India and the North-West Frontier: The First Afghan War," in *Great Powers and Little Wars*. Ed. A. Ion and E. Errington, pp. 31–51. Westport, CT: Praeger, 1993.

Kearsey, A. *A Study of the Strategy and Tactics of the Mesopotamiam Campaign, 1914–1917*. Aldershot, England: Gale and Polden, 1934.

Keegan, J. *The Face of Battle*. New York: Viking, 1976.

————. *A History of Warfare*. New York: Knopf, 1994.

Keegan, J., and R. Holmes, with J. Gau. *Soldiers: A History of Men in Battle*. New York: Viking, 1986.

Kennedy-Shaw, W. *Long Range Desert Group*. London: Collins, 1945.

Kosut, H., ed. *Israel and the Arabs: The June 1967 War*. New York: Facts on File, 1968.

Kühn, V. *Rommel in the Desert*. Tr. D. Johnston. West Chester, PA: Schiffer, 1991.

Lacroix, D. *Bonaparte an Egypte, 1798–1799*. Paris: Garnies, 1899.

Laurens, H., et al. *L'Expédition d'Egypte*. Paris: Armand Colin, 1989.

Lawrence-Archer, J. *The Punjab Campaign*. London: Allen, 1878.

Lee-Warner, W. *Life of Lord Dalhousie*. 2 vols. London: Macmillan, 1904.

Leonhard, R. *The Art of Maneuver*. Novato, CA: Presidio, 1991.

Leopold, A., and Editors of *Life*. *The Desert*. New York: Time Magazine, 1962.

Liddell Hart, B. H. *Strategy*. 2nd ed., rev. New York: Meridian, 1991.

Macksey, K. *Rommel: Battles and Campaigns*. New York: Mayflower, 1979.

———. *Tank versus Tank*. New York: Crescent, 1991.

McMahon, A., and A. Ramsay. *Report on the Tribes of Dir, Swat and Bajour Together with the Utman-Khel and Sam Ranizai*. Peshawar, Pakistan: Saeed Book Bank, reissue, 1981.

MacMunn, G. *Behind the Scenes in Many Wars*. London: Murray, 1930.

Martel, G. "Afterword: The Imperial Contract—An Ethnology of Power," in *Great Powers and Little Wars*, pp. 203–225. Ed. A. Ion and E. Errington. Westport, CT: Praeger, 1993.

Merk, W. *The Mohmands*. Lahore, Pakistan: Vanguard, reissue, 1984.

Michalon, R., and J. Vernet. "Adaptation d'une armée français de la fin du XVIIIe Siècle à un Théâtre d'Operations procheoriental (Egypte, 1798–1801), *Revue Internationale d'Histoire Militaire* 49 (1980), pp. 67–144.

Moberly, F., ed. *The Campaign in Mesopotamia*. Vols. 2 and 3, *Official History of the Great War*. London: HMSO, 1925.

Moore, M. *Fourth Shore: Italy's Mass Colonization of Libya*. London: George Routledge, 1940.

Moorehead, A. *The March to Tunis: The North African War, 1940–1943*. New York: Harper and Row, 1943.

———. *The Blue Nile*. New York: Harper, 1972.

Moran, Lord. *The Anatomy of Courage*. 2nd ed. London: Constable, 1966.

Napier, C. *Life and Opinions of Sir Charles Napier.* Vol. 4. Ed. W. Napier. London: Murray, 1857.

Neff, D. *Warriors against Israel.* Brattleboro, VT: Amana, 1988.

Neuman, S. *Military Assistance in Recent Wars.* New York: Praeger, 1986.

O'Brien, C. *The Siege.* New York: Simon and Schuster, 1986.

Perrett, B. *Desert Warfare.* Wellingborough, U.K.: Patrick Stephens, 1988.

Picq, A. du. *Battle Studies,* in *Roots of Strategy.* Book 2, pp. 27–299. Tr. J. Greely and R. Cotton. Harrisburg, PA: Stackpole, 1987.

Pitt, B. *The Crucible of War: Western Desert, 1941.* New York: Paragon House, 1989.

———. *The Crucible of War: The Year of Alamein, 1942.* New York: Paragon House, 1990.

Playfair, I., ed. *The Mediterranean and the Middle East,* Vols. 1 and 2, *Official History of the Second World War.* London: HMSO, 1954.

Pond, A. *Deserts.* New York: Norton, 1966.

Porch, D. *Conquest of the Sahara.* London: Jonathan Cape, 1985.

———. *The French Foreign Legion.* New York: HarperCollins, 1991.

Richards, D. *The Fight at Odds.* Vol. 1, *The Royal Air Force, 1939–1945.* London: HMSO, 1953.

Rommel, E. *The Rommel Papers.* Ed. B. H. Liddell Hart. Tr. P. Findlay. New York: Harcourt Brace, 1953.

Shadwell, L. *Life of Colin Campbell, Lord Clyde.* 2 vols. London: Blackwell and Sons, 1881.

Shazli, S. *The Crossing of the Suez.* San Francisco, CA: American Mideast Research, 1980.

Smith, D. *Mussolini's Roman Empire.* New York: Viking, 1976.

Sobel, L. *Israel and the Arabs: The October 1973 War.* New York: Facts on File, 1974.

Strawson, J. *The Battle for North Africa.* New York: Scribner's Sons, 1969.

Tennant, J. *In the Clouds over Baghdad.* London: Palmer, 1920.

Thornton, A. P. "Great Powers and Little Wars: Limits of Noier," in *Great Powers and Little Wars,* pp. 15–30. Ed. A. Ion and E. Errington. Westport, CT: Praeger, 1993.

Toase, F. "The Israeli Experience of Armoured Warfare," in *Armoured Warfare,* pp. 162–186. Ed. J. Harris and F. Toase, London: Batsford, 1990.

Vertray, Captain. *Journal d'un officier de l'Armé d'Egypte.* Ed. H. Galli, Paris: Charpentier, 1883.

Watson, B. A. *Sieges: A Comparative Study.* Westport, CT: Praeger, 1993.

Watson, B. W., et al., eds. *Military Lessons of the Gulf War.* Novato, CA: Presidio, 1991.

Wren, P. C. *Beau Geste.* New York: Grosset and Dunlap, 1926.

———. *Beau Sabreur.* New York: Stokes, 1926.

Yant, M. *Desert Mirage.* Buffalo, NY: Prometheus Books, 1991.

Index

Page numbers in italics indicate illustrations